INFINITE STEPS

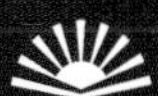

University Press of Florida

Florida A&M University, Tallahassee

Florida Atlantic University, Boca Raton

Florida Gulf Coast University, Ft. Myers

Florida International University, Miami

Florida State University, Tallahassee

New College of Florida, Sarasota

University of Central Florida, Orlando

University of Florida, Gainesville

University of North Florida, Jacksonville

University of South Florida, Tampa

University of West Florida, Pensacola

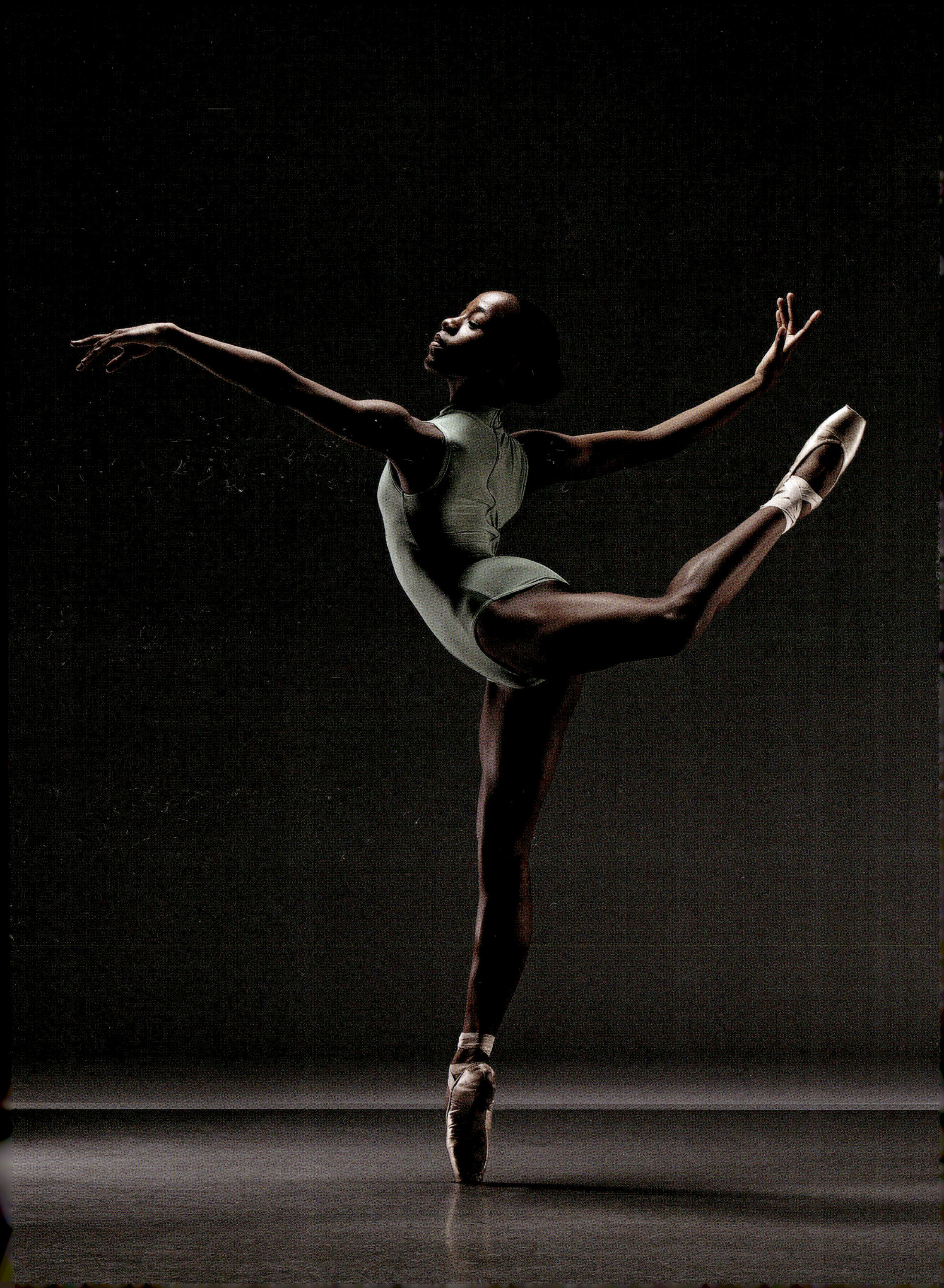

Gavin Larsen and Gene Schiavone

INFINITE STEPS

Thirty-Three Dancers and Their Lives in Ballet

FOREWORD BY KELLY RYAN

University Press of Florida

Gainesville / Tallahassee / Tampa / Boca Raton

Pensacola / Orlando / Miami / Jacksonville / Ft. Myers / Sarasota

Cover: Kylie Edwards, 2015. Photo by Gene Schiavone.
Design by Mindy Basinger Hill

Published in the United States of America

31 30 29 28 27 26 6 5 4 3 2 1

A record of cataloging-in-publication information is available
from the Library of Congress.

ISBN 978-0-8130-8150-2

The University Press of Florida is the scholarly publishing agency for the State University System of Florida, comprising Florida A&M University, Florida Atlantic University, Florida Gulf Coast University, Florida International University, Florida State University, New College of Florida, University of Central Florida, University of Florida, University of North Florida, University of South Florida, and University of West Florida.

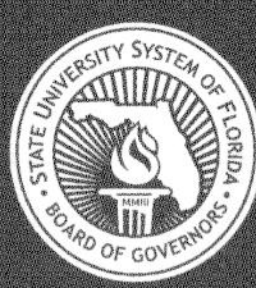

University Press of Florida
2046 NE Waldo Road
Suite 2100
Gainesville, FL 32609
floridapress.org

GPSR EU Authorized Representative: Mare Nostrum Group B.V., Mauritskade 21D, 1091 GC Amsterdam, The Netherlands, gpsr@mare-nostrum.co.uk

To my family,
past, present, and future.
With love,
GENE

To dancers everywhere, and to Gene Schiavone,
for making their brilliance eternal.
GAVIN

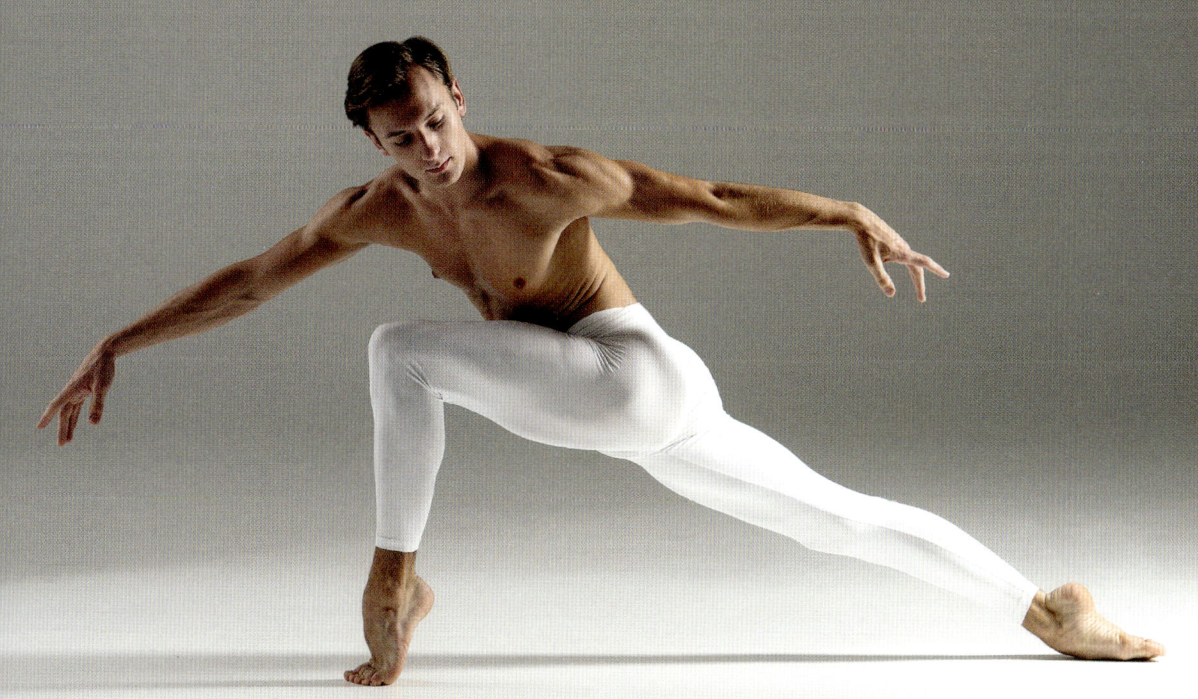

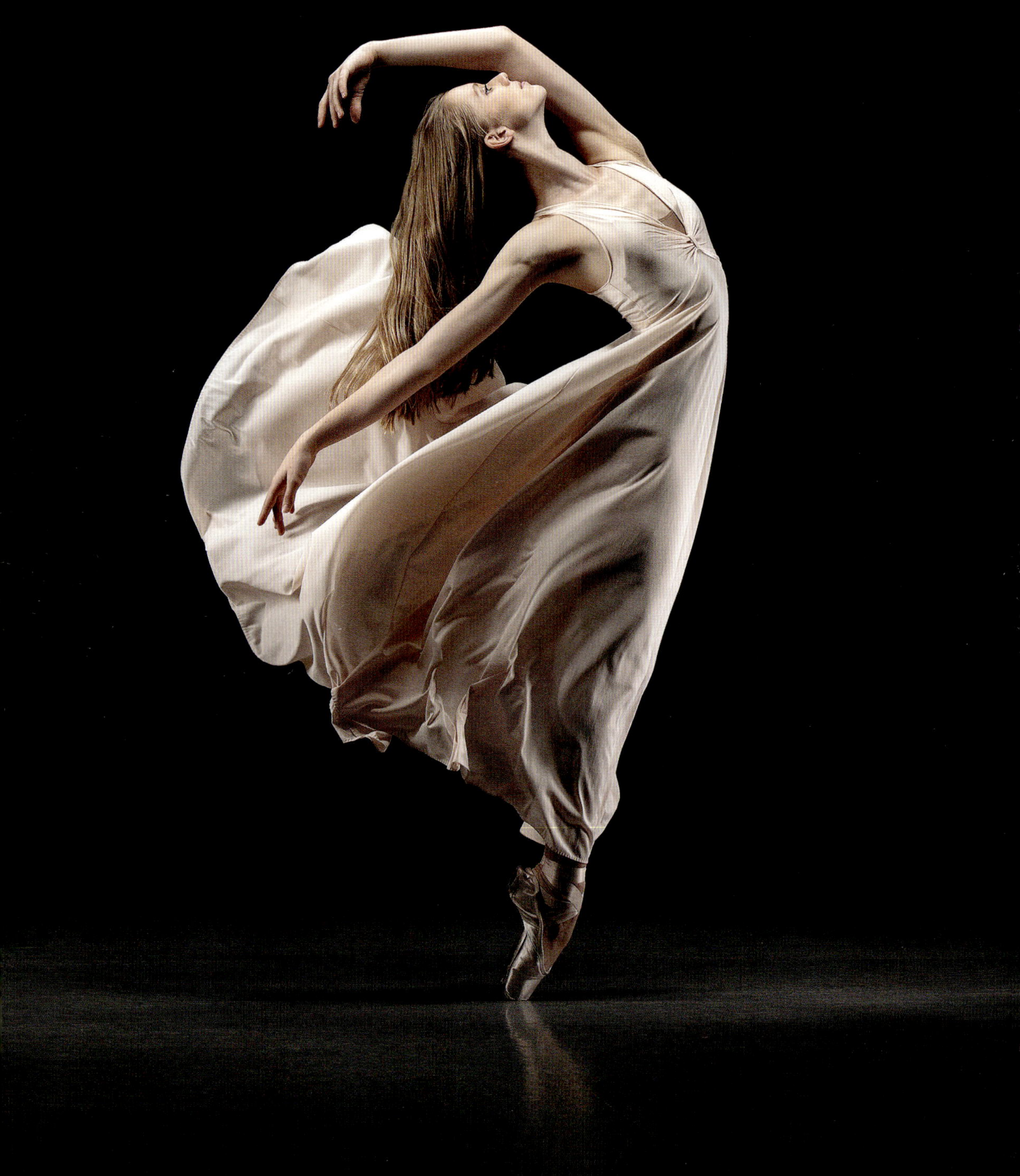

CONTENTS

FOREWORD

IF I'VE LEARNED ONE THING in more than three decades of working with some of the world's most magnificent artists, it is that dancers consider aspects of their art with seeming scientific exactitude. It isn't science, of course, but when it comes to photography, dancers regard images of themselves with an acutely critical eye. They apply special scrutiny to choosing the best photographic record of expression, extension, *épaulement,* and even the angle of a wrist.

As the press director of American Ballet Theatre (ABT) for more than two decades, photography and photographers were a constant. At times, it could seem that anyone who ever picked up a camera wanted to photograph ballet and ballet dancers. It was with some trepidation then that I began to work with a new performance photographer in 2004. Gene Schiavone was somewhat new to dance, though he had previously spent a few years photographing the Studio Company, ABT's pre-professional dancers. He had good skills and the latest equipment, and as I learned, he possessed curiosity, wonder, and a growing love for dance and ballet—the most important quality of all.

Gene gave tirelessly of his time and resources to ABT in order to master the technique of photographing dance. Others took notice. Soon, Boston Ballet, La Scala, Mariinsky Ballet, Martha Graham Dance Company, Radio City Music Hall, and countless young, hopeful dancers sought Gene's expertise. The result is a spectacular collection of photographs, spanning continents and dancers—pre-professionals to principals. His images of large-scale and sumptuous productions, as well as intimate, individual portraits, remain enduring remembrances of dancers for ballet companies and the admiring public.

As someone who works behind the scenes so that dancers may shine, I respect the selflessness required of the photographer. They exist in the dark—almost invisibly, in backstage shadows—yet what they produce is seen and appreciated by audiences far beyond the theater. Often, it's the only record of the ethereal, ephemeral, and evanescent moments of triumph on stage.

Gavin Larsen, a former principal dancer and author of her own memoir, offers context and fascinating detail to Gene's subjects. Her interviews with the thirty-three current and former dancers featured in the book provide keen insight into their endless pursuit of perfection. Above all, Gene Schiavone's photography exemplifies the exacting eye, quick reflexes, and genuine love that emanates from the artist behind the camera.

Kelly Ryan

FORMER PRESS DIRECTOR,

AMERICAN BALLET THEATRE

INFINITE STEPS

INTRODUCTION

Floating Down the Stream of Life

CENTER STAGE at the Metropolitan Opera House, two principal dancers are performing *Swan Lake*'s iconic Act 2 pas de deux. The audience is holding its collective breath, riveted by the tender, pliant, stoic choreography, evocative lighting, and Tchaikovsky's stirring music. Their eyes are glued to the pair in the spotlight, whose emotional tension is intensified by the twenty-four perfectly poised, equally dramatic swans framing the stage.

In a small, soundproof booth behind the last row of the theater's seats, a photographer knows exactly when to click his shutter—he's shot *Swan Lake* dozens of times. He follows the music, knowing that its crescendos mean the stars are about to hit an apex in the choreography that'll give him the great images the press department wants. He zooms in close to get pictures showing the dancers' sweat, the texture of their costumes, and the details of their expressions that are too far away for the audience to see.

But then he trains his lens on the corps de ballet standing in those precisely aligned rows along the sides and back of the stage: the beads of sweat on one dancer's forehead, barely visible below her white feathered headpiece; the arch of another's neck; the slight droop of someone's shoulders, hinting at how taxing it is to stay motionless, holding her arms in position for five minutes straight. To the audience, the dancers of the corps are anonymous figures, but the photographer knows them by name from years of watching them take class, rehearse, hang out backstage. Later, he'll give prints to a few of them, because a photograph is proof of their work and how much it mattered.

IN OCTOBER 2022, I had my first phone call with Gene Schiavone. It was the first of many calls, which often ran an hour or more, in which we'd talk about ballet, dancers, companies, photography, life . . . and how Gene, in middle age and with no previous knowledge of, exposure to, or particular interest in dance, came into a second career as eyewitness to and documentarian of the finest ballet performances and dancers of this century.

Very early in our relationship, I noticed that Gene preferred to reminisce about the countless less-stratospheric occasions when he showed up, camera in hand, to capture the work of dancers from the back line of the corps de ballet to the spotlight center stage, the hours he spent in rehearsal studios and behind the scenes, and, especially, the photo sessions held at his studio with excited, nervous, ambitious, and gifted (but often uncertain) student dancers. Along the way, he was not only accepted by these artists as part of their world; he became their friend. Young dancers on the road to professionalism, new and veteran corps members, soloists and superstars alike still think of Gene as their quiet champion, the unobtrusive, caring man who was always there, encouraging, supporting, and perhaps most crucially, making their dancing immortal.

When we first spoke, Gene's perspective on his twenty years' work as American Ballet Theatre's staff photographer, a position he'd almost stumbled into, thanks largely to his wife Ellen's interest in ballet, was starting to come into focus. By the time Gene retired from the business world in the late 1990s, Ellen had become an energetic key player in ABT's fundraising and volunteer initiatives, and in 2003, the couple hosted the dancers and staff of the ABT Studio Company following a performance near their home in Connecticut. Gene considered himself a hobby photographer at that point, interested enough to have taken some workshops over the years and invested in a good camera and equipment, and he felt especially drawn toward portraits—taking pictures that could, as he put it, tell a story. Meeting the Studio Company dancers and their director, John Meehan, Gene was struck by their combination of eliteness and realness and incredible talent. He inquired about photographing the Studio Company in rehearsal and performance, and although unsurprisingly ABT didn't welcome just anyone with a camera into their studios and theaters, Gene says it was because of the administration's respect for and trust in Ellen that he was granted permission. He learned the ropes of dance photography by watching the Studio Company dancers at work, getting an up-front view of everything that goes into making a performance happen. It's hard to overlook the beautiful symmetry of their trajectories as the Studio Company dancers and Gene evolved from newbies to pros at the top of their fields, despite the decades of age difference between them. His learning curve was steep. He was knocked down a lot at first by marketing and artistic staff who rejected images for reasons he'd not considered: mispositioned fingers or the broken line of a wrist, a jump not quite caught at its peak. Even the lumpy knot of a pointe shoe ribbon was cause to nix a photo. But despite never having studied ballet, Gene developed a keen eye and sense of timing that made his photographs valued by dancers and press departments alike. By 2005, he'd begun shooting the main ABT company, was officially on staff, and was spending most of his time in studios, backstage, and touring with the company around the world.

Gene's photos have appeared (and continue to appear) in publicity brochures, on posters and ads, and in newspapers and magazines everywhere, but after officially putting down his camera he found himself yearning for some way to tie together the incredible diversity of his photographic archives which, he realized, represented virtually every perspective on and way of being a ballet dancer. Through his camera lens, he'd seen many talented artists at work—but even more than their artistry, he saw their humanity. He watched as their careers and lives progressed, stalled, went in unexpected directions. And Gene wanted the world to hear the stories behind the people in his photographs.

I WAS A DANCER MYSELF. Throughout my career, I'd always felt that photos were the most revealing, poignant, and precious records of my dancing, much more so than videos. A picture, whether it was a studio or performance shot, told me a thousand things by taking me back to that specific moment while also giving me an outsider's view of myself. I could see who I was, in ways I did not at the time—even if the photo had only been taken a few days before. When I was a student, long before the internet made watching any dancer or ballet you wanted as easy as a click or a tap, books and photographs were virtually all I had. They were the only windows through which to peer at the vast, enthralling world of ballet. I spent hour after hour poring over photos of dancers, reading the captions, studying and analyzing the dancers' lines, expressions, positions, outfits. Those images were burned into my brain and completely informed my understanding of the art, technique, and culture of ballet. I was already in love with ballet, but through dance photography, I could see what it meant to be in the world those dancers inhabited. And I wanted to be there, too.

AFTER RETIRING from my performance career, I turned to teaching and writing about dance, and in 2021 my memoir, *Being a Ballerina: The Power and Perfection of a Dancing Life,* was published by the University Press of Florida. Gene, in thinking about how to produce a book of his own, read mine. He told me later that until he read *Being a Ballerina,* he thought he'd known everything there was to know about dancers. It seemed only natural that we collaborate on a project uniting photography and narrative to bring forth the stories of the dancers he had photographed. To make a picture more than an image, and an essay more than words.

In *Being a Ballerina,* I'd told my own story. Writing *Infinite Steps* was an incredibly exciting chance to talk to a huge panorama of other dancers, learning how our experiences differed, where we aligned, and teasing out the particular elements of their lives that, when pieced together with over thirty other mini-biographies, would paint a comprehensive picture of how many different definitions there are of being a dancer. Over the course of about two years, Gene introduced me to several of the artists he'd photographed. Many of them were famous names, a couple were friends or colleagues from my own past, and many were unknown—but now, they won't be. The process of conversing with them was, across the board, fascinating, moving, inspiring, and left me humbled by their trust in me to take on this weighty responsibility. Writing my own memoir was one thing, but writing someone else's was another. And doing justice to Gene's photographs added another consideration I'd not had before. Sometimes I felt like a choreographer, except instead of marrying movement and music, I had words and imagery.

"I ALWAYS SAID, LIFE IS LIKE A STREAM," Gene told me once. "Just constantly flowing, you don't know where it's going to end up. I feel the purpose of a photograph is to let the world know you were here. It is a point in the stream of life. Life continues, but this image exemplifies what you did at that point. That became very special for me, and I think it's something very special for the dancers. These dancers trusted me, and in return, I did my best to highlight their talent."

In collaborating on *Infinite Steps,* Gene and I wanted to highlight not only these dancers' talents but also the depth and breadth of what it means to be a dancer. In this book, we wanted to show that there are many ways a dancer can exist and yet, there is one defining characteristic: an insatiable need to dance. That's why there is no obvious organization to these chapters—in fact, categorizing the dancers by age or experience would do a disservice to their uniqueness and distract from the fact of their unity. These dancers have many differences, and if we brought them all together in one studio, only a few would have previously met. But they are undeniably bonded, as are dancers everywhere, across geographical zones and through the eras, by the utter conviction that they are their fullest selves when dancing. Our youngest dancer, Laina Mae Kirkeide, is just starting out in her career. A few, like Annalisse VeldhuyzenvanZanten, had only a few very intense years onstage. Susan Jaffe has gone from the very first rung to the top of the ladder at ABT, the company she joined as a teenager and now leads, but she made many bold decisions and chose adventure over safety along the way. Some of these dancers don't engage in ballet every day anymore (though it's always in their souls) but many, as of this writing, can still be seen onstage. Language, upbringing, opportunity, choices made, and experiences had—all these variables, taken together, illustrate the arc of a dancer's life.

WHAT MAKES A GREAT DANCE PHOTOGRAPH? Of course, a compelling photo could simply be the image of a brilliant moment of technical near-perfection. But some of the most arresting photos show a dancer in repose or introspection, caught on camera when they were alone in their thoughts, swept up in emotion, so connected to the movement, the moment, their character, and the music that the audience is forgotten and the world invisible. To dance in a way that reaches and resonates with an audience means performing with abandon—on top of meticulously built technique—and so completely losing oneself to the flow of choreography that conscious thought all but disappears. When that happens, the dancer's memory of their performance is blurred—sometimes it's almost questionable to them whether it even happened. Dance can't be mentally replayed like a video recording, but what does remain are snapshot-like fragments, brief snippets of clarity when the dancer's conscious thought did break through into their performance zone. As a former dancer, I know that photographs are representations of those mental snapshots—proof that the dancing was not just a dream. Perhaps because he spent so much time in their close proximity (although he says he initially felt awkward being in the studio with them while they were rehearsing, taking class, or just hanging out, every dancer I spoke to mentioned how low-profile and considerate he was and how seamlessly he fit in), Gene seemed to understand the intensity of every moment of a dancer's work. As vulnerable and fragile as they may seem, he saw the incredible strength of their effort. He wanted others to get that, too. "Ballet is all about emotion. What I tried to do was get very close-up, tight-in shots. I wanted to show the strain in their faces, the muscles, the sweat flinging off the forehead. Those were the most important shots to me. It's a depiction of what's really going on, not just what the audience thinks is going on, but what the dancer really feels."

HUMANS ARE ALWAYS TRYING to reclaim the past, to hold onto time even as it slips by us. Photographs allow us to do that. They allow us to immortalize ourselves, where we've been, what we've done. To a dancer, whose work evaporates the exact second it's made, these images are especially meaningful. And to a photographer who is documenting history through their own art form, recording individual dancers' careers has added importance. Roberto Bolle, who is no stranger to being in front of a camera, describes why dance photography feels especially meaningful. "The encounter between a dancer and photographer is precious. The dancer is an artist, the photographer is an artist; they create something unique together. Always with Gene, we were experimenting with different things, more creative than any usual poses. I felt the energy, the trust, and the result was very special."

Life is about education and the accumulation of experience. These dancers' memoirs-in-progress, painted with brushstrokes of reflection and photography, shine a light on the dancer's ever-present dilemma: What is my next step?

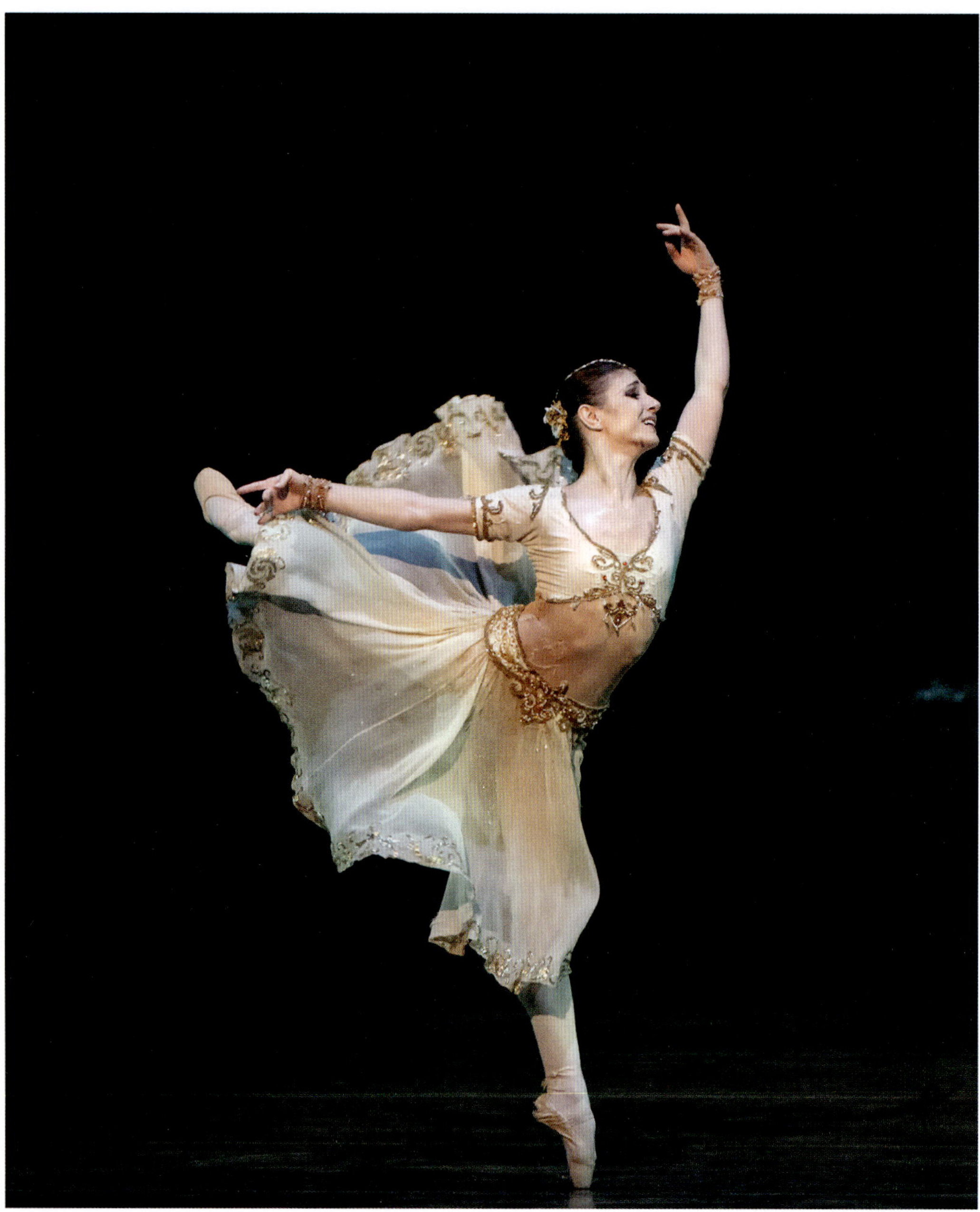

Alina Cojocaru in *La Bayadère,* 2014. Photo courtesy of American Ballet Theatre.

ALINA COJOCARU

If you learn how the heart and mind communicate with each other, then all doors are open. Because whatever life throws at you, you will be stronger, more resilient, and more understanding.

IT SEEMS THAT ALINA WAS BORN with a sense of purpose, even before knowing just what it might be. One of her earliest dance memories is of being taken to see a performance of *Don Quixote*. She was nine or ten years old and had just moved to Kyiv to train at the famous Kyiv Ballet Academy but had never seen a full-length classical ballet before. Her class was shepherded to the opulent theater for the performance, and at intermission, Alina slipped away from the group. She doesn't remember very much about that evening except that she was transfixed by the ballerina dancing the role of Kitri. "Apparently, I went to the front, down by the orchestra pit, and was leaning on the rail staring up at the stage saying, 'One day, I will do this role, and I will do it better than she does it.'" Six years later, Alina was performing Kitri on that very stage.

The doggedness Alina put into her relatively brief training years never let up. Over the course of her more than twenty-year long career (as one of the twenty-first century's most famous ballerinas, Alina performed around the world in her forties), she blended her natural independence with an equally intense urge to collaborate. She balanced her physical strength with mental fortitude, knowing that bravery often means having the willingness to let go.

Alina has been making bold choices for herself ever since declaring she'd be a superior Kitri. Her drive to continually self-improve was already evident back in those student years, when she'd write down all the notes she got in class and go over them every night with the goal of never getting the same correction again. (Hearing new critiques made her happy, because it meant she'd fixed the old ones.) She's never been without options in her career but has also rarely taken the most obvious or simplest path, starting with her decision to leave her first professional job as a principal with the Kyiv Ballet.

After only one season there, she moved to London to be a corps dancer in the Royal Ballet. The enticement of the Royal's much broader repertoire was enough to make her take the corps position, from which she worked her way up to principal within two years and very quickly captured the ballet world's attention and adoration. There would have been no reason to leave such a plum position, except for Alina's resistance to complacency. Her curiosity was sparked when she started accepting invitations to perform at galas outside the Royal Ballet. "When I saw other choreographers' work, it completely shifted my way of thinking," she said. "It made me want to search for different interpreters and repertoire, to work with different people." The experience of working with famed coach Sorella Englund on *La Sylphide* only emphasized

Alina Cojocaru in *Don Quixote,* 2011. Photo courtesy of American Ballet Theatre.

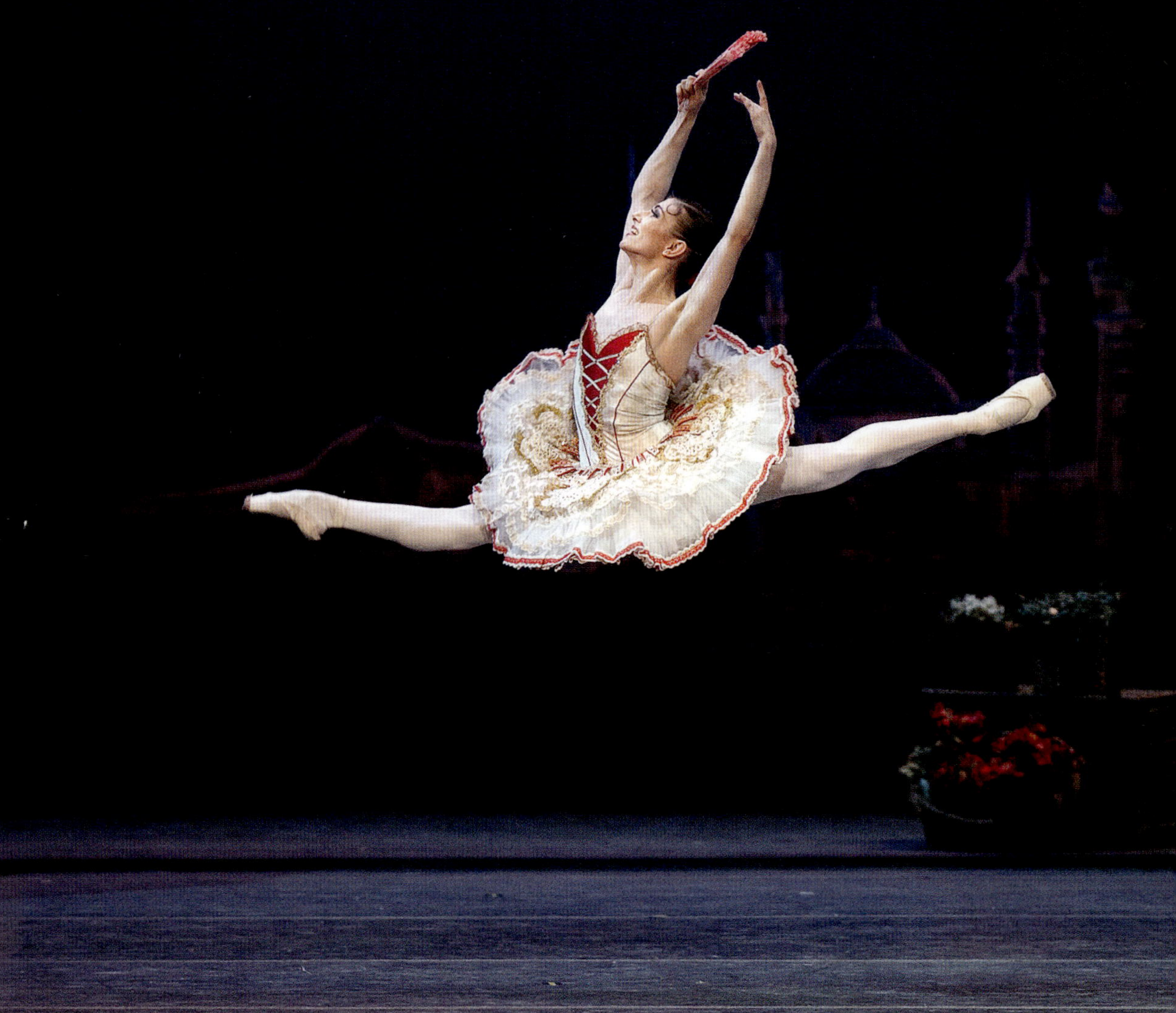

to Alina how desperately she needed to make a change. "I was always curious about the emotional side of a role, but had focused so much about the technical part," Alina said. "Sorella would come into the studio and say, 'How is your forest today? Is it sunny, rainy, in bloom? Can you smell the rain?' And I thought, 'Oh my gosh, my forest can be anything I envision.' The coaches I connect with more, will teach me more. I will be able to dance with all my senses open."

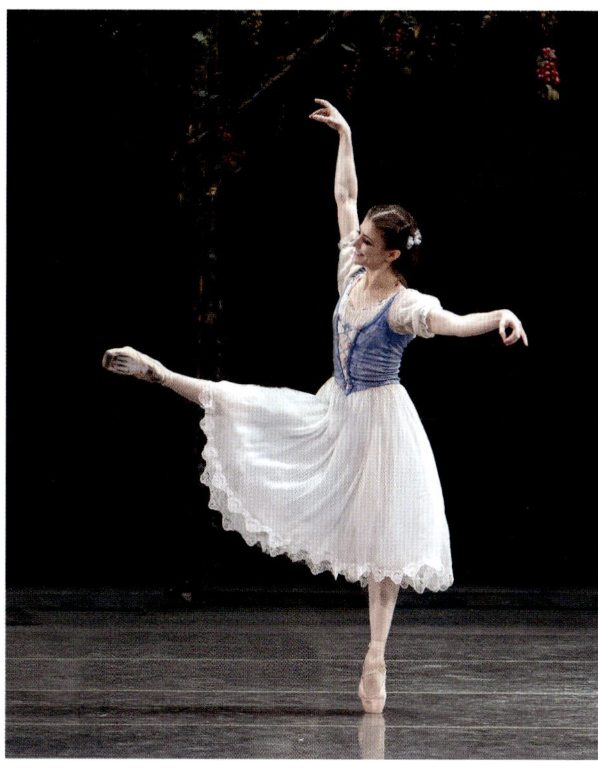

Alina Cojocaru in *Giselle,* 2012. Photo courtesy of American Ballet Theatre.

IN 2013, Alina left the Royal Ballet to freelance, splitting her time between English National Ballet and Hamburg Ballet, where she had found an artistic synergy with artistic director John Neumeier. Alina's awareness that her career could end at any time made her decision easy. "If you connect with someone, you have to put yourself in the position to work with them," she said. "It was a matter of taking it into my own hands."

Alina's sense of the fragility of a dancing career is heightened by the many times she's dealt with injury. Some problems were serious, some less so, but instead of taking away from her powers, physical dialogue became part of who she is as an artist.

If one injury treatment or therapy didn't work—or didn't work well enough—she tried something else, always looking for ways to heal. A process that would be dispiriting, exhausting, or frustrating to many has been empowering to Alina. All the information she collected only helped her get stronger, more sensitive, and better able to recover and accept her body's vulnerabilities. She doesn't think there's one route to longevity for everyone, and that's part of the point. "The answer is to get to know yourself and what

Dear Gene,

I hope you are well and still enjoying your busy schedule!
I am also busy and loving it, but very much looking forward to be in London and enjoy my home! In 1 week i will finaly be home after 6 month of traveling the world...!

Sorry it took me so long to send you, as promissed a pair of my shoes.

I want to take this oportunity to ones again Thank you for all photos you have so kindly given me. I love and treasure them.
With best wishes until we meet again,
Sincerely yours
Alina

Thank you note.

you need," she explained. "To know how much you can push, when to rest, how to rest. What does recovery mean for you? Is it more sleep, better nutrition, ice baths or heat? For me, it has been different things at various points of my career. Sometimes it was stretching at the end of the day, and sometimes recovery actually meant taking another class."

Alina's commitment to understanding and honoring her body is ironclad (she described setting an alarm to ice a sprained ankle every two hours throughout the night, and her doctor's subsequent astonishment at how fast she healed). But it's not all about being tough, nor is it only about the physical body. Young dancers act more naively and freely, she said, but the ability to filter information and listen to oneself comes with maturity. "There comes a point when we can do more analyzing, and more trusting. The key is to not be afraid to try things, don't be afraid to learn, but always listen to yourself. Because we have the right instincts in ourselves."

HER OWN EXPERIENCES in seeking, trying, finding, and filtering have been epic. Alina has sought out legions of therapists and trainers from both inside and far outside the ballet world not only for injury help, but to optimize herself in all ways. After a severe neck injury that required surgery, she didn't feel she was healing quite right. Through a chance encounter she found sports trainer Patrick Rump, who convinced her to revamp her entire routine from exercises to nutrition to maintenance, and helped her realize that misalignment is often the root of pain, even more than weakness. Her constant pursuit of knowledge feels like daily renewal. "Every day I go in with curiosity—what more can I discover, what more can I learn?—and the sense that I can find a way. If we always go in the same circles, we stay the same."

In 2012, Alina came to New York to dance *La Bayadère* with American Ballet Theatre. Gene had photographed Alina many times before in London and New York and, as he often did, presented her with prints after the performance. Although Alina almost never gives away her worn pointe shoes, several weeks after the close of the season, a package arrived for Gene: a note from Alina, and a pair of her signed pointe shoes.

John Meehan
and Cory Stearns,
2004.

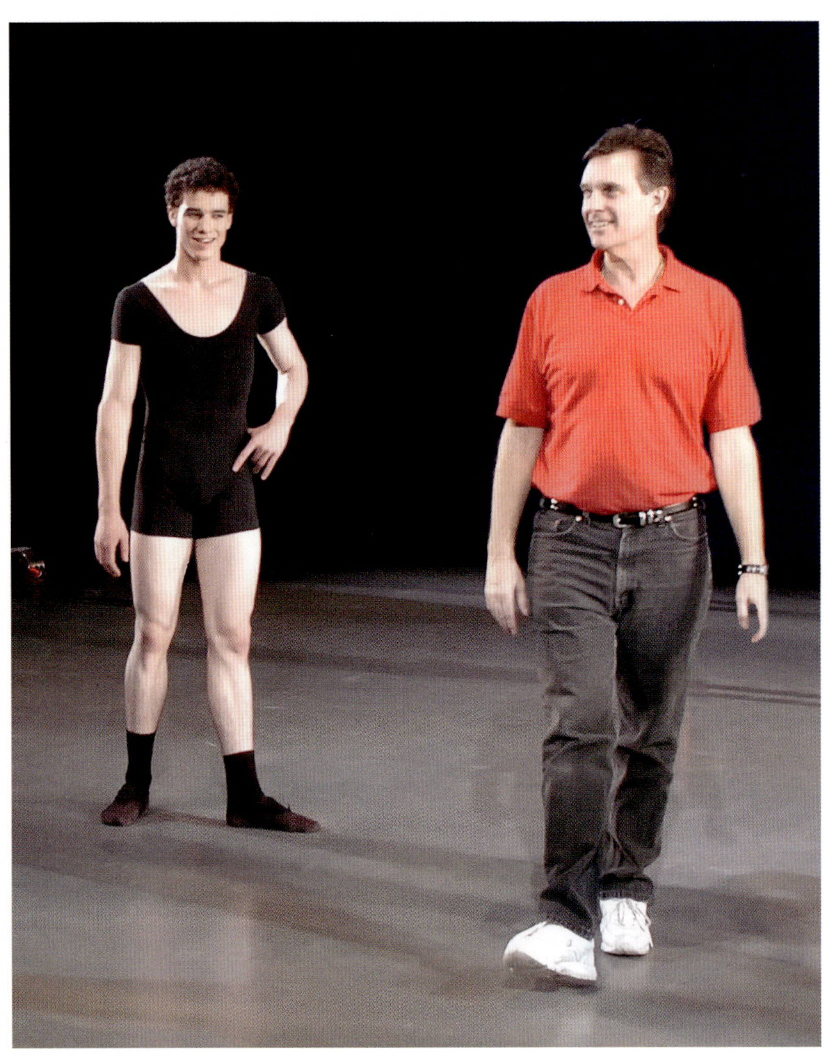

JOHN MEEHAN

Photography is very important for dance. They go hand in hand, because both are all about imagery. It was wonderful to have Gene on board with us; he became a real friend of the company. He cut his teeth on the Studio Company, so to speak. Seeing images of themselves in rehearsals and performances helped the dancers feel the weight of what they were doing. Gene's work made a big difference to us.

A NATIVE AUSTRALIAN, John trained at the Australian Ballet School and had become a principal with the Australian Ballet by the time he was twenty-four. A few years later he moved on to American Ballet Theatre, also as a principal dancer. By the end of his nearly twenty-year stage career, John had partnered iconic ballerinas like Natalia Makarova, Gelsey Kirkland, and Margot Fonteyn in repertoire including every major classical ballet and many important contemporary works, and had guest performed around the world.

John's performance career was legendary, but his influence offstage and in the studio in the years afterward may leave an even more lasting and significant mark on those who live, love, and watch ballet.

In 1997, following his retirement from the stage and after three years at the helm of the Royal Winnipeg Ballet, John became the artistic director of the ABT Studio Company, a small group of elite young dancers on the cusp of professionalism. Over the next decade he would shape the lives of dozens of the world's most talented young dancers, most of whom have gone on to have significant impact in theaters and studios around the world.

John resists touting just how important he was to the dancers of the Studio Company during his tenure, and he does not claim, as many teachers do, to have "made" any of them. His pride does show, though, when he remembers rehearsals, tours, and performances; group dinners in foreign cities; and cheering the dancers on at exciting moments and helping them through difficult ones. Those days were filled with the energy, laughter, emotion, and equal parts strength and fragility of ambitious, precocious young dancers. With only twelve members and a structure and schedule equivalent to that of a fully professional company, the Studio Company became tight-knit. John's role was much more than simply to be a teacher and coach to these teenagers who, while living away from home and their families—including some from overseas who had to learn English along with their choreography—were given major responsibilities and faced high expectations. In many ways, he was a special sort of dad. He focused on each dancer individually, trying to custom-fit his teaching to each one and create an atmosphere where they felt encouraged, trusted, and excited about taking responsibility for themselves. He wanted to make them ready for the rest of their lives.

Joseph Gatti's season in the Studio Company launched him into a career as a soloist and principal with major companies around the world. When he became the director of a company of young professionals himself, he said that being in the Studio Company was a major stepping stone and that John's influence lasts to this day. "One of the main things was that in the studio, he brought order. It wasn't a place to chit chat or goof off—even though we wanted to; we could be a rowdy bunch! He instilled in us that this was going to be a job. It's not going to be sunshine and roses all the time. You have to be there, be attentive, and give it all you have. That's something he explained so well. And that's something I try and want to emulate."

Craig Salstein left a corps de ballet position with Miami City Ballet to take John's offer to join the Studio Company. His two years there were formative, and John was the perfect leader at a crucial time for him and his peers. "He was our artistic overseer, but also sort of our chaperone and mentor," Craig recalled. "He wasn't pretending, he wasn't putting on any airs. You always knew what you were doing; you never felt lost. He opened the door for us."

John's job can't have been easy, even though he had the gratifying task of training the best of the best. A spot in ABT's Studio Company was, and is, as prestigious as a contract with the main company, and the dancers John chose already had high levels of technique and polish. He knew that what they needed—and what he could give them—was the sensibility of a professional dancer, an amorphous concept not everyone, no matter how talented, instinctively understands. "I tried to keep us focused on our mission, which was our guiding star: artistry. Artistry has to be developed in a safe environment and, if possible, a fun environment. And that's what we tried to do. We were pretty happy, as a group. I think those dancers look back on it as a joyous time."

According to Craig, it *was* a happy time, one that still holds a bit of a golden tint in his memory. Even after he and the other Studio Company members moved up and out, they knew they could still go to John for advice and support as they found their footing in a new phase of life. "I still felt I was working for John," Craig said. "Not only was he riding the bicycle with me, he's the person who pushed me off."

John understood the delicacy of preparing dancers who were likely to become the stars of tomorrow but were anxiously stepping onto the bridge between youth and maturity. Studio Company dancers performed principal-level repertoire and likely had illusions of grandeur for themselves, but John had important words to temper their expectations. "I will never forget that he told me that it was more important to be an ensemble member than to stand out," Craig remembered. "He would also say, 'No matter what, never stop working hard.' That was so helpful for the rest of my career. He was setting me up for reality, and that could not have been a better piece of advice."

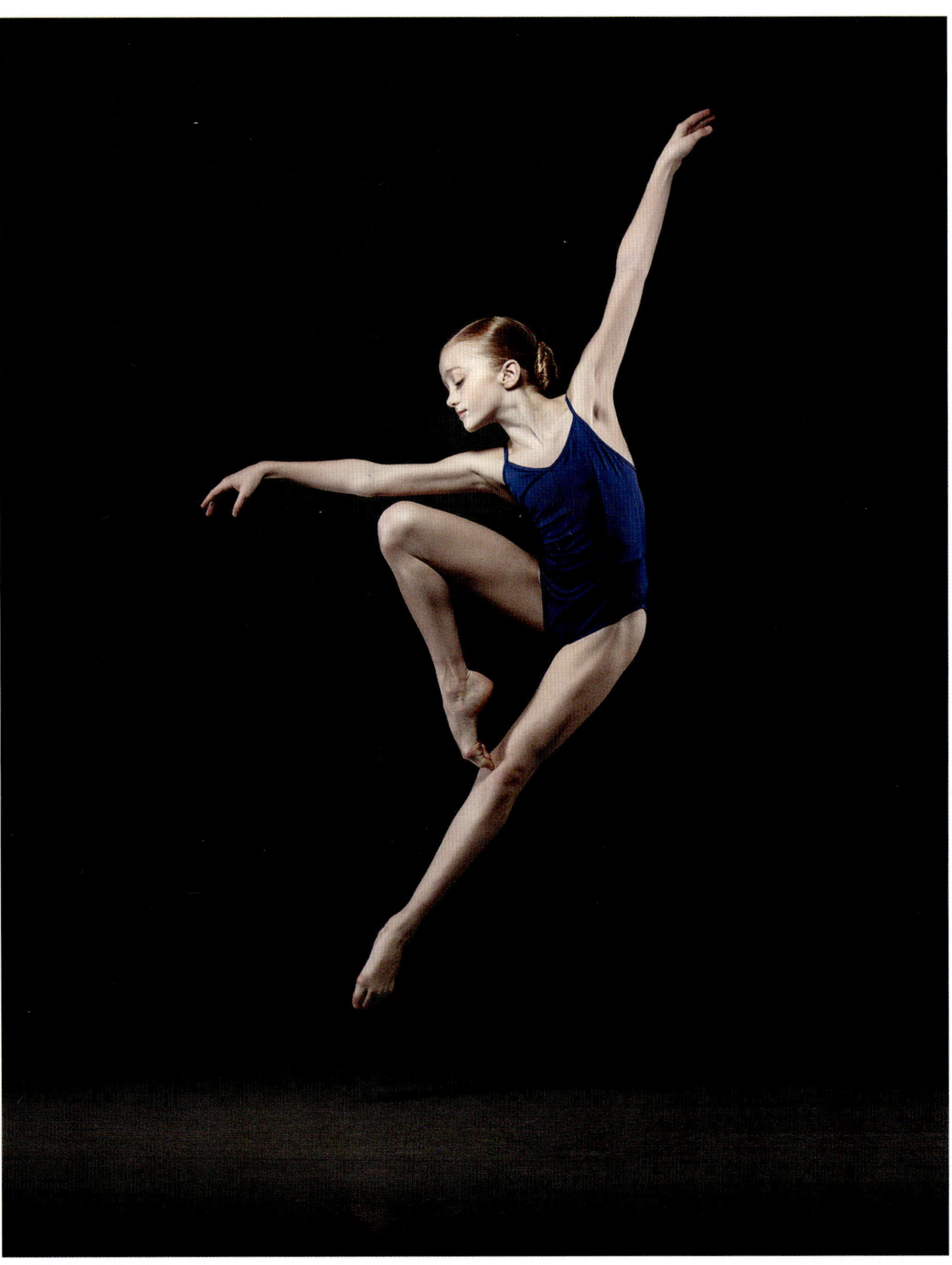

Laina Mae Kirkeide, 2013.

LAINA MAE KIRKEIDE

Wherever I end up, I want to be able to express myself and be appreciated. I want to embrace being an artist first before being a dancer.

WHEN LAINA MAE did her first photo shoot with Gene, she was just ten years old and on the fence about ballet. Laina Mae's early start in gymnastics had led her into the world of dance competitions where she performed in multiple styles, and although she took a once-weekly ballet class that was required by her studio, the rigid structure of the Cuban style in which it was taught didn't really inspire her. But a summer at the School of American Ballet when she was twelve did. Five weeks immersed in ballet the "Balanchine way" left no question in her mind about what she wanted to focus on. From then on, ballet was everything.

It wasn't just ballet that really lit Laina Mae's passion, but the particular quality of how dancers in New York City Ballet and students at SAB moved. Her teachers' encouragement to be expressive in class, even with the most basic steps, was thrilling and freeing. The emphasis on individuality and bold movement from a foundation of technical precision was empowering.

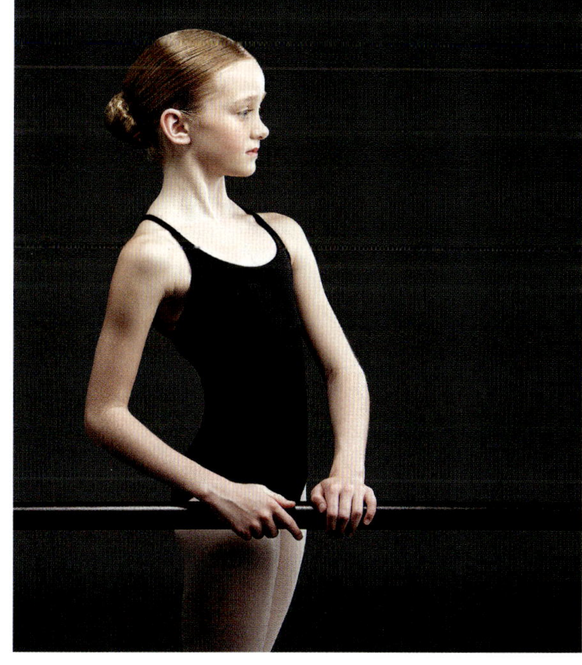

Laina Mae Kirkeide, 2013.

After waiting impatiently while training hard at the Ballet Clinic in Arizona, Laina Mae turned fourteen, finally old enough to accept an invitation to join SAB's year-round program in 2021. Over the next three years, Laina Mae's commitment to ballet only deepened and her goal became clear: New York City Ballet was her first choice.

Being an SAB student meant days filled with dance classes from 10:30 in the morning to 4:00 or later each day, plus Pilates training and rehearsals. At the same time, the academic load she carried as she worked through online high school added additional pressure. But Laina Mae loved learning and was equally passionate about education and dance, so she squeezed in schoolwork before breakfast and in between classes throughout the day. She dug deep and put in the effort needed. It was a lot to handle. There were ups and downs in living a life as active as a professional dancer, like fatigue and the pain that sometimes goes along with it.

Since she lived in the SAB residence hall, just a few flights up from the school's studios, Laina Mae's academic, dance, and social lives all blended together. It would have been easy to never leave the building, since even the cafeteria was right there on the ground floor, but she realized that working *too* hard could backfire. Going out to dinner with friends on weekends, finding a shady spot in Central Park or the Lincoln Center Plaza to do homework in nice weather, and surrounding herself with what she called "good energy" were the release valves that allowed her to stay focused without burning out.

In Laina Mae's last year at SAB she was cast to learn several roles, including solo and principal parts, in the school's end-of-year Workshop. These annual performances are a big focus for months beforehand not only because they offer students valuable and exciting stage experience, but also because NYCB often selects apprentices to join the company after the Workshop. As much as she has always loved taking class, being on stage is where she's in her element. "I think my competition experience made me able to be so comfortable onstage," she said. "Performing, projecting to the audience, and being in tune with the artistic side of my dancing has always been one of my strengths, ever since I was a kid."

Laina Mae didn't know what would happen after her Workshop performances, so she prepared mentally for lots of scenarios. "NYCB was my dream, but it didn't end there," she said. With her love of contemporary dance (instilled in her from training for the dance competitions she did as a kid) as well as ballet, she eyed some European companies with diverse repertoires and planned a summer intensive at the Dutch National Ballet. "Sometimes when it feels like there are so many factors pushing against what I want so badly, I think it's important for me to remember the big picture and why I dance, which is because I can express myself, give the audience insight and

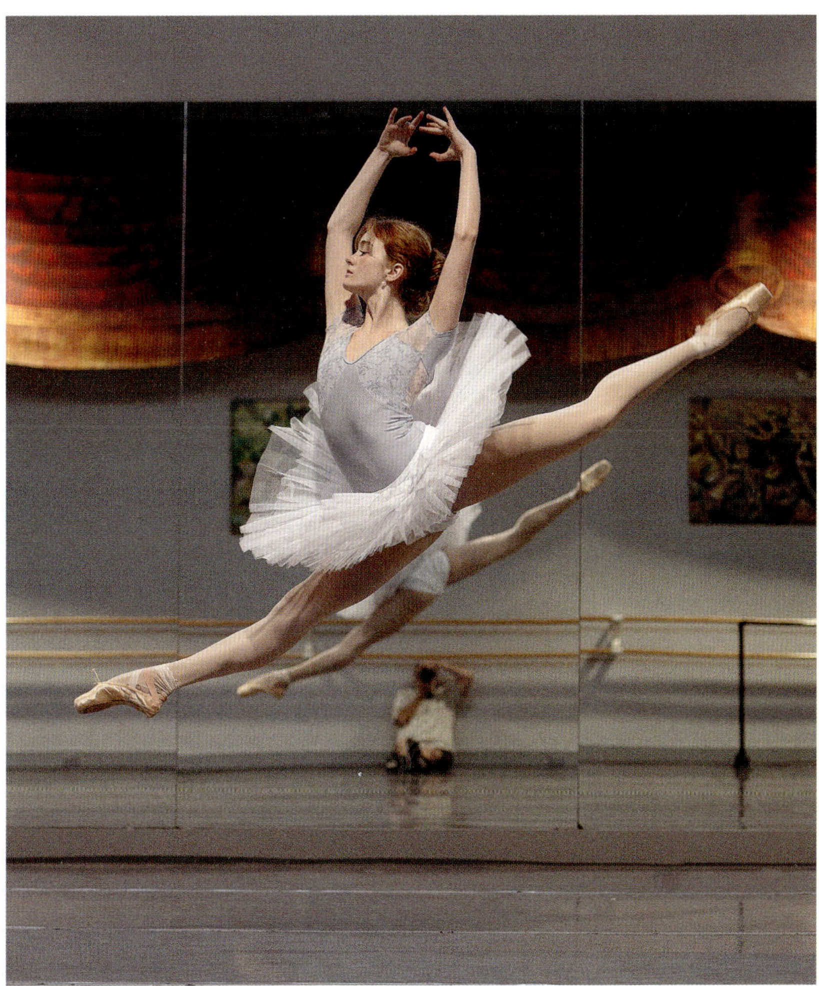

Laina Mae Kirkeide, 2024.

help them feel something. There is a light at the end of the tunnel. No matter where my journey takes me, where I end up or what I do, I'm learning from these steps. That's what keeps me motivated and pushing through."

In 2024, Laina Mae was offered an apprenticeship with NYCB, bringing her to her longtime goal and making her dream a reality.

Even though she's still at the very beginning of her life in dance, Laina Mae already has something to say to that younger version of herself. "Trust the process. Everything happens for a reason. And make sure to always remember why you dance, which is because you love it."

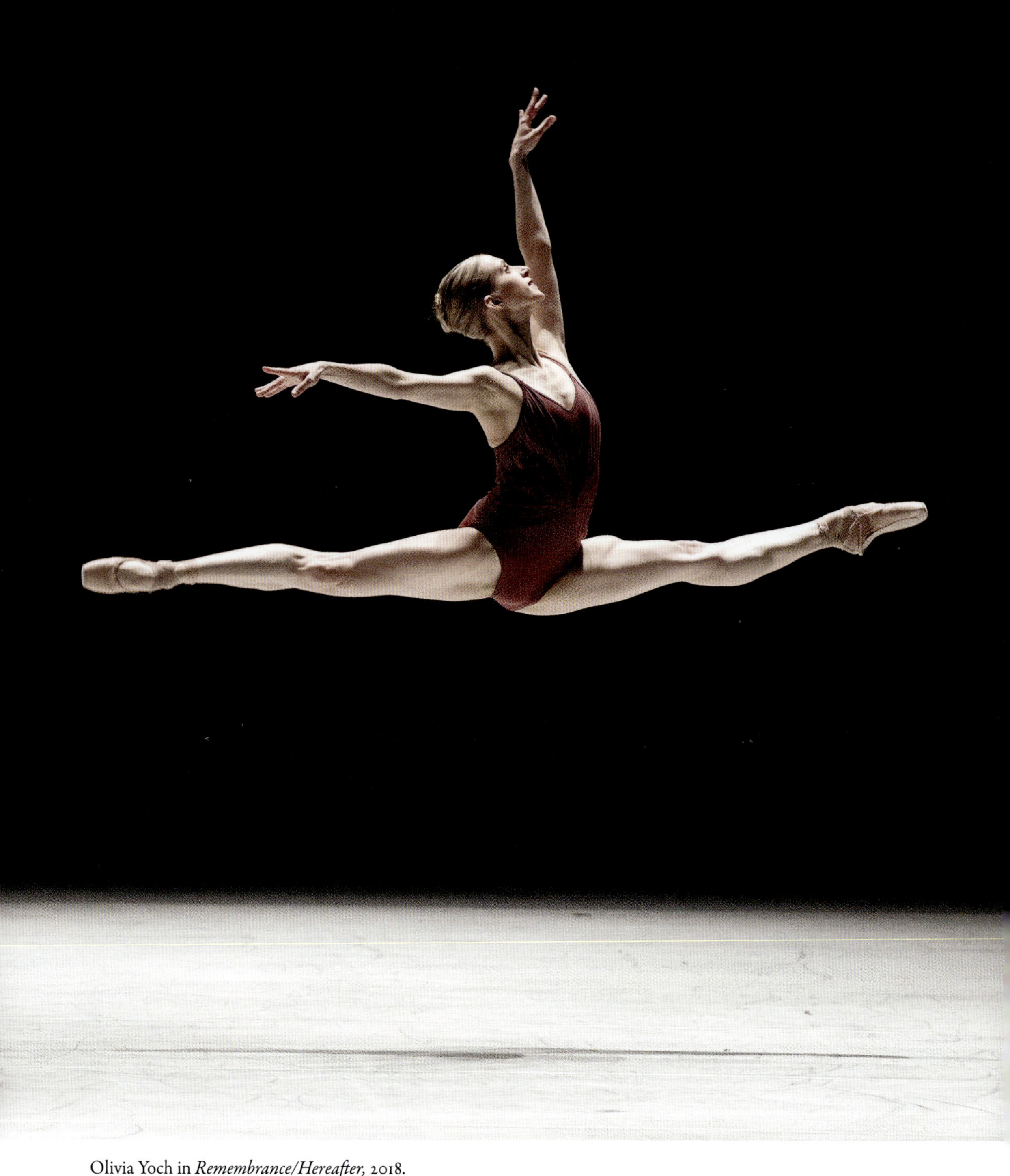

Olivia Yoch in *Remembrance/Hereafter,* 2018.

OLIVIA YOCH

These experiences taught me that when people expect hard things of me, I am able to rise.

OLIVIA YOCH DOESN'T REMEMBER quite what it was that drew her into ballet in the first place, but from her first classes at the YMCA in her hometown of Richmond, Virginia, to a small local studio and eventually to the School of Richmond Ballet, something kept her coming back. Despite competing interests in writing and publishing as she got older, she knew she could do those things later in life. Ballet kept winning out.

As a child, Olivia had a very romantic view of ballet, which of course is not unusual. She had a natural aptitude for it—easy flexibility and a dramatic flair—but she always sensed there was more to dance than that. She loved how the physical aspect of continually learning new skills with her body led to endless ways to use steps to express something. "You can always explore more," she said. "You can be interested in ballet with your body, your brain, and your heart."

Olivia went on to dance professionally, first with Tulsa Ballet and then with Atlanta Ballet, but from season to season, her next move was not always clear. She faced rejection and more than once felt the uncertainty of not having a job offer. It shaped her mindset, luring her into a sort of underdog mentality where she seemed only to focus on what hadn't happened for her, what she hadn't achieved.

But one experience helped her find a sense of purpose and self-empowerment. When she was in Atlanta Ballet, the choreographer Craig Davidson cast her in a principal role in his ballet *Remembrance/Hereafter*. The ballet was hard, but Olivia felt trusted. When there was a technical challenge in the choreography, she was given the space to work through it. Olivia felt capable and more in control of her body than ever before. "What Craig did was very special to me. He trusted that I could do it, so I did. And if I couldn't do something at first, he said, 'OK, figure it out,' and would move on. I was able to rise," she remembered.

This 2018 photograph of Olivia in *Remembrance/Hereafter,* mid-grand jeté, is more than a beautiful moment of dance. It represents Olivia's powers both physically and spiritually, and what she considers the triumph of her life in ballet. "I loved to jump and always considered that one of my strengths. For Gene to have captured me doing a grand jeté, one of my favorite steps in one of my favorite moments in the ballet . . . it was incredibly meaningful to me. I don't have many photos of me dancing, and this is the only one I have ever hung on my wall."

Olivia retired in 2020. Her last performance, in an excerpt from a ballet choreographed by Juliano Nuñes in which she had the rare opportunity to dance a lyrical role, was not supposed to be her farewell. The occasion was an Atlanta Ballet gala, as festive and celebratory as a tribute to her career should have been. She turned to her partner, Jacob Bush, afterward. "I said to Jacob, 'Even if we never end up performing the full ballet, I'm glad I got to do this with you.' I must have had some sense . . . and of course, it was the last performance I had."

Shortly after that performance, Olivia was considering a move to another company when theaters went dark due to the COVID-19 pandemic. Day-to-day life as a dancer had become increasingly hard, as it inevitably does, and the timing seemed right to make a life change. Olivia decided to retire. She started teaching ballet but also discovered an interest in the nonprofit sector. She found work in donor management, where her boss called her the

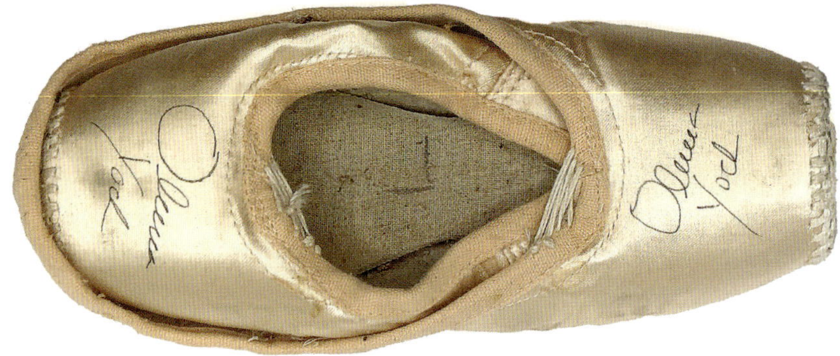

Olivia Yoch's signed pointe shoes.

most detail-oriented person they'd worked with in forty years, and has balanced her career with parenting her two children. Both roles play up Olivia's analytical skills, something she hopes to use back in the dance studio someday as a rehearsal director. But for now, she said, "Life has been good to me."

Olivia recognizes that it was the times of friction and roadblocks that shaped her career and brought out her strengths. "When one director didn't renew my contract, at the time I was angry—but now I'm grateful, because it was so helpful in finding my next steps. I felt like people were continually saying *no* to me and I had to work so hard to change that to a *yes*. I was always struggling to attain the next thing I wanted. I'm proud that I didn't give up, and that I kept going, and working, and asking, until the *no* turned into the *yes* that I wanted."

3-26-18

O Y B

Dear Gene,

I was both mystified and delighted to receive your package in the mail. Your photos breathe with life, and, yes, those were all of me. I am flattered and touched that you took the time to send me these treasures with such a thoughtful note. From the bottom of my heart, thank you. Thank you for the photos, your sweet words, and especially for your time. You made me feel so special. I will treasure them always!

Sincerely, Olivia

Handwritten note from Olivia Yoch to Gene Schiavone.

Olivia is one of the very few dancers who Gene photographed but never met. He described how a single performance and the beauty of pure chance brought them together nonetheless.

"Sadly, professional ballet dancers rarely receive photographs of themselves," he recalled. "It's not unusual for some to end their career with no tangible evidence of the beauty they created. When reviewing work at the end of a performance, I sometimes select an image or two to print for a dancer. Such was the case on March 15th, 2018, after photographing an Atlanta Ballet performance. Although the dancer in the photo I chose was unknown to me, by carefully studying the cast directory and program I later identified who I thought she might be. During intermission that evening, I wandered through the lobby and randomly purchased a pair of signed pointe shoes from the company's gift boutique. I believe it was serendipity to later discover they belonged to Olivia Yoch, the dancer in the photos. I sent her the prints and received this lovely note in return."

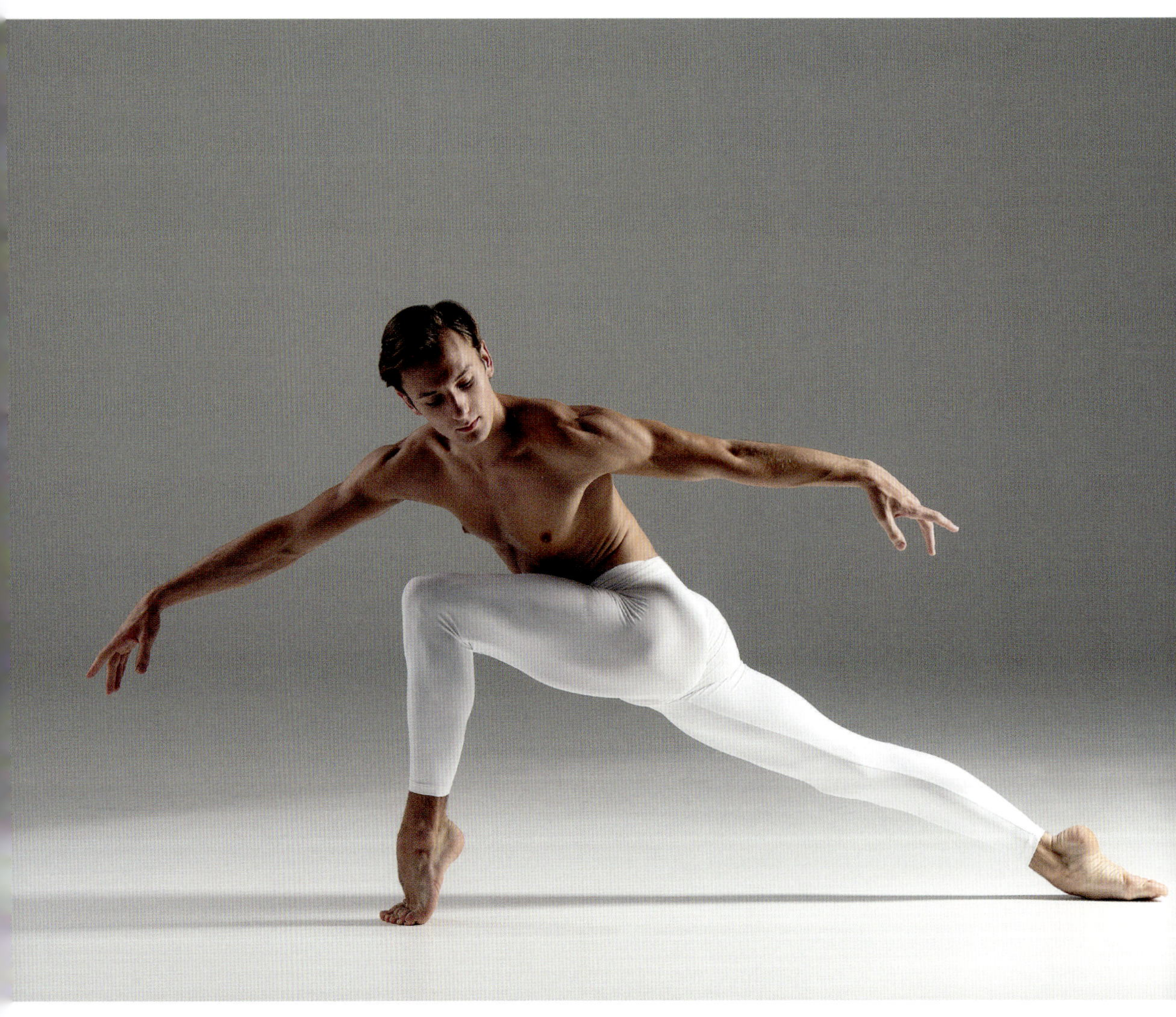

Jacob Hughes, 2014.

JACOB HUGHES

I don't know why I was so critical of myself.
It's like I was blind.

WHEN YOU'RE TRAINING to be a ballet dancer, you're always told to do more. More turnout, more extension, more arch, more stretch. No one ever—or rarely—says, "Lower that leg," or "Can you turn out less?" During Jacob's six years with Sarasota Ballet, he worked hard. Really hard. Rehearsals ran from 9 to 5, and he did Pilates, gym workouts, and extra classes during his off time. He was at the top of his game, but somehow still felt that he was not measuring up. His focus was on what he lacked, what was wrong.

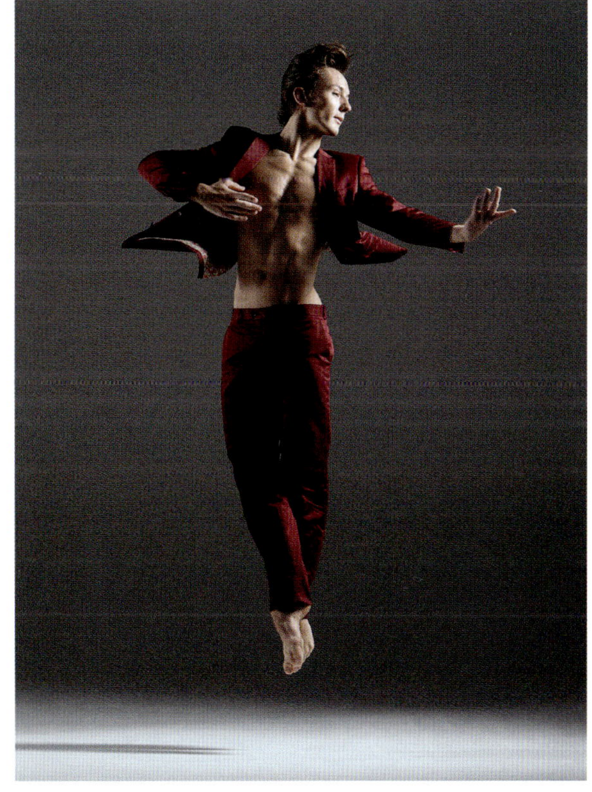

Jacob Hughes, 2014.

And then came a severe ankle sprain. The forced downtime was an eye opener. With an unfamiliar sense of freedom, Jacob explored Florida, where he'd lived for years but hardly knew, and realized something needed to change. "I wasn't living my life," he remembered. "I still loved dance and wanted to be onstage, but something had to be different."

When Jacob recovered, he seized a chance to make that change in a big way by auditioning for *Phantom of the Opera*—the Copenhagen production—and landed the job. Going into musical theater from classical ballet was a big gear-shift, but the differences between those two worlds revealed where his frustration and sense of "not enough" had come from. In doing eight shows a week of the same choreography (unless

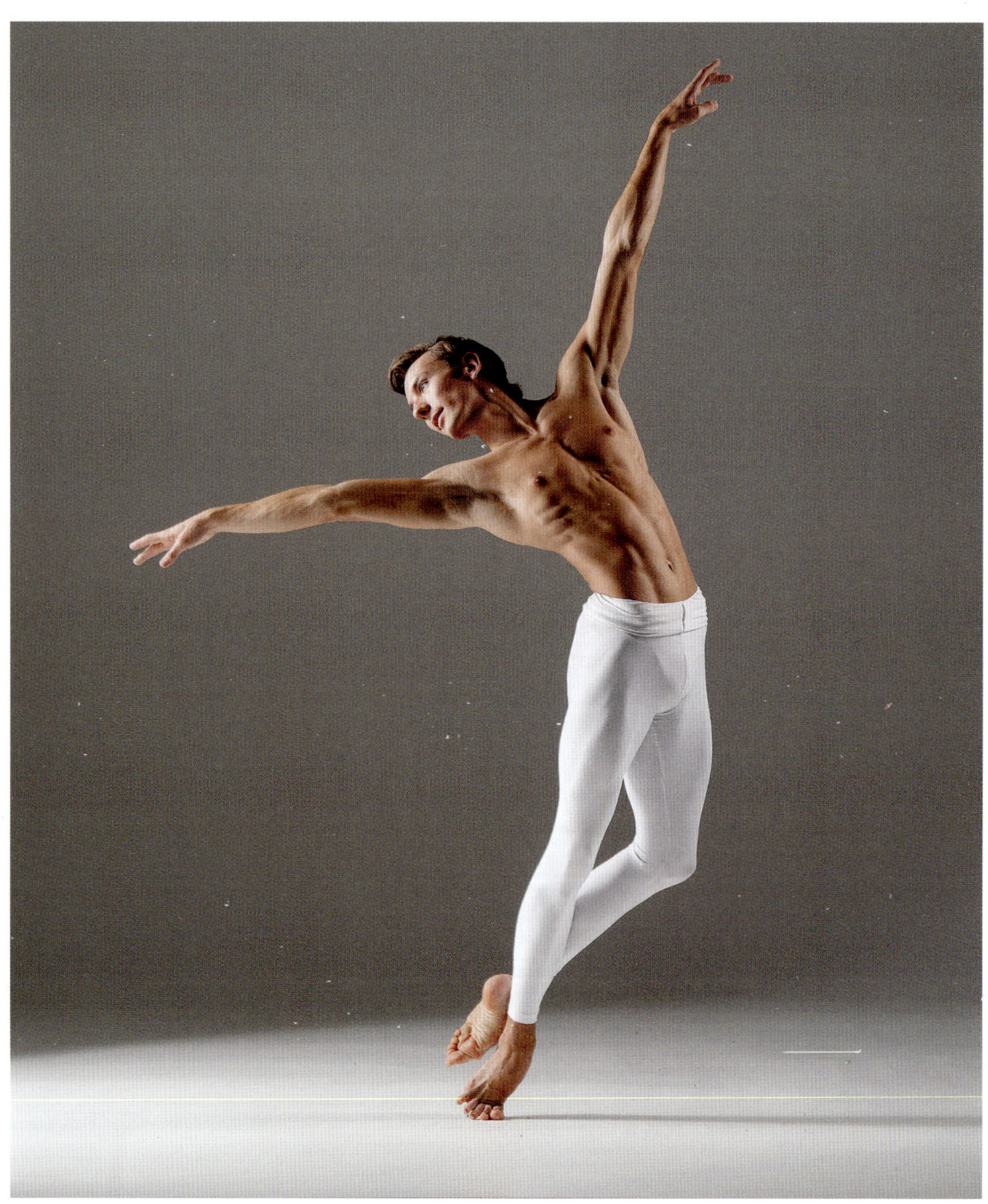

Jacob Hughes, 2014.

he was called on to step into another dancer's track), week after week, he found freedom, not drudgery or boredom. The repetition was the base from which he could experiment night after night, knowing that tomorrow was another chance to try a new angle to his character, add new flair to his choreography, tweak the way he interacted with the rest of the cast. He shifted from a "play it safe" mindset to a "say yes and give it a go" attitude. "I approach life as a dancer differently now. When I'm onstage, I'll try anything. There's a moment in the show when we can basically improvise, and if someone asks me to try some crazy pirouette, I'll say okay. It doesn't matter if it goes wrong. Tomorrow's another day and another show. I'm happier knowing I tried."

Jacob's hyper-criticism didn't completely go away, but his self-perception changed. He reminds himself that he is capable, ready, and that much of a dancer's career is out of their control. "I don't regret anything about my ballet career," he said. "I wouldn't do anything more or differently. I worked really hard and was really hard on myself, thinking it wasn't enough—but it was. And if anyone wasn't happy with it, then that's their own fault for being blind to it. Analyzing yourself in the mirror every day, you always want to do more, be more. But photos capture a fleeting moment that you can't see in a mirror. They show that you *are* achieving it."

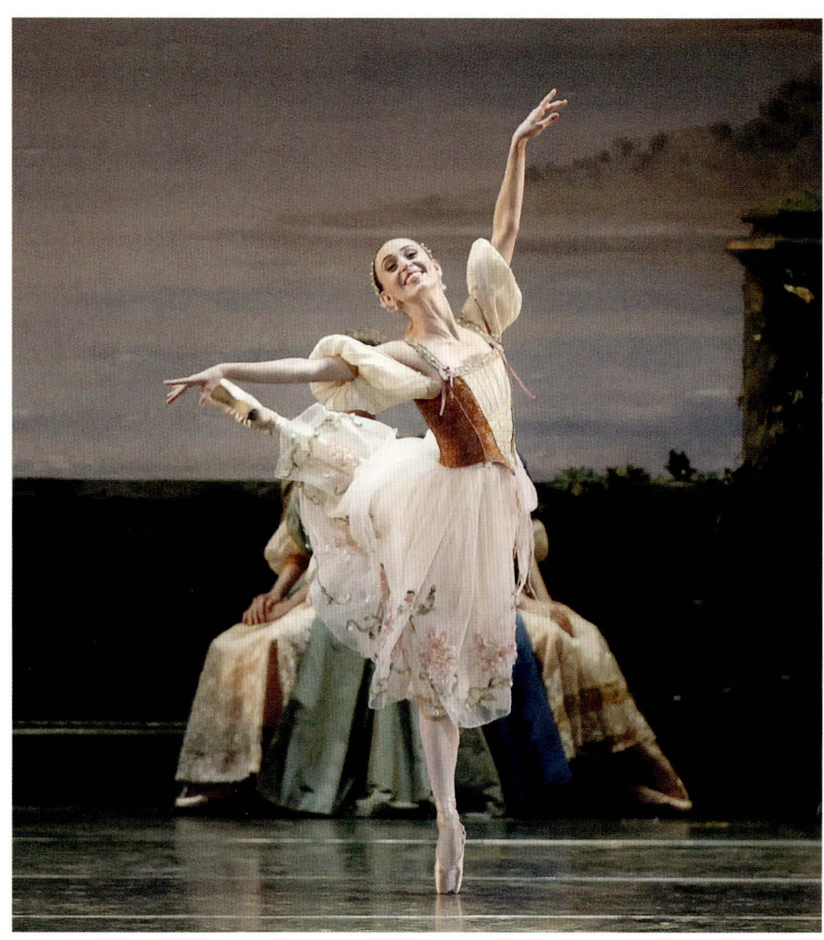

Skylar Brandt in *La Bayadère,* 2014.
Photo courtesy of American Ballet Theatre.

SKYLAR BRANDT

Looking back at the photos from years ago, I can see that I've made strides in my technique, my aesthetic. I still have a ways to go, but I can appreciate the timeline of my progression.

FROM HER VANTAGE POINT on the glittering roster of American Ballet Theatre principals, Skylar still feels the amazement of living her childhood dream. As an eight-year-old, Skylar had devised her plan: she'd train hard, get into ABT's junior company, then become an apprentice and work her way up to principal status. She never doubted that she'd see her plan through, but she also didn't anticipate how much more there was to success than just working hard. When she joined ABT II (as the junior company was called at the time) in 2009 at just sixteen, she was younger than most of the other members. As a self-described "innocent, sheltered kid who loved ballet," it was a jolt to have to suddenly grow up, fast. ABT II toured internationally and operated much like any professional company, but Skylar had never traveled anywhere without her family. She wanted to fit in but felt awkward, uncomfortable, and insecure as the youngest in the group. "Those couple of years makes a big difference," she remembered. "Getting comfortable took some faking. Eventually I realized that you don't need to fit into a box. Just be who you want to be." And that's what Skylar has held true to ever since.

Skylar's talent and strength quickly caught attention, and standout opportunities started coming her way soon after she became an ABT apprentice at seventeen. In those early years of trying to establish herself, her characteristic determination was her weapon against inexperience. She knew she could handle the bigger roles she wanted so badly but hadn't anticipated that working her way up the ladder took more than talent, ability, and readiness. "As self-critical as I am, I felt ready for the responsibilities," she said. "But not how challenging it would be to get where I wanted to go."

A ballet company is just that: a company, with structures, hierarchy, and complexities that can often feel they have less to do with art than with the

Skylar Brandt with ABT coach Franco De Vita, 2005.

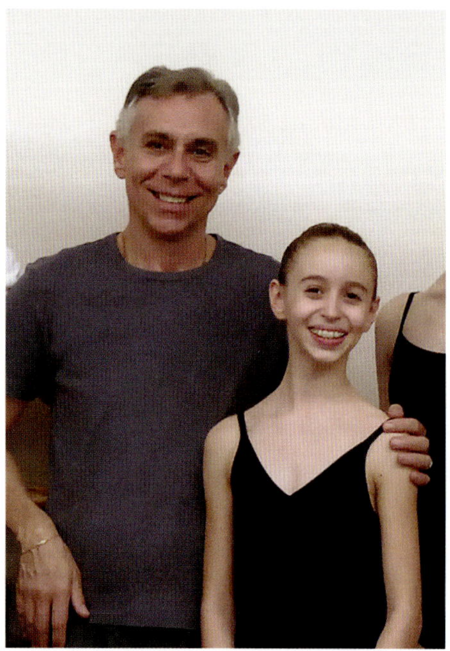

business. And in a company like ABT where every dancer has star potential, excellent dancing is just one part of the job. Skylar began learning about the politics of a ballet company, where the meritocracy she wanted to believe in wasn't always the model. "ABT has the best dancers in the world," she said. "I had to learn to advocate for myself, because if I didn't, nobody was going to push me forward."

As a very quick study with rock-solid technique and natural artistry who stayed calm under pressure, Skylar was a go-to when casting emergencies arose. Her first performances of several major roles happened because she was tapped to fill in for an injured dancer at the last minute. She learned *Le Corsaire* (her first full-length ballet) in three days and was thrilled to have been chosen, but she soon saw a pattern happening. "I was only going onstage in emergencies," she said. "And I didn't want to build my career based on my friends' misfortunes."

Gratitude and excitement for the big opportunities that came her way—despite the sting of not being cast in those roles in the first place—kept Skylar going for a while. But as she accumulated more and more repertoire

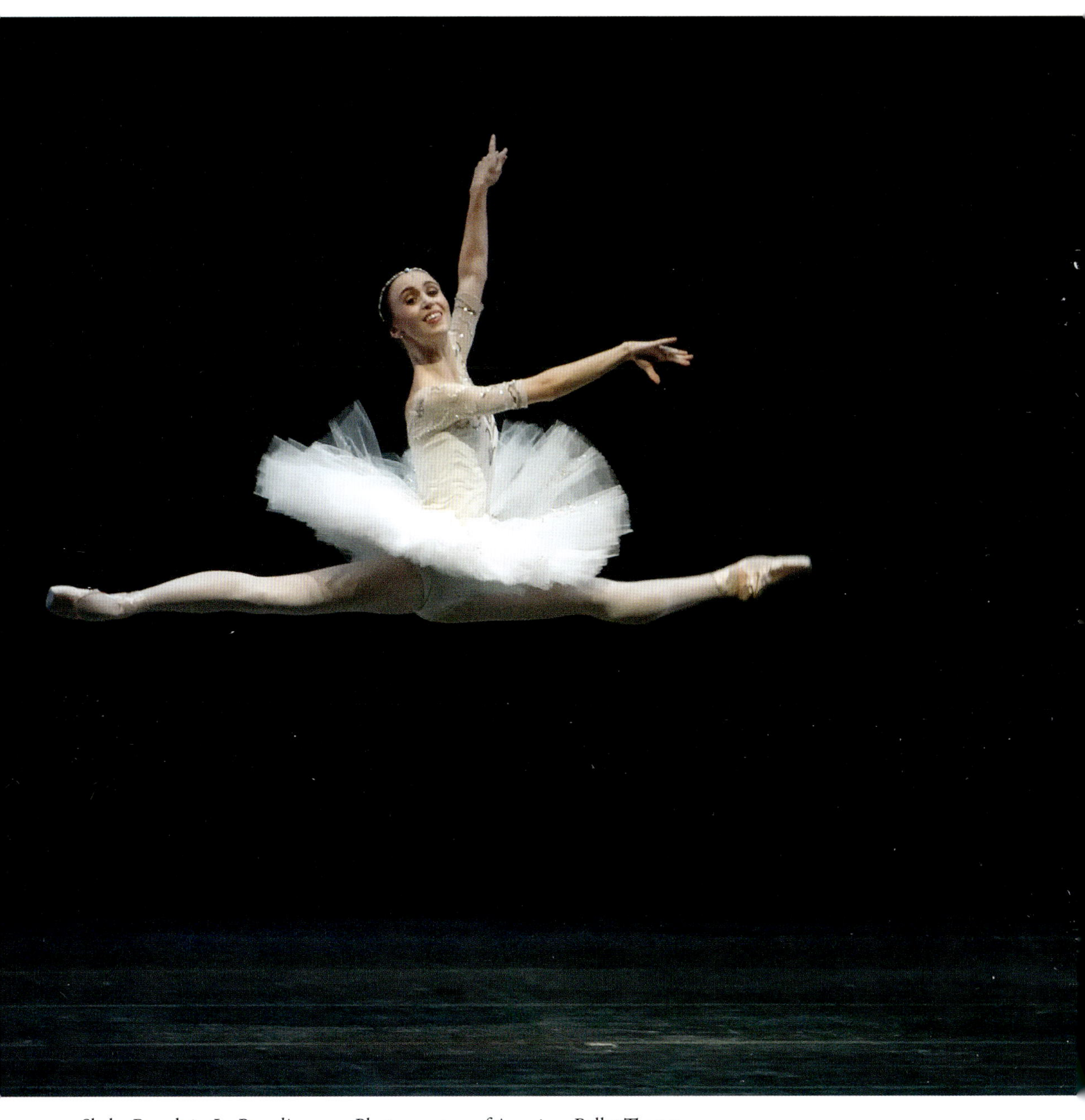

Skylar Brandt in *La Bayadère,* 2015. Photo courtesy of American Ballet Theatre.

and accolades for her pinch-hitting successes, a bit of indignation crept in. She felt she deserved to be chosen in advance, instead of as a second thought. The diligence and obedience entrenched in the silent art form of ballet conflicted with Skylar's frustrations, but she still hesitated, not wanting to be seen as pushy.

Throughout her corps and soloist years, Skylar had regular end-of-season meetings with Kevin McKenzie, ABT's then-artistic director. Hoping to be chosen for leading roles, instead of landing them in the next emergency casting situation, she'd ask if there were any ballets she should work on by herself during the company's layoff, in preparation for the following season. Usually she'd get an encouraging but nonspecific response. But finally one year, McKenzie indicated that the title role in *Giselle* was likely in her future. She was thrilled, and rehearsed herself to the point of stage-readiness. But when the season began, she wasn't cast. Finally, she spoke up. "I went and asked Kevin to reconsider. There was one performance without a name yet, and I asked if that could be mine. And it was."

That was a turning point in Skylar's career. From then on, she started making her feelings known more often, ignoring any of her previous doubts about using her voice. But she did so in her own way, with appreciation for the complexities of a large company, so it felt right. "I'm not the person to kick and scream," she said. "If you don't ask, you don't get, but there's a way to do it that is respectful, professional, and exhibits the integrity you want to maintain. And Kevin understood. That's why we had mutual respect, openness, and honesty."

Skylar doesn't take for granted that her voyage to ABT principal has been relatively smooth—a supportive family, excellent training, a natural facility for ballet—but she wants people to know that even for someone who appears to have it all, she's just as human as anyone else. Well aware of how many aspiring young dancers are watching her, she says they should know that everyone has days when they're unmotivated, exhausted, and would rather relax than go to class. But going to the studio when it feels extra hard builds the mental stamina you'll need to perform under difficult circumstances. And not every day brings big gains. "I think it's comforting to know that even your worst rehearsal day is making you better. You can always learn something, even if it's just one small thing from a two-hour rehearsal. It's still worthwhile."

As a top-tier dancer, Skylar is familiar with the specific kind of pressure that comes from being there. The expectation—especially for a dancer known for astounding technical feats—to always be "on" is an ironic hardship, but it's real. Skylar knows now that machine-like consistency is unrealistic and, ultimately, not desirable. The most important thing is always artistry.

"Even though I work every day to be more flexible, to jump higher and turn more, I feel at peace knowing that those abilities are really not the most important qualities. I hope other dancers, younger ones especially, understand that what's really important is artistic expression. Being a storyteller is what inspired me to be a ballet dancer, and what I look forward to developing as the years go on. I want to take on more roles, more challenges, explore my artistic range and depth. For the rest of my career, I will always be searching for more."

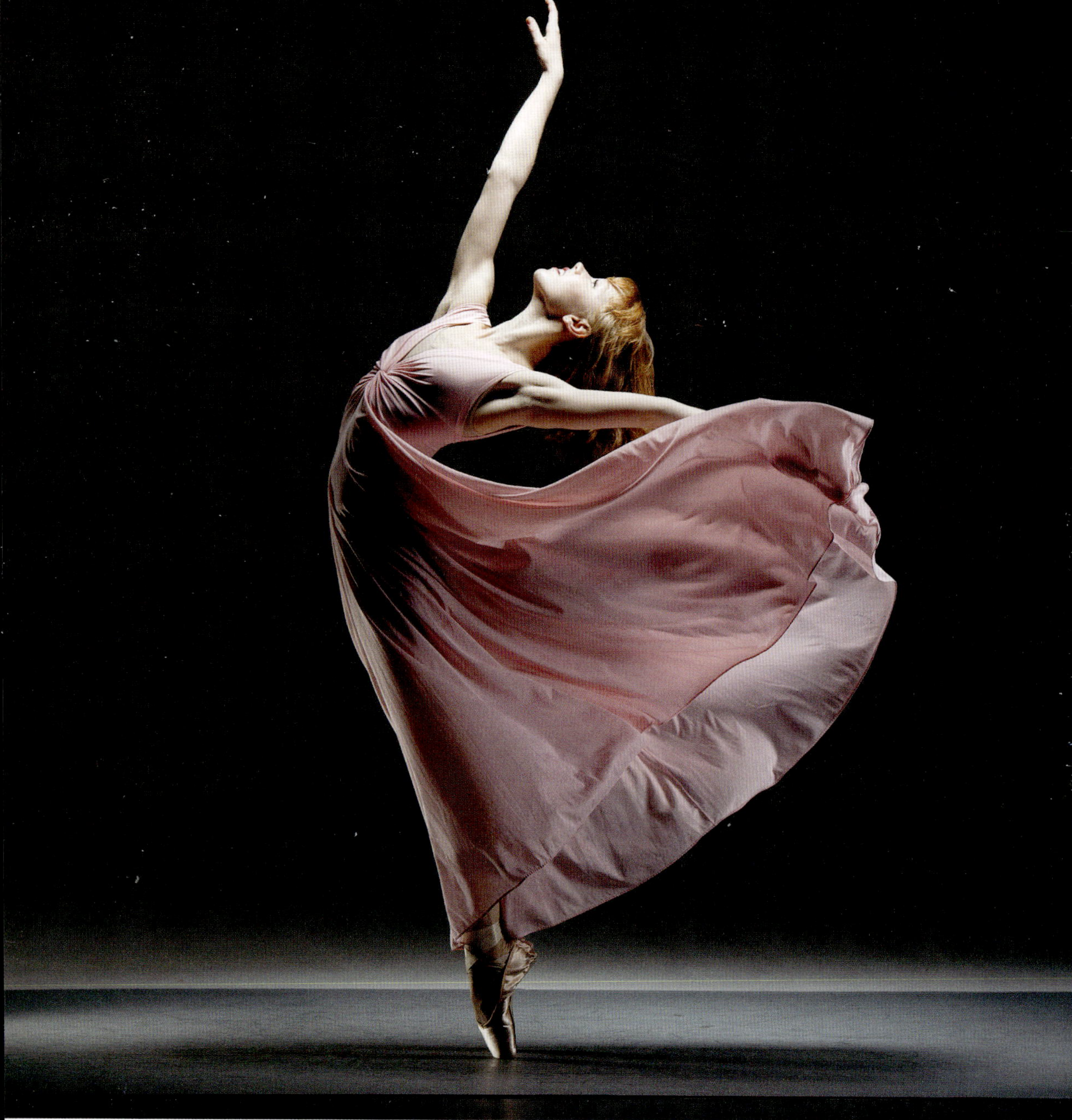

Kylie Edwards, 2015.

KYLIE EDWARDS

In acting, the sense of competition is very different from ballet. Everyone is so individual that there's no way you can really compete for anything. That total and complete self-acceptance is a different foundation from the ballet identity, where it's really difficult to be your own authentic self.

KYLIE IS A TRIPLE THREAT who's performed on stage and screen in productions ranging from *Anastasia* and *An American in Paris* to *The Marvelous Mrs. Maisel, The Gilded Age,* and *Law and Order,* but classical ballet was her first love. It took years for her to listen to the whispers in her head saying that it was okay to take her self-described "leap of faith" away from her ballet foundation, but her taste for drama and flair for becoming someone else in front of the camera were always there. Now, "it's like living my dream."

It all started with the Barbie *Nutcracker.* Like so many little girls, Kylie watched the movie over and over until her parents enrolled her in ballet classes at Vermont Ballet Theater near their home in Essex Junction, Vermont. Real-life ballet was just as engrossing to Kylie as the Barbie version. "It just clicked," she remembered. "I think I knew I was serious about ballet because I kept choosing it over anything else. It wasn't forced. It was my identity, my life, my purpose." Kylie spent hours watching ballet videos on YouTube, where she discovered that one of her favorite dancers, ballerina Whitney Jensen, had trained with the famous coach Valentina Kozlova. With the dream of following in Jensen's footsteps, Kylie spent the next two summers at Kozlova's elite school in New York City, immersed in Vaganova technique and taking additional classes in contemporary dance, Russian language and culture, even rhythmic gymnastics. The atmosphere was strict but nurturing, and Kylie wanted nothing else.

When Kozlova explained that if she wanted a chance at a ballet career, Kylie needed to keep up high-level training, Kylie spent her freshman year of high school commuting between Vermont and New York to continue

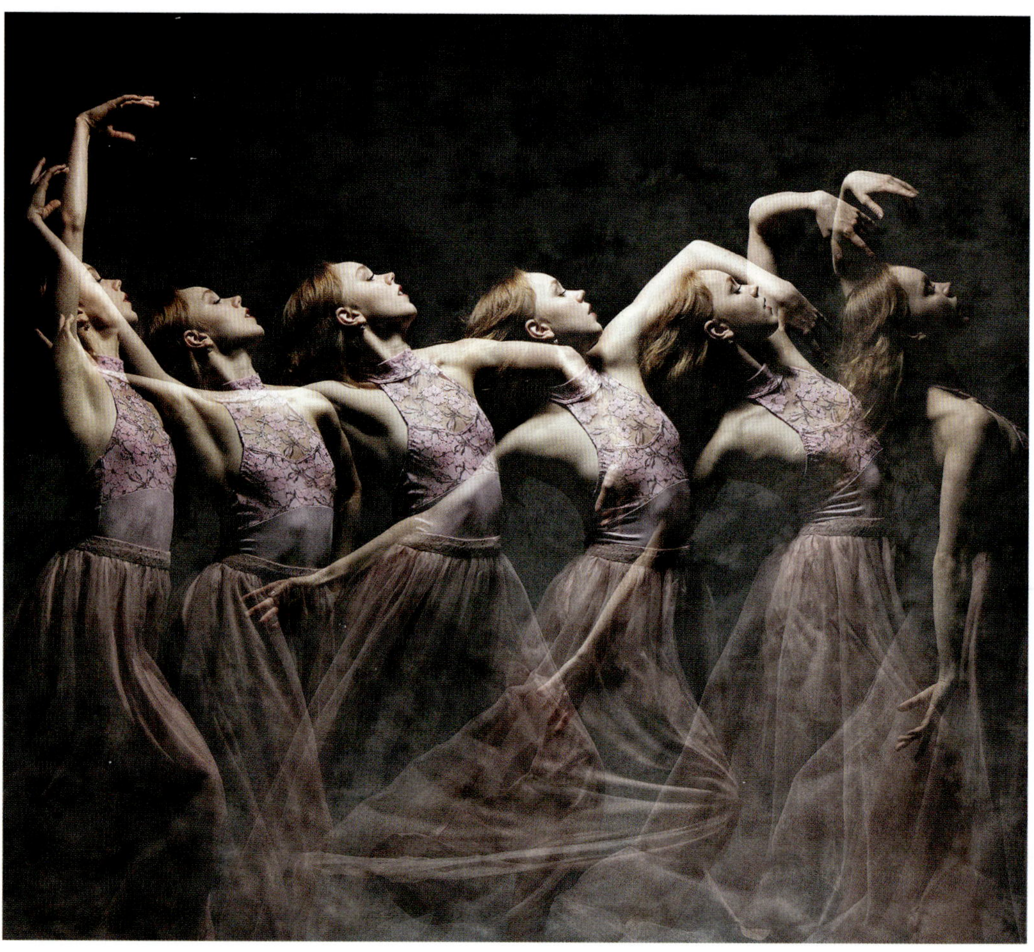

Kylie Edwards, 2017.

studying with her. Within the next year, Kylie moved on her own to New York.

The next couple of years were heady and exciting, but also hard. Kylie roomed with another ballet student and a chaperone, enrolled at the Professional Children's School for academics, and danced every day at Valentina Kozlova's Dance Conservatory of New York. It was everything she wanted, but the arrangement soon put a strain on her always-supportive parents. If Kylie was to stay in New York, they had to find a more financially feasible way to do it. While she was devastated to leave Kozlova's school, Kylie

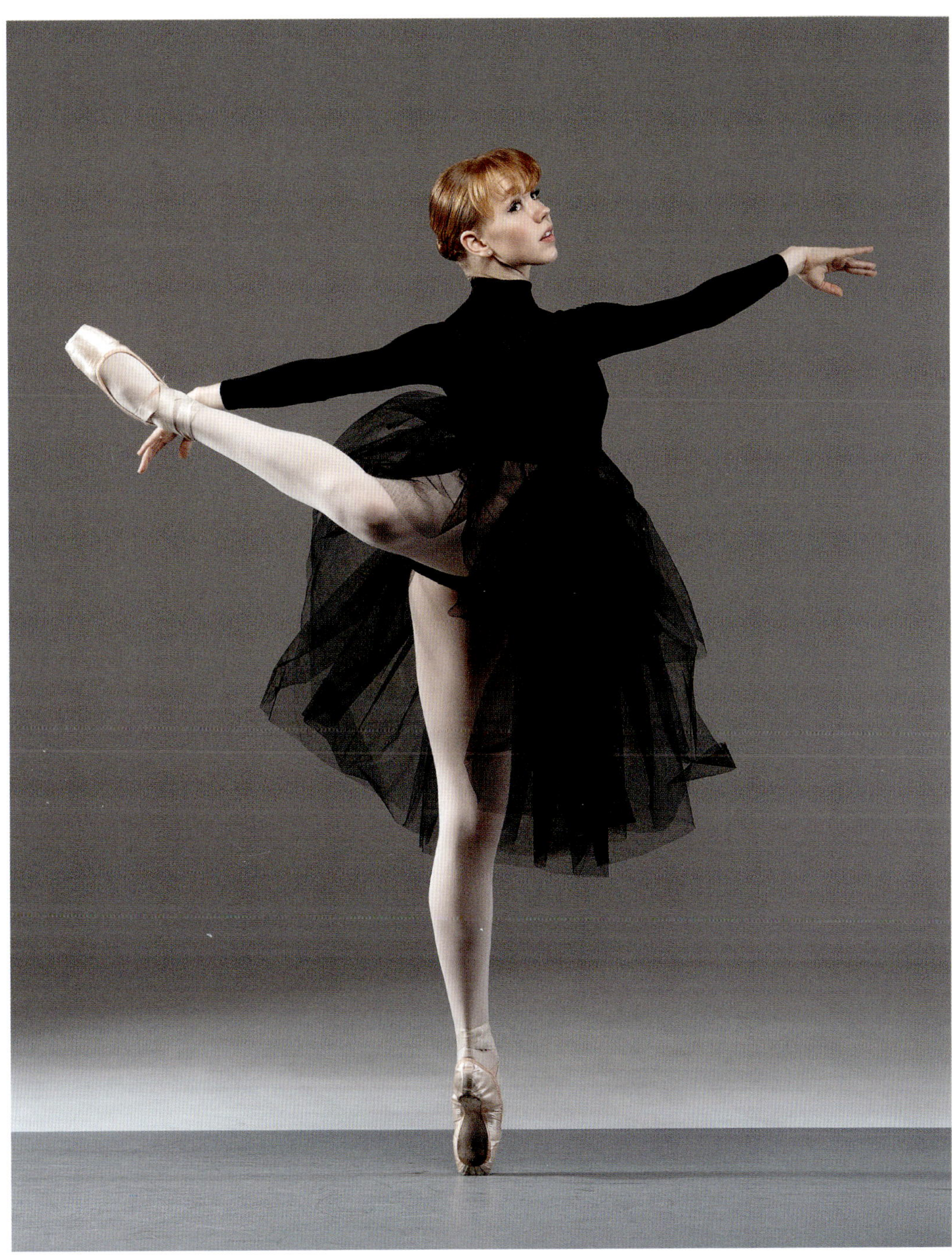

Kylie Edwards, 2015.

understood. She switched to the more affordable but no less rigorous SLK Ballet, run by Sara Knight, who became something of a mother figure to Kylie.

After her high school graduation, Kylie deferred her college acceptances (highly driven academically, she'd applied to pre–physical therapy programs), giving herself a year to stay in New York, keep training at SLK, and focus 100 percent on landing a ballet company job. Her plan worked, and Kylie was offered a corps position with City Ballet of San Diego for the following season.

But during that time, and without hedging on her determination to dance professionally, Kylie felt a flicker of curiosity about alternatives. Throughout her high school years in New York, she'd taken some private lessons with another famous ballerina that she'd revered since childhood, Irina Dvorovenko. Irina, who'd segued her own ballet career into stage and screen acting, was appearing in a revival of *On Your Toes* when she coached Kylie. The two had developed a close mentor–mentee relationship when Irina suggested that Kylie consider Broadway herself. The "ballet blinders" were too strong for Kylie to make a pivot, but before heading to San Diego to start her ballet career and with Irina as her role model, she did connect with a theatrical agent and audition for a few Broadway shows that featured ballet, like *Phantom of the Opera.*

During Kylie's first season with City Ballet of San Diego, she danced her first Balanchine ballet, *La Source,* experienced getting thrown into a part at the last minute—and juggled ballet dancer life with periodic flights back to New York when the agency lined up show auditions. Edging into the theater world triggered memories of Kylie's childhood loves of movies and soundtracks, school chorus and plays. Ballet overshadowed it all, but her itch for theatrics never left.

At the end of her first season in San Diego, Kylie was offered and accepted a contract to return for another one. With a free summer before the next season was to start, she returned to New York to take dance classes and be ready for any theater auditions that might come up. She got a part-time job working the front desk at a physical therapy clinic that treated lots of Broadway performers and threw herself into contemporary, jazz, and theater classes at Broadway Dance Center, which she describes as a "crash course" in different dance styles. She felt the pull of this new world she was becoming part of, where the structure and strict aesthetics of ballet fell away. Kylie's confidence grew, as did her curiosity to see whether she could be more than a dancer who acted. Boldly, she started auditioning for nondancing projects instead of only those calling specifically for ballet dancer types. When she returned to San Diego at summer's end, something didn't feel right anymore. "It was a complete leap of faith, to be perfectly honest," she said, thinking about the day she made her big decision. "I went into the artistic director's office to tell her, 'I love being here, but I think I need to be in New York and pursue theater.'" The company's director was supportive, and Kylie moved back to New York, permanently this time.

Auditions became a regular part of Kylie's daily life, but in an unexpectedly positive way. The different balance of agency and vulnerability in an actor's life versus a dancer's took away much of the sting of rejection she'd felt in the ballet world. The motivation was different, too. Ballet auditions felt inherently competitive, but in the theater world, Kylie realized that being better than anyone else wasn't the point. "Even if someone looks like me or has a similar background, what we bring to a part will differ. It can be liberating, and for me as a ballerina going into that space, it was also scary. But it's been a wonderful exercise in relinquishing control, and every time I do it, it gets easier."

Kylie felt a hint of how she might evolve from ballet dancer to actor way back when she did her first photo shoots with Gene. During her ballet training years in New York, Kylie (an avid American Ballet Theatre fan) needed photos for the company auditions she was planning to do. She'd seen Gene's photos and although she was intimidated, she decided to contact the person who'd photographed her idols. But Kylie felt completely at ease at Gene's studio, where he put on show tunes instead of classical music and encouraged her to try multiple costumes and outfits, stretching her imagination to create dramatic, cinematic poses and scenes. She felt the freedom of choice and creative input to become a character, something she'd never felt in the ballet studio, where critique and judgment were more dominant.

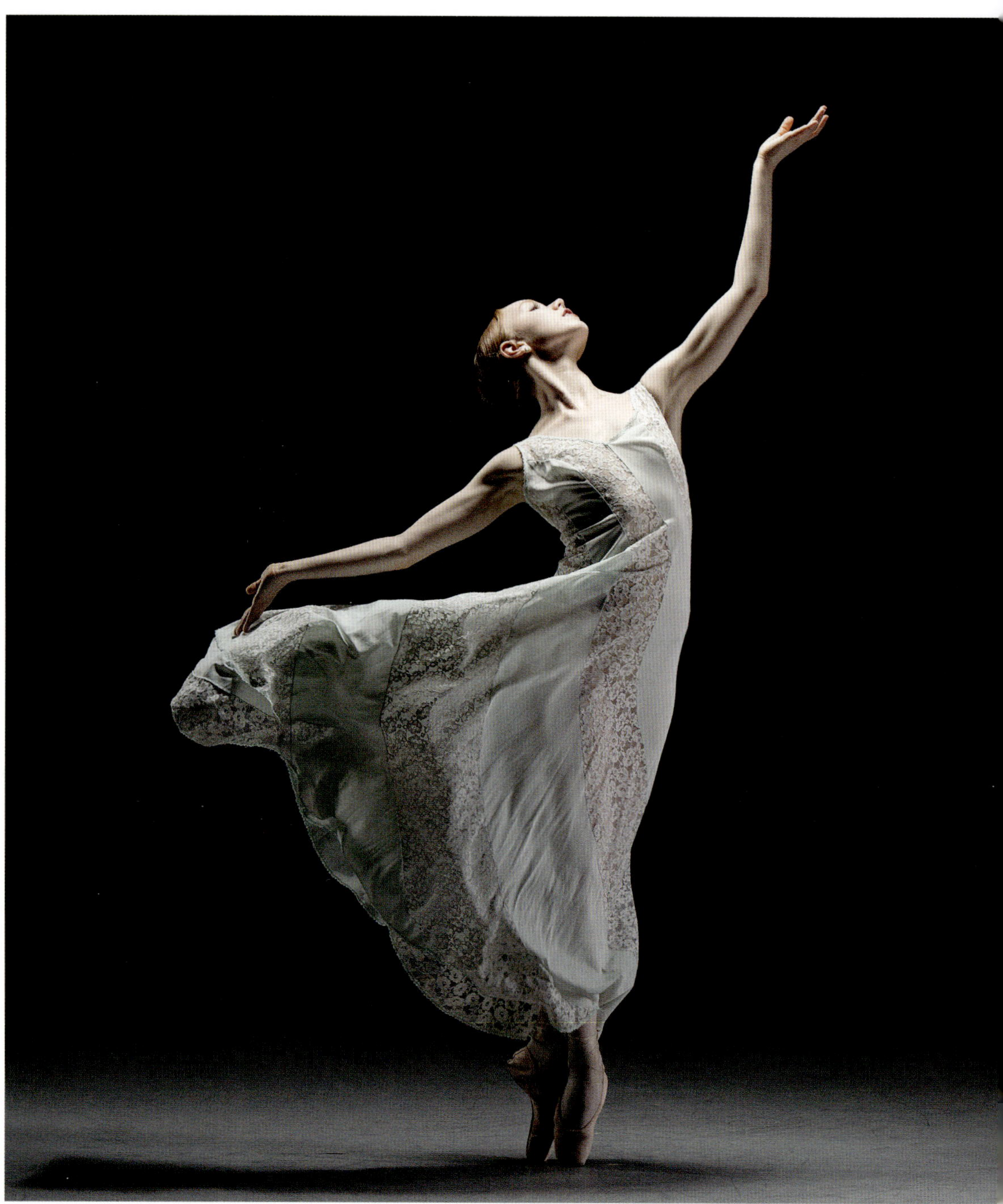

Kylie Edwards, 2016.

The two did more shoots together over the next few years, each one like a milepost marker along the way from Kylie's shift from a pinpointed focus on ballet to a wider vision of herself as an actor. "I was able to find, refine, and be the fullest version of myself," she said. "There are not a lot of places that give you that much space artistically."

Kylie still sometimes has the urge to take ballet class, but not being at her previous skill level is painful, even though she knows that what she's doing now is, for her, a richer and fuller life. Self-reflection is necessary to be a great actor, and Kylie's perspective on the script of her life so far is useful for anyone looking at their own. She recognizes how scary it is to question yourself when you've already gone so far down a specific road, and that veering off could be seen by others as a failure or quitting. "We're so committed to the pride of hard work that for a long time, I did feel like I was giving up," Kylie said. "But I was actually seeing shades of who I am. Because now, I'm first and foremost an actor who happens to have a strong background in classical ballet. It feels like a secret weapon now, rather than one I'm holding against myself."

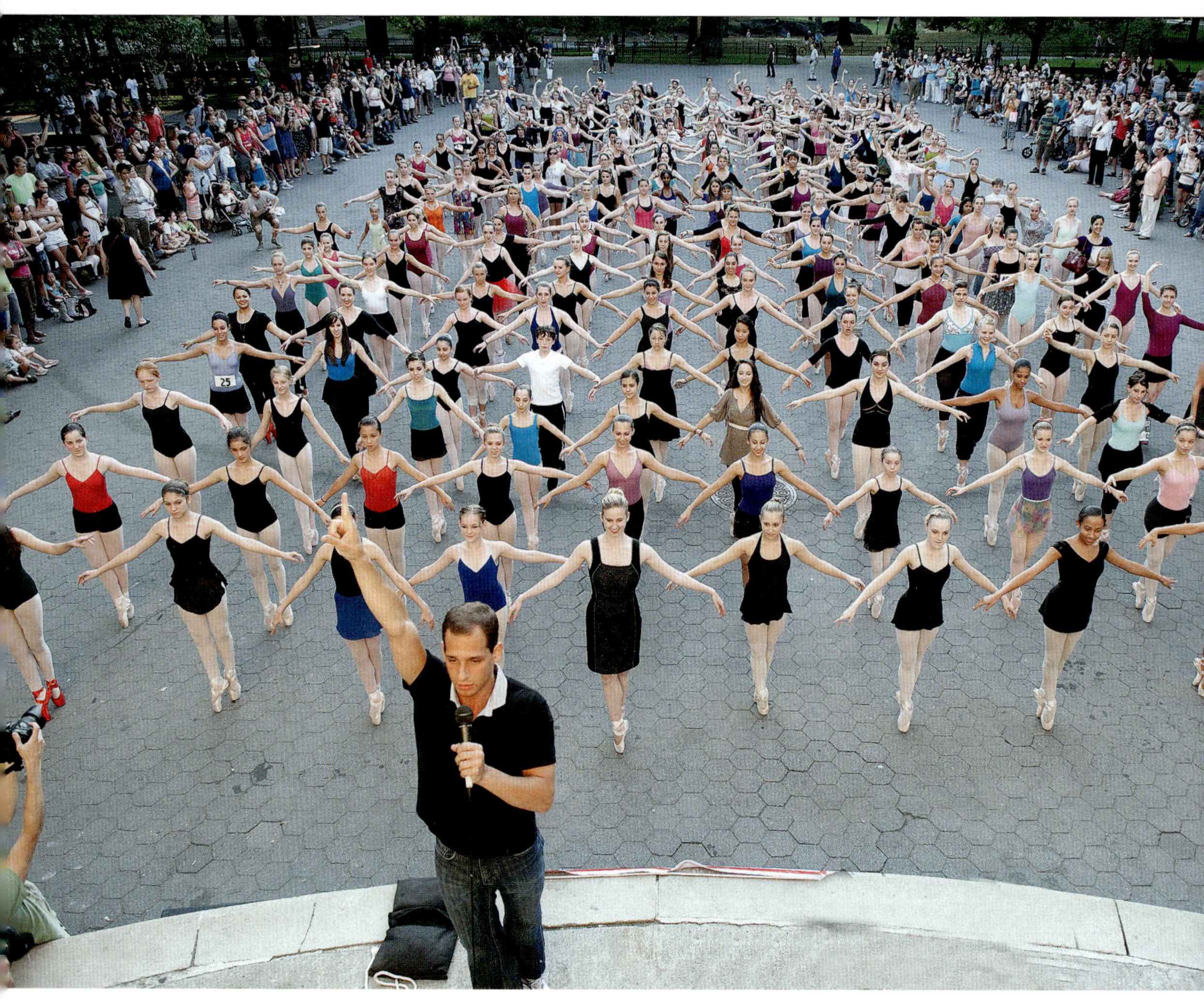

Craig Salstein leading dancers to set the Guinness Book of World Records for most ballerinas on pointe, Central Park, 2019.

CRAIG SALSTEIN

For me, dance is like Camus's myth of Sisyphus. It's a task that you have to do every day. You can either fall in love with the task and all its nooks and crannies, or go out hating it. But I think you have to accept it and do it. And that's your reward.

ON AUGUST 2, 2010, Craig stood on the stage of the Central Park bandshell, looking out over a gathering of more than 200 dancers. They were there to break the Guinness Book of World Records for "The Most Ballerinas On Pointe." The day's event was the brainchild of Gene and his wife, Ellen, who'd had the idea to bring together dancers from across the city not just for the thrill of making history, but to showcase and perhaps even reinvigorate the concept of how bonded and tight-knit the dance community is, even across the divides of rank, prestige, fame, achievement, and opportunity. Gene and Ellen decided that the event, which took three years of planning, organizing, recruiting volunteers, and navigating New York City bureaucracy, would also be a fundraiser for the Kips Bay Boys and Girls Club, which sent four young girls from its ballet program to perform.

When asked if he'd emcee the event, Craig enthusiastically agreed, and a more gregarious, energetic, and motivating cheerleader you will never find. He led the eclectic group of dancers—from tiny to retired, beginner to professional, unknown to famous—through a short but just-long-enough-to-qualify-for-the-Guinness-Book's-tabulators pointe combination, and his pride was evident when he was able to announce to the crowd that they'd done it. They'd officially broken the world record and earned a place in the Guinness Book of World Records.

Craig's own performance that day was a triumphant and characteristically generous addition to an illustrious dance career full of experiences and accolades reflecting his unusually wide versatility. Craig grew up in Florida, where he trained at the Ballet Academy of Miami and later at the Miami City Ballet School. His ballet career, first with Miami City Ballet and then as an American Ballet Theatre soloist, later expanded into Broadway and

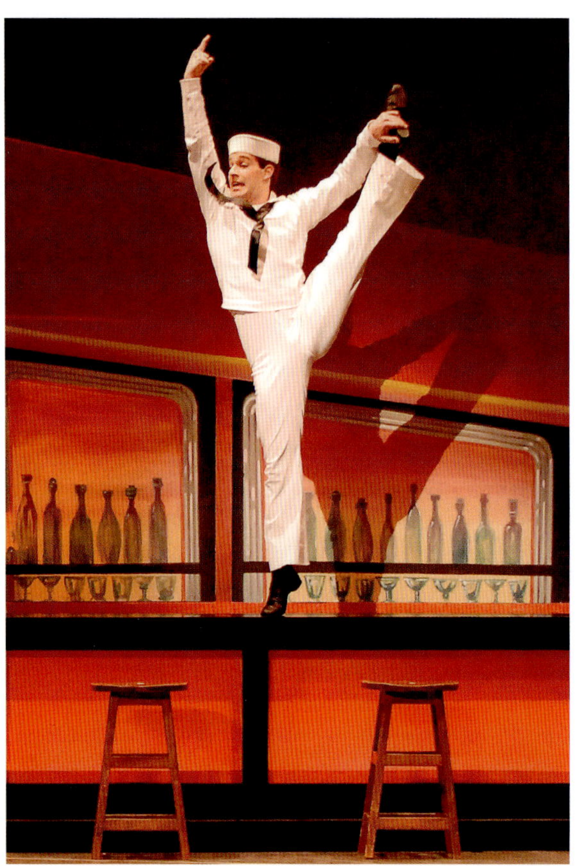

Craig Salstein in *Fancy Free,* 2006. Photo courtesy of American Ballet Theatre.

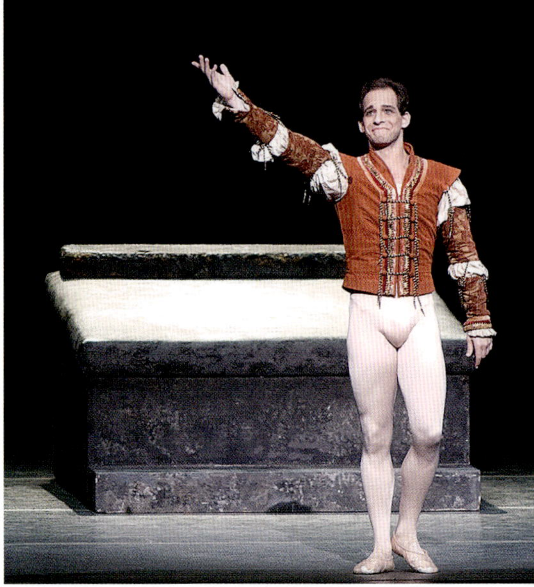

Craig Salstein in *Romeo and Juliet,* 2009. Photo courtesy of American Ballet Theatre.

film, capturing the hearts of a devoted fan base along the way with his charisma, charm, humor, and magnetism.

It's hard to imagine someone like Craig living life anywhere but on the stage. But all performers know that the amount of time and investment they have to put in behind the scenes far outweighs the number of performances they'll ever give, and that the adrenaline rush of showtime never pays lasting dividends. An actor or dancer may love performing, but there has to be more. In a somewhat unusual response to a common question that's surprisingly hard to answer, Craig said that hard work itself, offstage and to no applause, is a big part of his motivation to dance.

"As a kid, I started dancing just because whenever music was on, my body would move," he recalled. "It was like when your parents see that you might need braces, they take you to the orthodontist. They saw me moving around, and said, 'Well, there's this thing called dance, and maybe you should go into it.'" And so he did. But then, he fell in love with the hard work. It felt good, and its satisfaction wasn't dependent on other people liking, necessarily, what he produced. "If you are seen as a hard worker . . ." He laughed. "That's a good thing."

Craig's addiction to putting in the effort was a necessity and an asset in a career that included signature roles that are notoriously difficult, including the Bronze Idol in *La Bayadère, Fancy Free,* and Mercurio in *Romeo and Juliet.* Challenge was something he faced constantly, which may be why he's so frank about what he says were his, and most performers', constant companions: dread, nervousness, and the hope to do well with no guarantee that you will. He took solace in knowing that if he was feeling those fears, others probably were, too. It is a silent, unspoken bond between performers.

After leaving ABT Craig became a sought-after teacher, coach, and artistic collaborator. Although he "sort of" stopped performing in 2018, he was coaxed out of retirement by his frequent colleague, choreographer Justin Peck, to dance in Peck's show *Illinoise* in 2023. But even before that, he'd never really quit dancing. For someone like Craig, the compulsion to work one's body is fundamental to life. He loves doing class, he says, even if just a little, so he goes through classwork inspired by his mentor, the late, famous teacher David Howard, every day.

There's a different psychology to having to take class for one's job and doing it purposefully—and alone—for its quiet payoff. That Craig has found the place where satisfaction, pleasure, pain, and effort have called a truce speaks to his philosophical approach to dance and to life. His years circulating through so many parts of the theater world have made him ponder what it is that makes performers tick, and how they cope with the anxieties, insecurities, and metaphorical brick walls they face on a near daily basis.

"You sit in it. You sit with it. Because there's no other way. You can try transcendental meditation, you can try yoga, and to a certain extent, yes, you can sort of silence the voices telling you negative thoughts. But in the end, you have to accept it and keep going. And yes, it's going to sting. I think that's why a lot of people leave the career early. They can't handle the insanity that ensues inside. But you just have to accept it. You have to feel nervous. Radical acceptance. And then you just go out there and do it.

It seems so simple, but it's not."

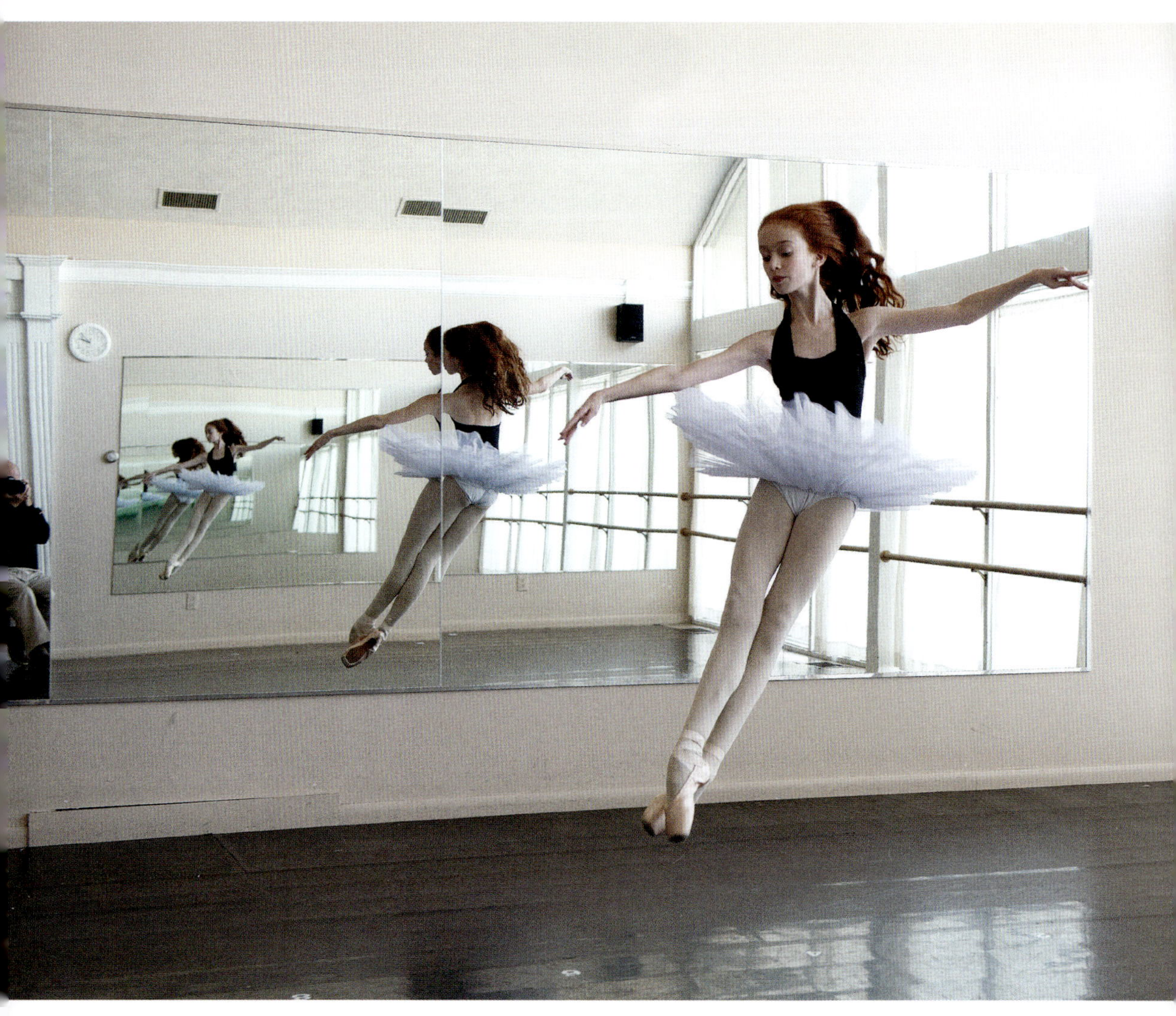

Connor Hamilton, 2014.

CONNOR HAMILTON

I'd never imagined this for myself.

EVEN THOUGH SHE STARTED CLASSES at age two and her father had been a professional dancer, Connor didn't consider ballet as a career for herself. She didn't even like dance all that much, until she was old enough to perform—and from then on, ballet was a compulsion instead of a hobby. But even so, Connor's route to professionalism wasn't immediately clear, even with her talent, family history, and her newfound discovery of how much more there was to ballet than classes and exercises. But she moved from one stepping stone to another, each new phase seemingly inevitable but unforeseen. By the time she became a corps dancer with the National Ballet of Canada, Connor had already felt the fear and pressure of injury, the uncertainty of the job market, and the emotional challenge of becoming an adult when just a teenager.

Connor's family moved around a lot when she was growing up, but her parents made sure she got solid training wherever they were. Her teachers encouraged her to participate in ballet competitions, which fueled her love of the stage and where she regularly placed very high, catching the attention of the many school directors who judged and attended. At thirteen, after a great finish at Youth America Grand Prix, Connor was invited to visit the National Ballet School in Toronto for a test drive. A ballet career still wasn't necessarily her goal, but spending a few days embedded with the NBS students, taking dance classes and sitting in on academics with them, was "insane—in a good way," she remembered. Her life changed from there on out. "It opened up whole new world for me," Connor said. "Even though I was kind of scared and shy, I wanted nothing else but to be there." She enrolled in time to start her eighth-grade year.

Boarding school would be a huge change for any adolescent, and since Connor had been homeschooled up to that point, she was especially nervous about leaving home for Toronto. But her parents made frequent trips

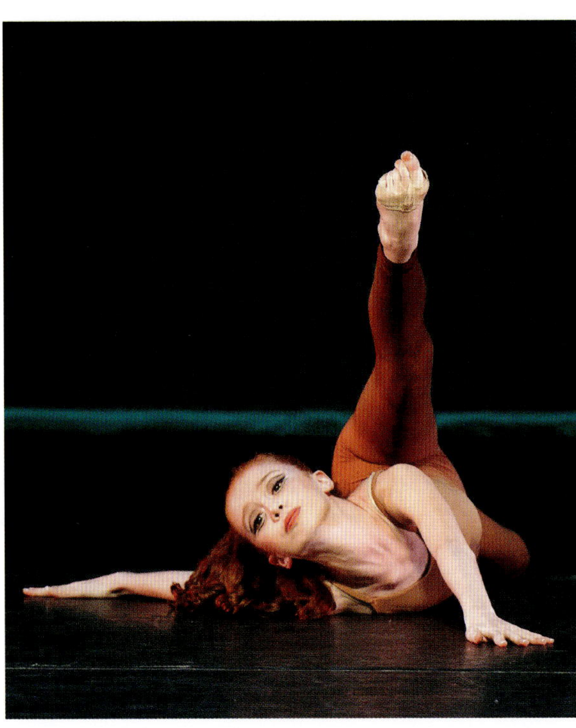

Connor Hamilton, 2015.

to visit, and Connor's roommate in the dormitory became her "best friend for life," as she put it.

Connor and the other students were well taken care of at NBS. The counselors treated them like family, but even so, being so young and away from home, she remembers how intense it all felt. With academics and dance every day from morning until evening, she wavered sometimes, questioning if this was what she really wanted to do. But her doubts were never enough to make her stop. She always knew she'd stick with it.

In her twelfth-grade year, Connor was invited along with a few other dancers from her class to audition for the National Ballet of Canada. She'd been getting positive feedback from the NBS director and faculty but had also been injured recently and was unsure what would happen. Being accepted as an apprentice was an overwhelming relief, but even then, a future with the company wasn't guaranteed. The usual two-year apprenticeship period was extended to three for Connor's cohort because the COVID-19 pandemic stalled their first season, and when it came time for contracts to be offered Connor was again working with an injury, this time a sprained ankle. She remembers that during one of her regular meetings with the artistic staff midway through her final apprentice season, the conversation was not entirely positive. The staff told her she needed to gain a lot of strength. Connor took on the challenge, and by the end of the season, she heard that the company and school directors noticed her progress. She was invited to join the company's corps de ballet.

Connor soon realized that company life poses very different challenges than those faced by a student. Staying inspired through endlessly repetitive days—without individual attention and encouragement from a teacher—was

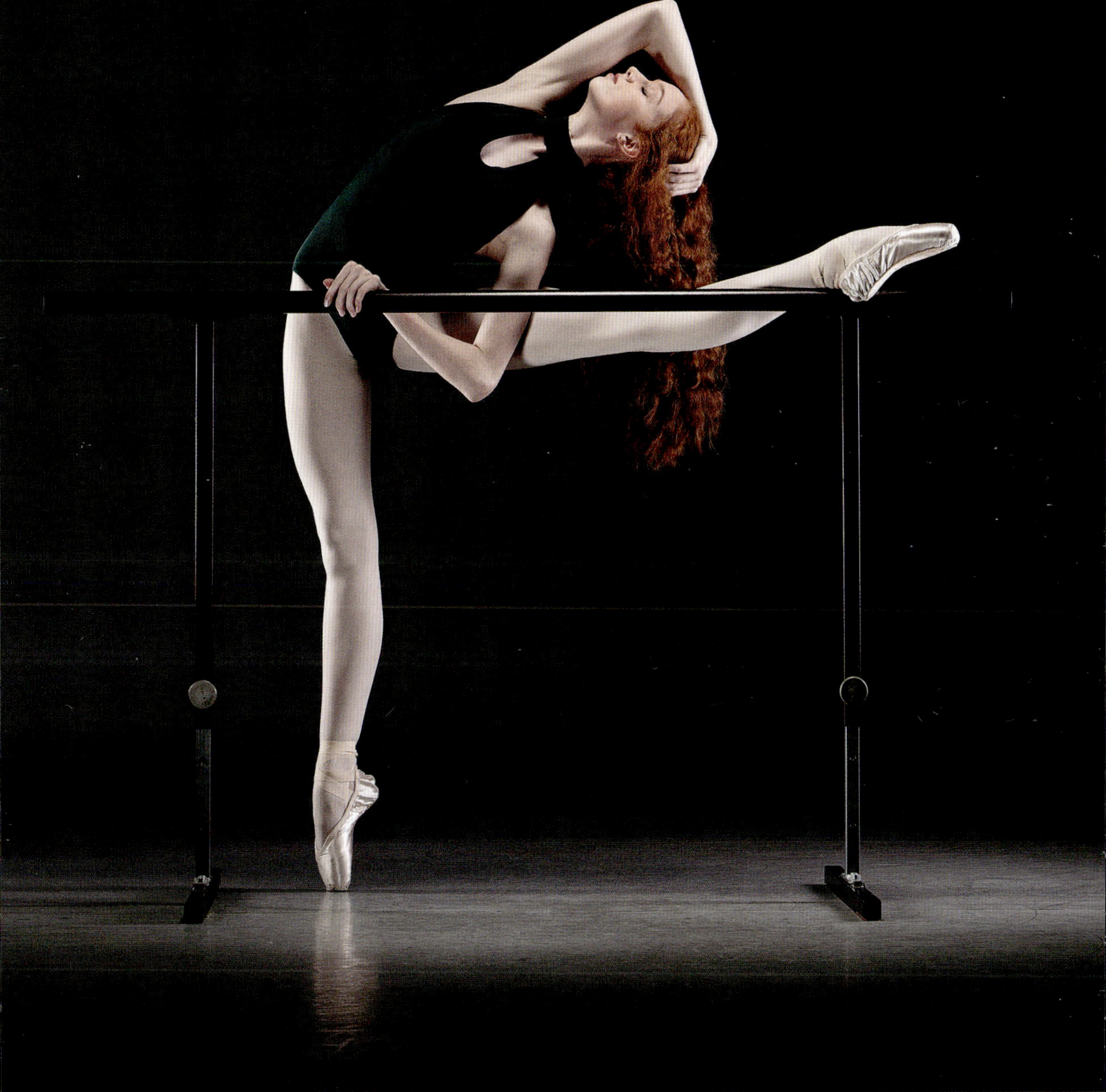

Connor Hamilton, 2018.

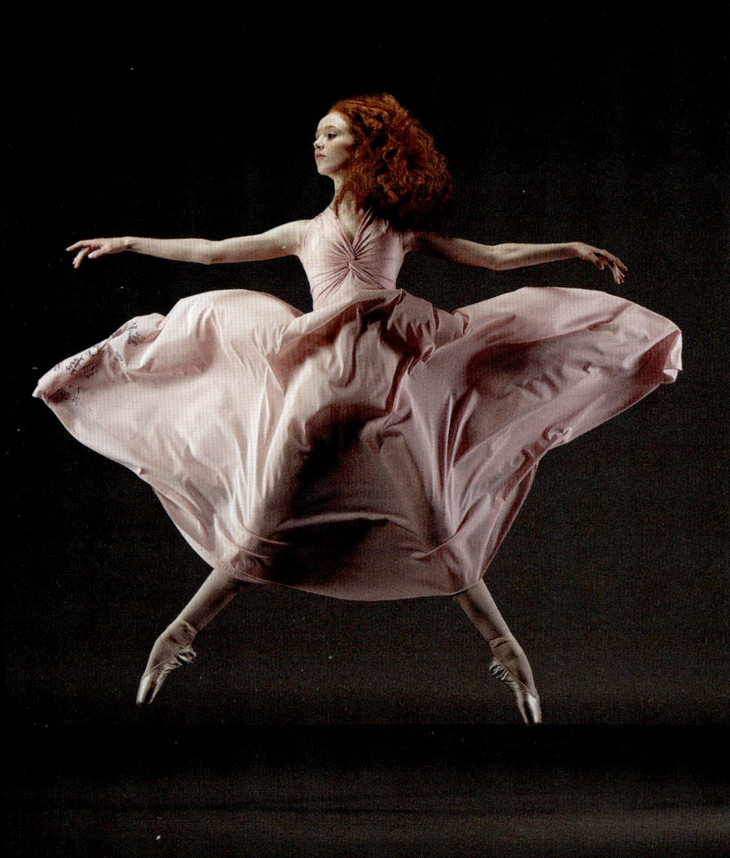

Connor Hamilton, 2018.

hard, and on top of the monotony of life in the corps were the already-familiar pressures, pains, and fears about the future. She finds motivation to push herself onward by watching the deeply diverse, talented dancers she's in the studio with every day, recognizing how strong she's become, and relishing her time on stage, where letting her natural presence shine has never been an effort.

Connor has also let go of the mindset from her competition days. Instead of worrying about being the best or "making it," she focuses on today.

"When I was younger, I thought that if I wasn't the best, I didn't want to do it. But right now, I just want to keep enjoying dancing, rather than focusing too much on rank," she said. "Because that's when you start to lose the passion. I want to stay in the moment, enjoy performing, because at the end of the day, that's my favorite aspect of being a dancer."

"It's an amazing feeling to be so comfortable and at home onstage," she continued. "Your individual traits and quirks are what make you a special dancer, and you don't have to apologize for that. I think that's really cool."

VJOLA HAJATI

You never lose if you follow your heart.

IN 1990, Vjola had just entered the Ballet de Tirana, the national company in Albania, where she was still completing her training, when the Communist regime that had been running the country toppled. Vjola was sixteen. She and her parents fled Albania, searching for stability. For two months they traveled, not knowing where their new home would be, until landing in Belgium with friends. Vjola's parents were determined that their daughter not lose all the work she'd done to become a dancer, so she entered the Athénée Royal de Fragnée in Belgium, graduating two years later with a medal of honor from the Belgian government. She danced with the national ballet company in Brussels before briefly moving to the Royal Ballet in London, but concern over her nationality papers brought her back. Her parents proposed she try something completely different: go to Paris and audition for the legendary Moulin Rouge.

Ready for a new chapter in her dancing life, Vjola agreed. She went to Paris.

GROWING UP IN ALBANIA, Vjola was a happy, energetic, adventurous, and athletic child who was also "unique," as she described herself. She was surrounded by a loving, extended family of grandparents, aunts, and uncles, but was especially close to and protected by her parents, who were both artists (her mom was a comedian and musician and her father a film director.) The three traveled throughout Albania during her childhood. "I felt as if I'd seen the world even though the country was completely closed off," she remembered.

Even with artistic parents, Vjola was more into sports, often winning school competitions. But one fateful day when she was nine years old, playing outside the National Theatre building in Tirana while waiting for her mother, a man approached her. He asked if she studied dancing. No, she

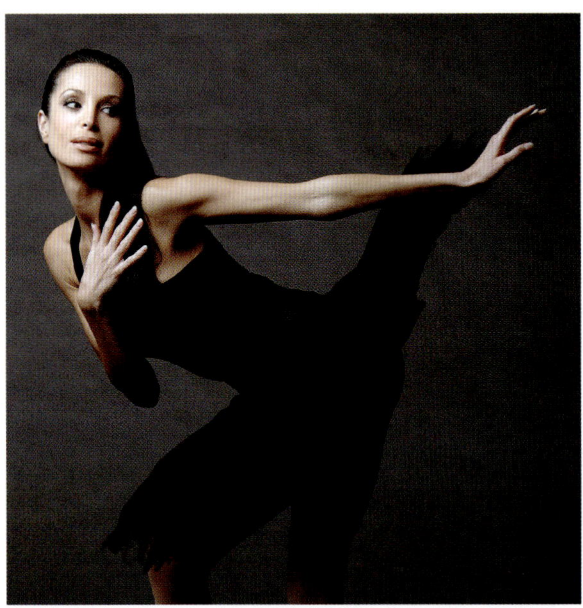

Vjola Hajati, 2009.

replied, and she had in fact only seen dance on TV on rare occasions, since the Communist regime limited access to things like classical ballet. The man who'd spotted her natural athleticism and dance-ready physique turned out to be a star with the Albanian Opera. When Vjola's mother returned to pick her up, he suggested the entrance exam for the Opera's dance academy.

For reasons she can't quite remember, Vjola did want to give ballet a try. But even though she was only nine, because she had no experience whatsoever, she had to enroll in basic lessons before attempting the Opera audition. The moment she walked into the dance studio and saw the other students, she was transfixed. "The perfection of their movements, their eyes, the way they held themselves . . . I wanted to be like them. It wasn't about tutus or dresses or color. It was beyond that. Something very pure and powerful, very unique. It took only one lesson for me to make the decision to dance."

Vjola's keen ability to concentrate and focus on a task, along with her compulsion for physical exertion, was perfect for the very tough training she needed to prepare for the Opera entrance exam. In order to learn in six months what normally took a few years, Vjola took hours of classes every day. Discovering what her body could do through ballet technique was thrilling. "It matched me physically and emotionally," she said. "It fed me like oxygen."

Six months later, Vjola took the entrance exam for the Albania Opera School and was accepted. From that day forward, she said, everything changed. "It was the beginning of a very long adventure. I lived for dancing."

IT'S HARD TO IMAGINE going from classical ballet to the flash and dazzle of a Parisian cabaret. But Vjola says her love of dance in any form, plus the experience she'd had over the years with varied styles, made this potential

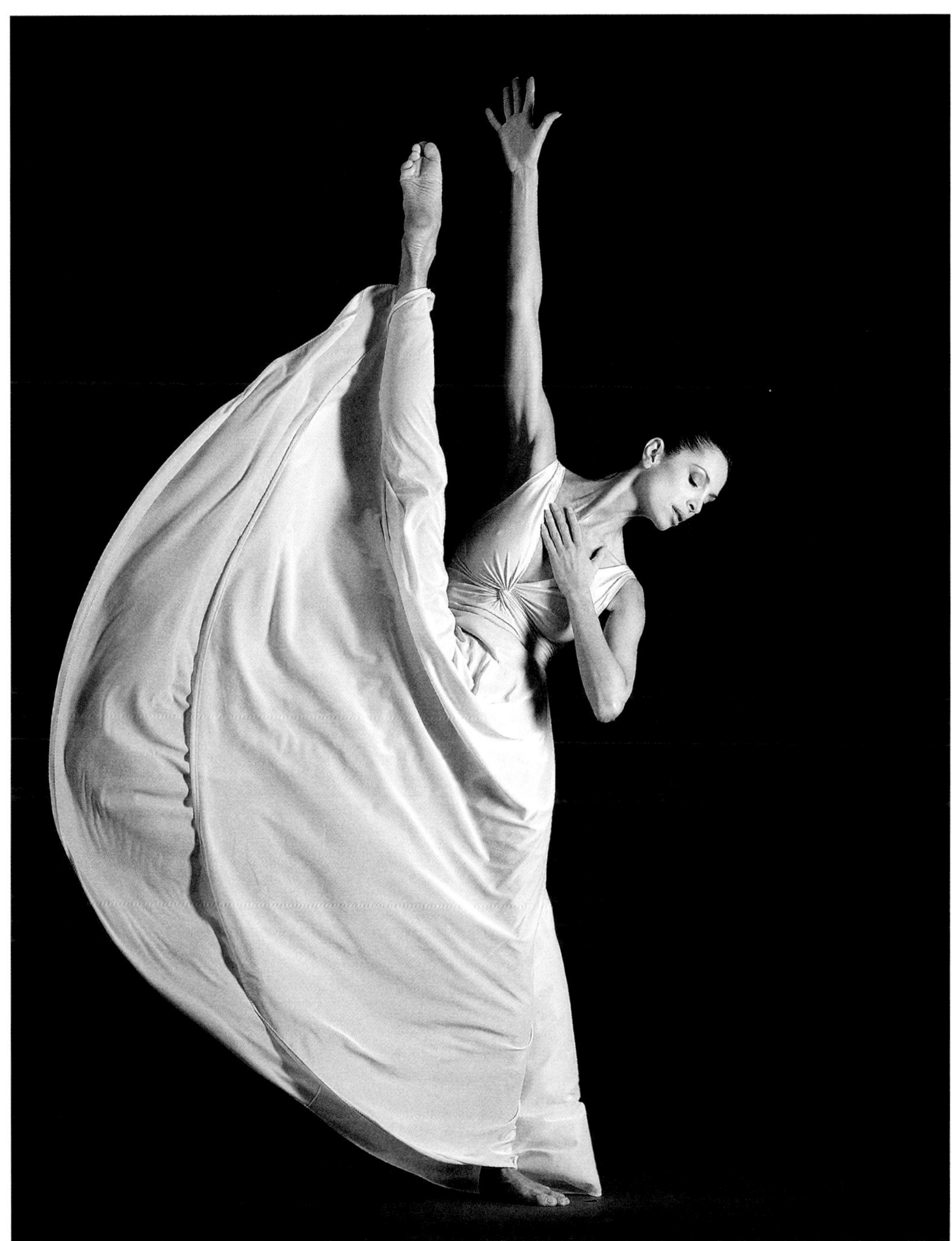

Vjola Hajati, 2009.

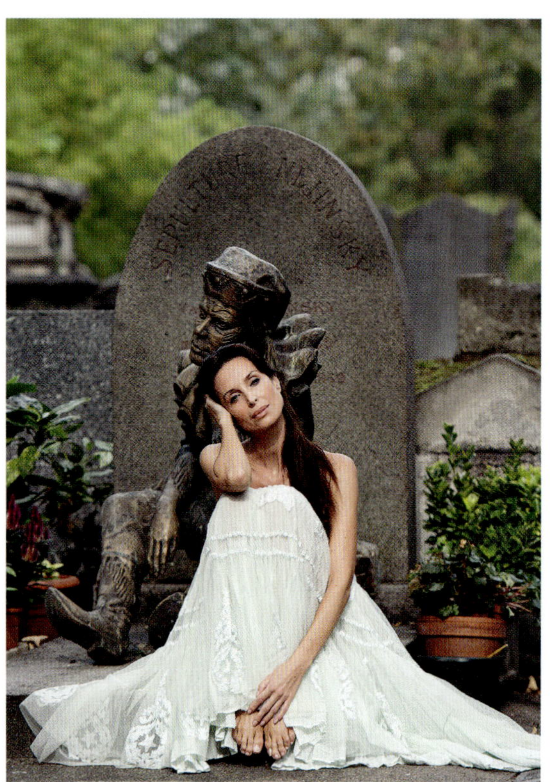

Vjola Hajati at Nijinsky's grave in Paris, 2013.

segue feel, if not totally natural, very fun and fulfilling. She arrived at the Moulin Rouge audition in her black leotard and pulled-back bun, only to find herself surrounded by young women in colorful outfits, high heels, sheer tights, and lots of makeup—so she quickly pulled her hair down and changed into sneakers (she didn't have heels). Although she still stood out as the "ballerina," the management of the cabaret loved her technique and polish and wanted to work with her.

Vjola moved to Paris and began working in the ensemble of the Moulin Rouge as cancan dancer, even though the management had offered her a principal dancer position. "It was a very hard decision to make, because being a principal meant being topless, and for me, coming from ballet and used to a tutu and pointe shoes . . ." she remembered. "That was a complete change for me. So I said I would be a cancan dancer, in the corps de ballet, because those dancers are always covered."

Vjola fit so easily into life in the cabaret that after three or four months, she started to rethink her decision to turn down the principal dancer position. She wanted to dance more than the ensemble allowed, even if it meant wearing the revealing costume. The company's management wanted her to stay and be a long-term dancer with them, so they urged her to begin learning the main roles in the show. Vjola did, and became a principal after all. As she became a renowned, respected, and revered figure in the Moulin Rouge, Vjola felt accomplished, full, and happy. "I don't regret any moment. I loved it. There were difficult times, drama, lots of stories, but I want to keep the best memories in life and learn from all the rest. It all made me grow, as a dancer and as a person."

By thirty-six, Vjola had married and was ready to start a family. She

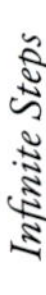

decided to retire from the Moulin Rouge, although the theater management tried to convince her to stay, saying she could dance another ten years there if she wanted to. But Vjola felt she'd progressed as far as she could. Her focus had shifted. "I didn't want to be a slave to my first passion," she said.

In 2009, not long before retiring, Vjola traveled to the United States and, after an initial connection via social media that sparked mutual interest in working together, met Gene for their first photo session at the American Ballet Theatre studios in New York. The collaboration felt seamless and fruitful for both of them. They met again a few years later, when Gene had embarked on a photography project exploring the drama and mystery of cemeteries. He went to Paris, and thought of Vjola. Their second photo shoot together took place one drizzly Parisian afternoon at the Cimetière du Montmartre. Vjola, by then pregnant with her second daughter, described the cemetery shoot as one of the most freeing, fulfilling artistic experiences she'd ever had. "For once, no one was asking me to do anything related to dance—turn your leg out here, put your arm here—it was only me, only emotion. The pictures were spontaneous. It was like a performance with no dancing, and I loved it."

VJOLA REALIZES HOW RICH HER LIFE HAS BEEN. She feels she hasn't missed out or sacrificed anything, despite her uprooted adolescence, difficult training, and bold choice to leave her familiar world of ballet behind for the cabaret. She wants her children, who love music and dance already, to make all of their own choices so they, like her, will have no regrets.

"If you listen to your heart and your head, follow what you feel, you are never wrong. And maybe get something you'd not imagined. Even if at first you don't get what you want, you are going to learn and grow stronger. It was physically hard, but inside I was very, very happy."

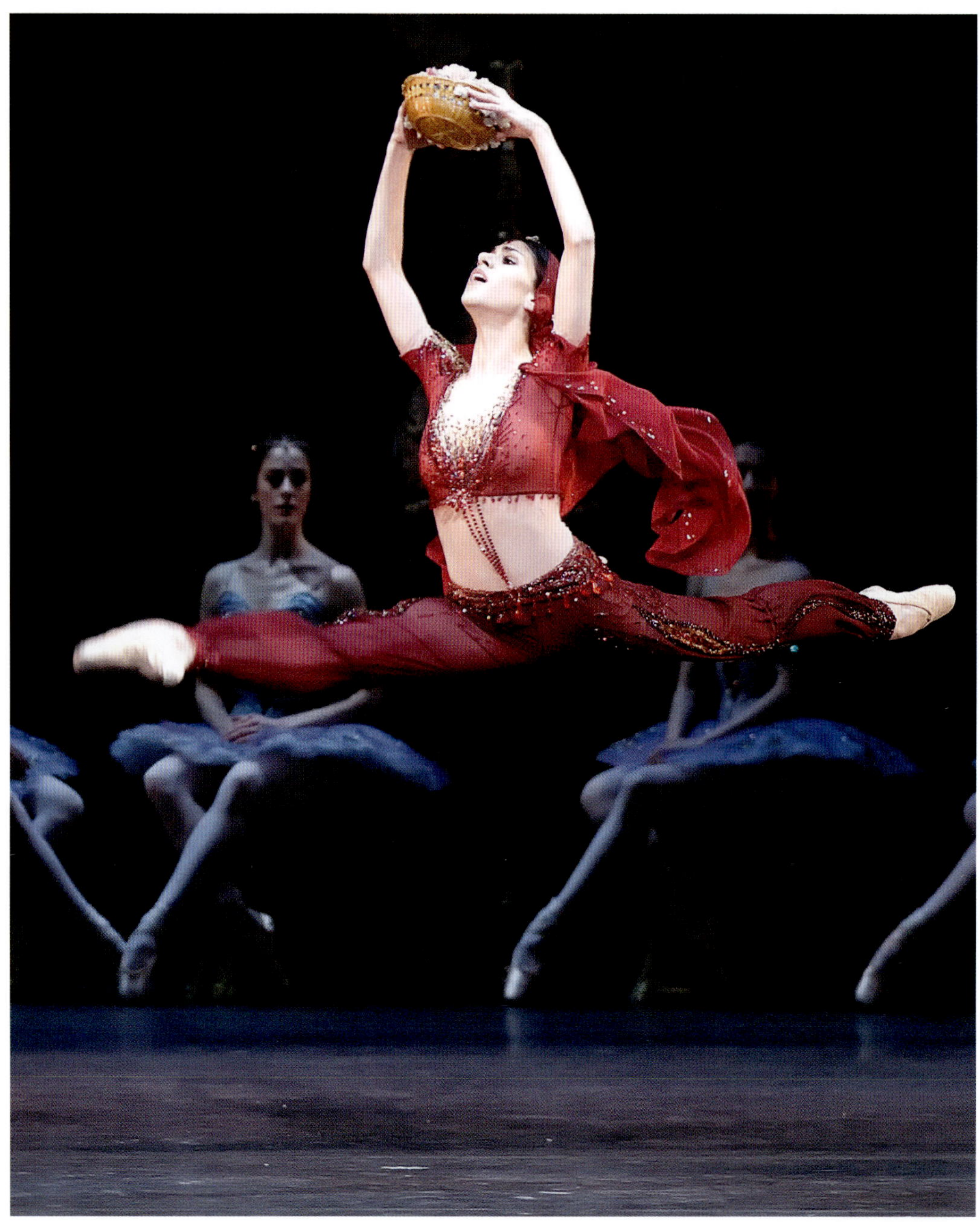

Paloma Herrera in *La Bayadère,* 2007.
Photo courtesy of American Ballet Theatre.

PALOMA HERRERA

The higher you set the bar for yourself, the more you have to do to stay there.

SHE JOINED AMERICAN BALLET THEATRE at age fifteen. At seventeen, she performed the *Don Quixote* pas de deux at the Kennedy Center and soon after, she appeared on the cover of the *New York Times Magazine.* And by nineteen, Paloma was an ABT principal dancer.

Paloma's place in the American ballet scene is legendary. Born in Argentina, she came to the US when she was fifteen for what was supposed to be six months of study at the School of American Ballet. Despite the radical difference between the SAB style of dancing and her staunchly Vaganova training (and the fact that she spoke virtually no English and was thousands of miles away from her parents, with whom she was extremely close), Paloma wasn't fazed. Dance was all that mattered. She felt inept in the SAB classes but tried to do whatever the teachers asked of her. Her love of dance was so intense that it outweighed any discomfort. "I was lost, but I had the world of dance," Paloma remembered.

Stylistic differences didn't seem to matter to the teachers at SAB either, who immediately saw her talent and put her in the highest class with older girls, and then cast her in a lead role in the end-of-year Workshop performances. It was wonderful, but Paloma still planned to return to Argentina as soon as the school year wrapped. But then something completely unexpected happened that changed her life.

While at SAB, Paloma frequently went with her classmates to see New York City Ballet performances and had acquired a love for and appreciation of that company. But ABT, across the plaza at the Metropolitan Opera House, had always been her true dream. She got to see them perform several times, too, when her host family took her to see the legendary Sylvie Guillem in *Don Quixote,* as well as a Twyla Tharp program and *La Bayadère.* It was magical to see ABT live, on stage, after watching videotapes of the company for years.

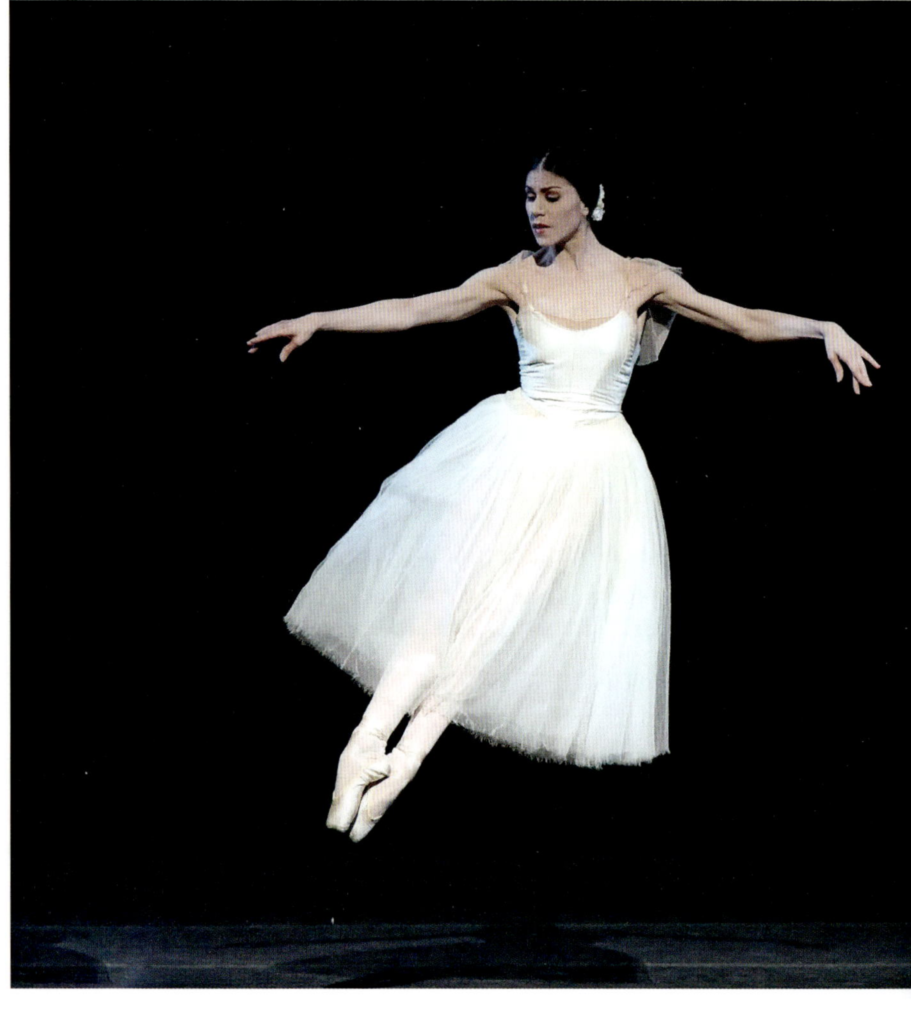

Paloma Herrera in *Giselle,* 2011. Photo courtesy of American Ballet Theatre.

When Paloma overheard some SAB classmates talking about an ABT company audition that was being held the day before she was due to fly home to Argentina, she thought . . . I wonder if I could go, too? "There was no way, in my mind, that I would get in. I just wanted to take that class, be in that studio, look around at those dancers. I had no expectations," she said. "My suitcase was packed to go back to Argentina."

After the audition class, she was called into the Green Room and offered a corps de ballet contract. She said yes on the spot.

Paloma danced, screamed, sang her way down the street back to her residence, where she immediately called her parents to tell them what had just happened. There was no doubt in her mind, no hesitation, about moving to a foreign country to start her career at such a young age. "A lot of people asked me at the time, 'Are you sure you want to join a company now? You are only fifteen.' But I knew it was right. It was my dream."

She did board her flight to Argentina the next day, but with her ABT contract in hand and a new plan to secure her work visa, learn English, and return to New York in time for the fall season. Her usual fear of flying was completely gone. "On that flight, I vividly remember thinking, 'It's okay, with an ABT contract, I can die now, it's fine!'"

Paloma Herrera in her American Ballet Theatre farewell performance, 2015. Photo courtesy of American Ballet Theatre.

Paloma didn't stay in the ABT corps for long. Major roles and important premieres came fast, as did success. Some observers questioned the wisdom of placing so much pressure and big responsibilities on such a young talent. What about burnout? Many prodigies might freeze in the face of relentlessly high expectations, despite the thrill and excitement of it all. Plus, when you reach the top of your profession at the beginning of your career, what's left?

She did feel the pressure, but the people closest to her—her parents, ABT artistic director Kevin McKenzie, and her coach Irina Kolpakova—gave her the support and guidance she needed to nurture a belief in herself. As the years passed, Paloma developed an outlook she hadn't had as a teenage phenom. Previously, if a show had gone badly she was frustrated, but if it went well, that only meant she had to do even better next time. There was no winning. But when she turned thirty, Paloma realized there was no point in such harshness. She began to relax and relish the process of working with her coaches and mentors, who were so important to her, on continually refining roles even after she'd done them many times. She says she stopped worrying so much about the steps. "I just enjoyed dancing again," she said. "It felt fantastic."

IN 2015, Paloma decided she was ready to retire. She had danced professionally for twenty-four years and loved every minute of it, but just like making the decision to join ABT at fifteen, the choice to retire at forty was clear and firm in her mind. She wanted to leave her career feeling happy, not tired or struggling. She wanted to remember loving what she did up to the very end, without anything to taint her gratitude and sense of amazement at all she had.

As fiercely passionate as she was about her performing career, leaving it behind has not been painful. Paloma looks at photographs from her thousands of performances with happiness, but not sentimentality. Maybe that's because she appreciated her moment-to-moment dancing life so much. There's no need to be nostalgic now. She danced to her fullest every single day, she says, knowing how unpredictable life is and how quickly it moves. She doesn't need to go back in time, only forward.

After her final performance, Paloma began teaching and coaching around the world from her home base in Buenos Aires. She's as passionate, energetic,

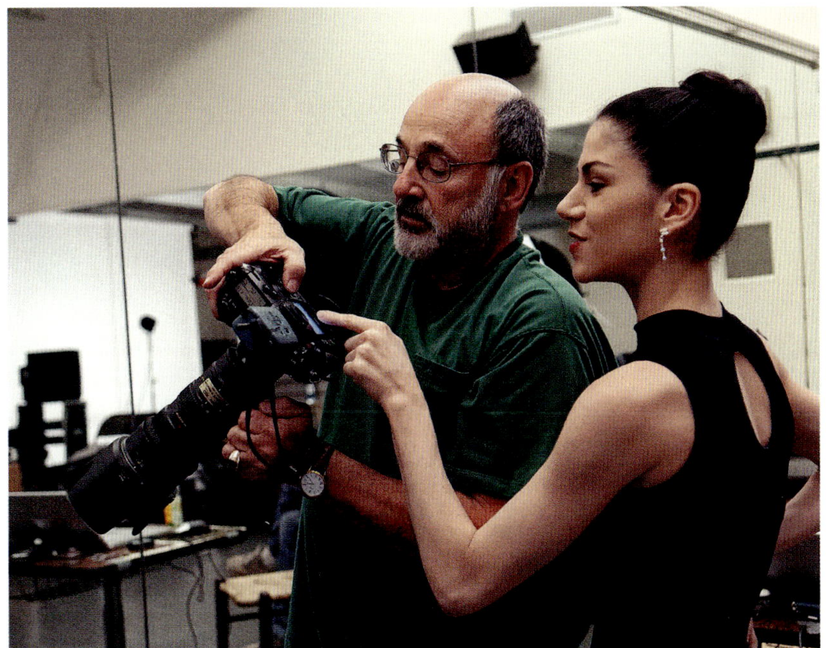

Paloma and Gene critique a shot, 2007.

and devoted to teaching as she was to performing. She wants to pass on her trademark conviction that beyond technique and hard work is consistency: you have to show up, for yourself and for the art. "That was my secret, I guess. I never missed a class, I never missed a rehearsal. I was the first one to the theater and the last one to leave. But it was because I loved it. It was my passion."

"I never had a Plan B. From age seven, when I started dancing, I knew what I was going to do. There was never a doubt, never a question. And that's why I was the happiest person. If you ask me now, I would do everything exactly the same."

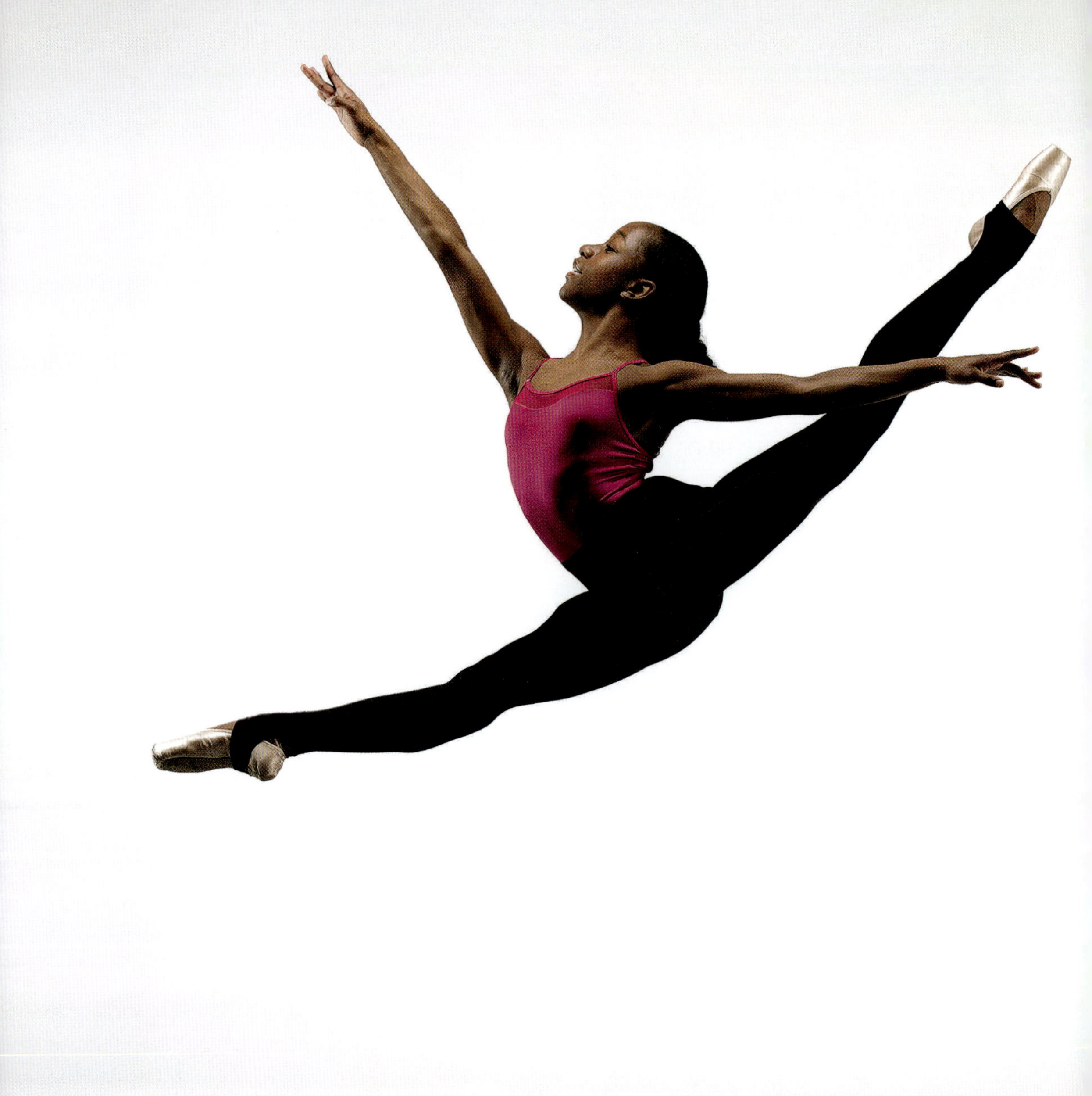

Marja' Quaqua, 2018.

MARJA' QUAQUA

There's no point in staying the same. Art has to change. As an artist, you should do whatever you feel—with good technique of course!—but being genuine and authentic is really important.

NEARLY ALL OF MARJA'S LIFE has been in the dance world, where she feels most at home, yet sometimes also the most alone. She felt very early on that the specific beauty and expressive power of ballet called to her more than any other style (she'd started dancing at age three, taking tap, jazz, and gymnastics in addition to ballet), but it took some time to get herself to believe that it could be her voice. Now Marja', who describes herself as "just your average nineteen-year-old," is on a mission to make her personal stamp on the ballet world.

At first, ballet was just a fun way to move and let out emotions that were hard to grapple with. Since Marja' has a stutter, which makes verbal expression challenging, she loved that she could show feelings like stress or anger more effectively through dance than in words. But even with movement as her voice, Marja' internalized another difference that dance couldn't change. As the only Black girl in her dance school, she had no role model to look up to or bond with. From the beginning, and for a long time, Marja' had to be her own inspiration.

As strong as her love for ballet has always been, Marja's relationship with it has morphed over the years, much like two lifelong friends whose lives diverge, changing their understanding of each other. The first shift happened when Marja' entered her first ballet competition. At only ten years old and without much exposure outside her South Carolina town, she surprised herself by finishing near the top of her age group. A few years later, she had another top finish. But even though by any measure she'd triumphed, the competitive atmosphere shook Marja's self-assurance. The excitement and attention she got for winning—and the inherent pressure to keep going—made it seem like being the best was more important than her reasons for dancing and her

Marja' Quaqua, 2018.

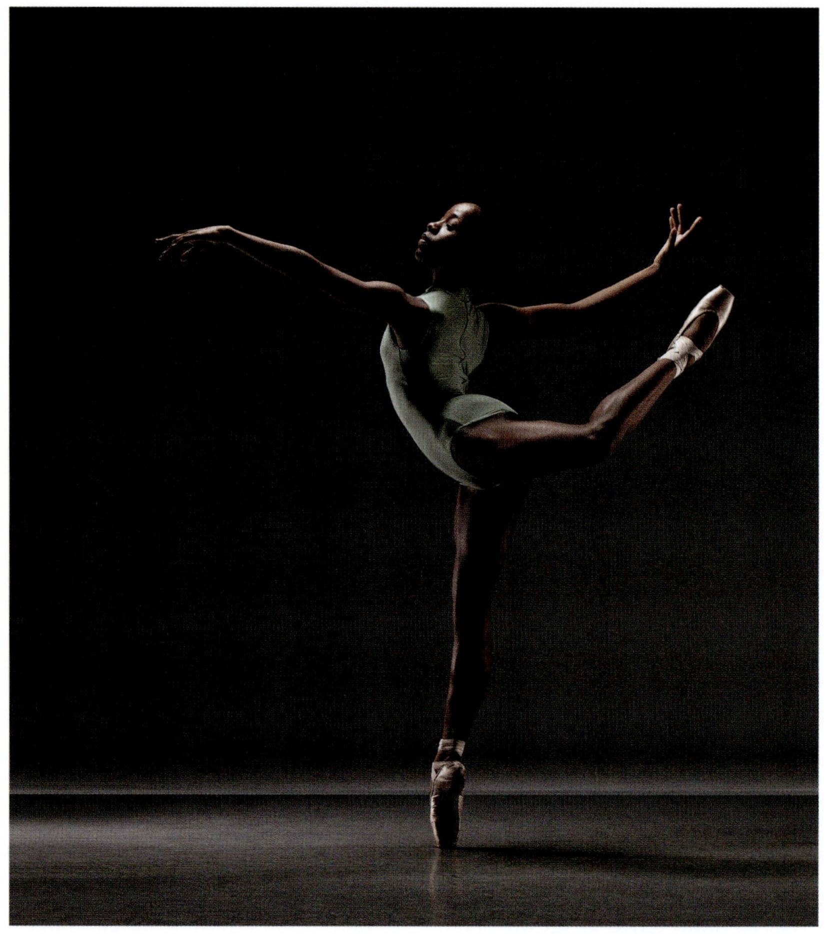

love of it. She was thirteen and felt burned out. "I didn't know what I wanted for *myself*," Marja' said. "My teachers were saying things like, 'You have to be a dancer, you have to do X, Y, Z.' But I didn't feel any growth or progress. I didn't have the passion and fire I used to. I thought I might as well quit."

But she didn't.

WHAT'S OFTEN MISUNDERSTOOD about dancers is that the need for validation is not about ego. It's not about applause. It's about finding and maintaining perspective on something you'll never be able to see for yourself. Marja's story shows how critical it is for young, ambitious dancers to have

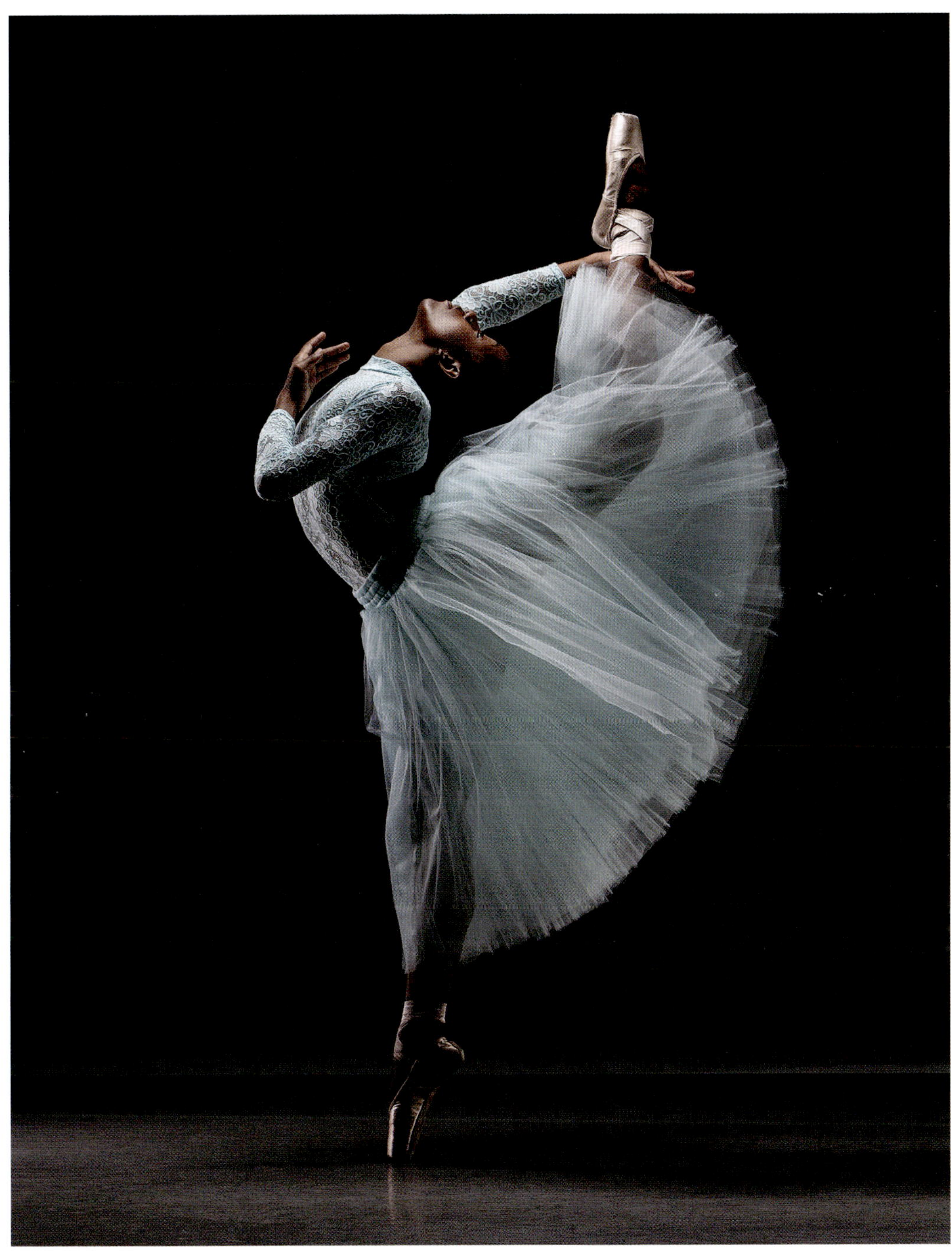

Marja' Quaqua, 2018.

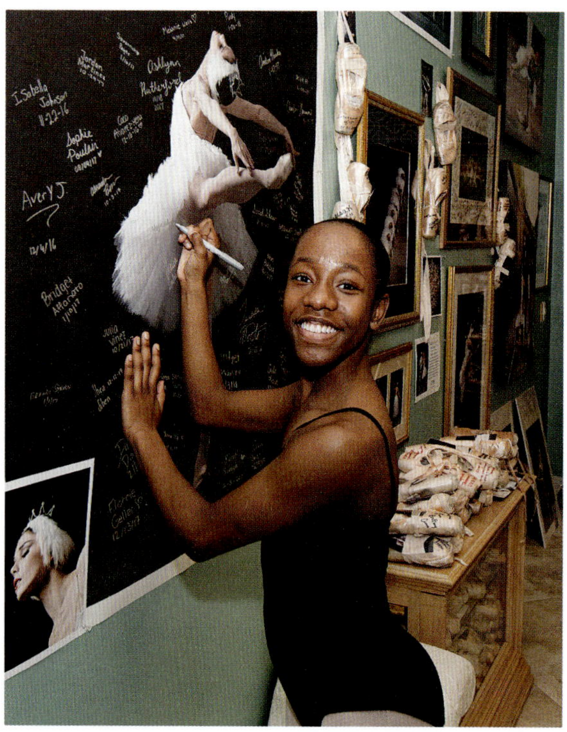

Marja' Quaqua, 2018.

ongoing support and communication with a trusted voice both in the studio and outside. She found herself measuring her own work by whether her teachers corrected or commented on her in class. When she perceived they weren't interested in her, she felt lost. "If they didn't show they were invested in me, I thought I'd done something wrong," Marja' said. "I need to know I still matter."

Through those very hard periods of burnout, Marja' turned to her very supportive parents and reignited her energy to keep going. She realized that what she'd invested in herself was more important than anyone else's ideas or attention. When she returned to the competition scene a few years later, she performed a trio with two friends in the ensemble category. They made it to the final round—and then, by the competition's end, finished near the top. This time, Marja' had a different approach to competing. "I switched my mindset from 'I'm here to win' to 'I'm here to perform,'" she remembered. "That helped me be less nervous when I saw other people doing twelve pirouettes on pointe. I can't do that, and it's completely fine! I'm here to put on a show, because that's what I like to do."

A MAJOR TURNING POINT came in 2018 when Marja', at the urging of her mother, applied for the annual scholarship awarded to an African American female dancer by Ballet in the City, an organization co-founded by Misty Copeland. Just like her last competition experience, Marja' went for it, but without pinning her hopes on a win. And again, she was shocked to learn that she had, in fact, won. The honor had special meaning because Marja' had been looking up to Misty Copeland from afar for years. Getting the scholarship meant even more than the money it came with. It was recognition of her talent, her potential, and for persevering and excelling despite tough odds. In an interview after receiving the award, Marja' summed up why that particular kind of recognition is so important. "It lets us know that we're not hidden or forgotten. The ballet world is harsh, and being a brown ballerina I have to work ten times as hard just to be noticed, while others may have it easier. I used to want to fit in and be like everyone else, not attract too much attention. But now I realized that sticking out is amazing! I've learned to love myself."

Marja's next steps in life will surely be big. She's already become the person she needed in her own early dance life, a role model for her 19,000 followers on Instagram, who are wowed by her displays of technical virtuosity and flair. She engages with everyone who comments, which fuels her as much as them. She wants to continue to be a leader in breaking down stereotypes about how ballet dancers should look or who can be one. What needs to change for that to happen? "Oh, so many things!" she said with a laugh. "People assume there's a 'ballet body,' but I don't want to be told that you can't dance because you're too big or too muscular. If you have a body, you can dance. That's just how it is."

What she reminds herself, and all the dancers whose passion risks being stifled from the strain of trying to fit into a mold, is straightforward. Show yourself, and others, what you're capable of and don't hold back. "It's going to be hard, and it's going to be discouraging, but don't lose yourself. Keep your goals clear and follow the path of amazing brown ballerinas who have a name in this industry—but also make a path for yourself and others to follow. Make something new."

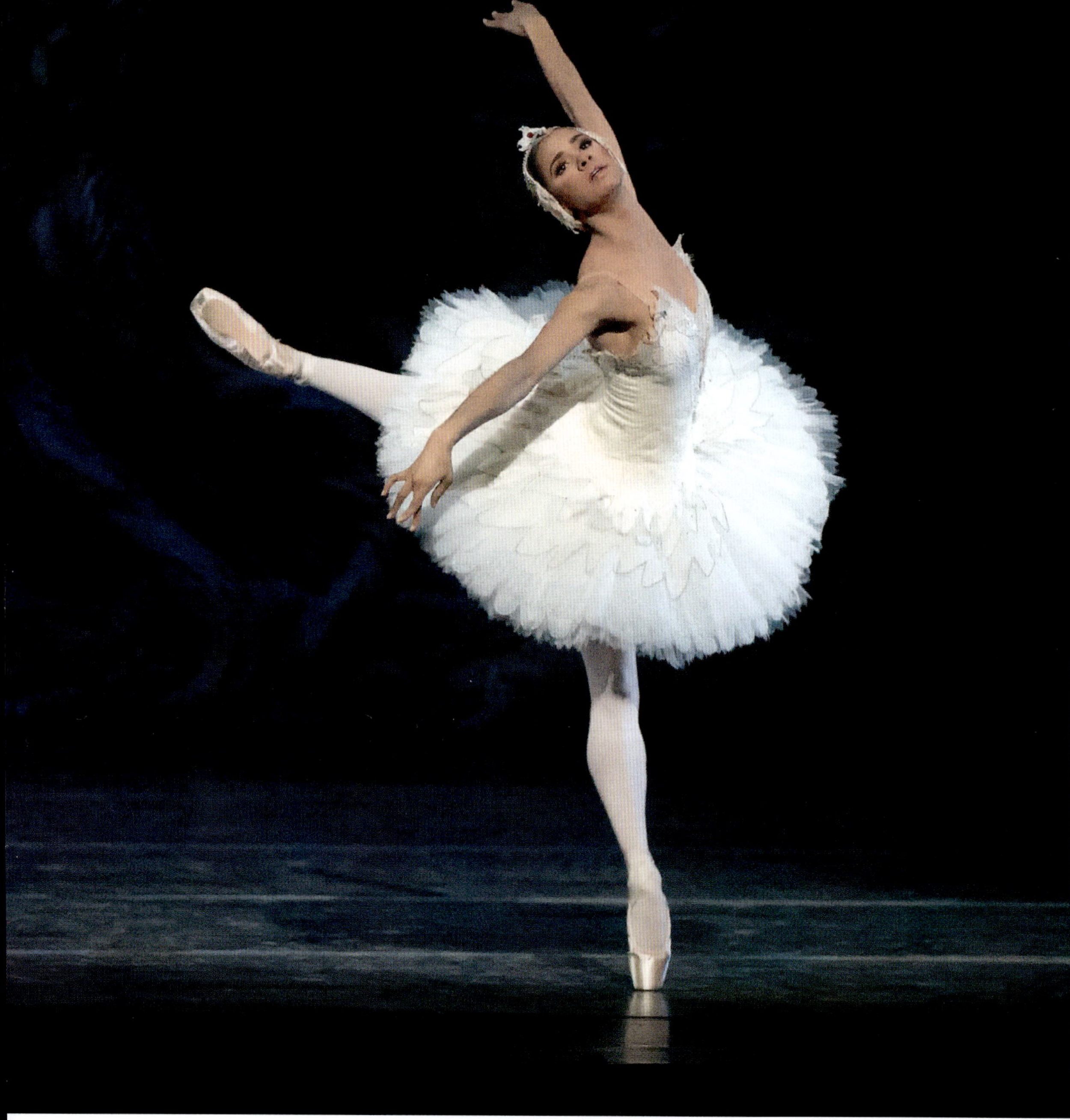

Misty Copeland in *The Sleeping Beauty,* 2015. Photo courtesy of American Ballet Theatre.

MISTY COPELAND

I look back at these photos, and I see the joy in my face. I see the freedom that I feel when performing, and also the community we had within the company. To have those things captured, reminding you of what you felt and also why we do what we do, is really special.

SIFTING THROUGH a handful of the many photographs taken of her during her ascent through the ranks of American Ballet Theatre, Misty tries not to let her eye focus on the technicalities that she, like all dancers, is trained to pick out. Instead, she lets the strong memories the images bring up take her back to each ballet and role. There's a lot of emotion attached to going back in time like this, but the feelings aren't only about her. The pictures are reminders of the deep understanding and bonds between dancers, something many people outside of dance don't realize about life in a ballet company. In full-length story ballets, the soloists and principals often perform their variations surrounded on stage by other dancers, onlookers in the scene. Whether they're onstage with her or watching from the shadows, dancers' shared energy keeps them going, like when fellow ABT dancers Maxim Beloserkovsky and Irina Dvorovenko would silently cheer Misty on from the wings every time she performed a particularly hard *Don Quixote* variation, even if they weren't cast that night and could have been at home resting.

"As often as I can, I try to express the camaraderie between us," she said. "I've been at ABT for twenty-three years now and have grown up with a lot of my colleagues. We've traveled the world together. It's not as cutthroat and competitive as people assume it is."

Support systems have been critical to Misty throughout her life. She's vocal about the many people who gave her ways to find her footing, from her unusually late start in dance classes and an unstable family life to the very different types of uncertainties she faced when she became professional. Ballet dancers assume unusually big responsibilities at ages when their nondancing friends are probably still trying to figure out their interests. But even though they may know exactly what their life's purpose is—to dance and perform—how to make their way forward on a daily basis is not always so clear. Today, having reached the peak of the profession and broken through many barriers to get there, Misty is fervent about the concept of mentorship. Without her own mentors, both on the way up and today, as she branches out from the stage, she knows her life would have been much, much different. She's seen others get derailed, despite massive talent and opportunity, when self-doubt spoke too loudly, and for too long.

As the only Black woman in ABT for a long period of time, Misty sometimes thought about quitting. She didn't feel supported and wondered why she was trying too hard to be seen as both an equal and a singular ballerina. "I thought, why am I doing this?" Misty remembered. "But I had people who kept pushing me, telling me to just put one foot in front of the other because of how much I love it. I know for sure that if I hadn't had that support from outside the ballet company, I would not have gotten to this place."

An image that is sure to become iconic is the photograph of Raven Wilkinson, one of Misty's most important mentors, presenting her with a bouquet of flowers at the conclusion of Misty's first New York performance of Odette/Odile in *Swan Lake.* Raven's pioneering status as the first Black ballerina to join a major ballet company, the Ballet Russes de Monte Carlo, had been—and remains—a point of reference for Misty, which she heavily relied on when the opportunity came to break a barrier herself. The time leading up to her *Swan Lake* debut, which she knew would be scrutinized by audiences and critics, was fraught with pressure that most other dancers wouldn't face. She was still a soloist at the time, and felt the role was an unspoken test of her potential to become a principal—and therefore be the first Black dancer of that rank at ABT.

When the performance came, despite the buzz, she found her usual solace onstage, which is always her safe haven. Seeing Raven emerge from the wings during the curtain calls was a complete surprise. Through the swirl of emotions and still caught in the other world of the performance she'd just given, Misty was struck by the significance of the moment and the gesture. "It was an opportunity she should have had in her career—to dance Odette/

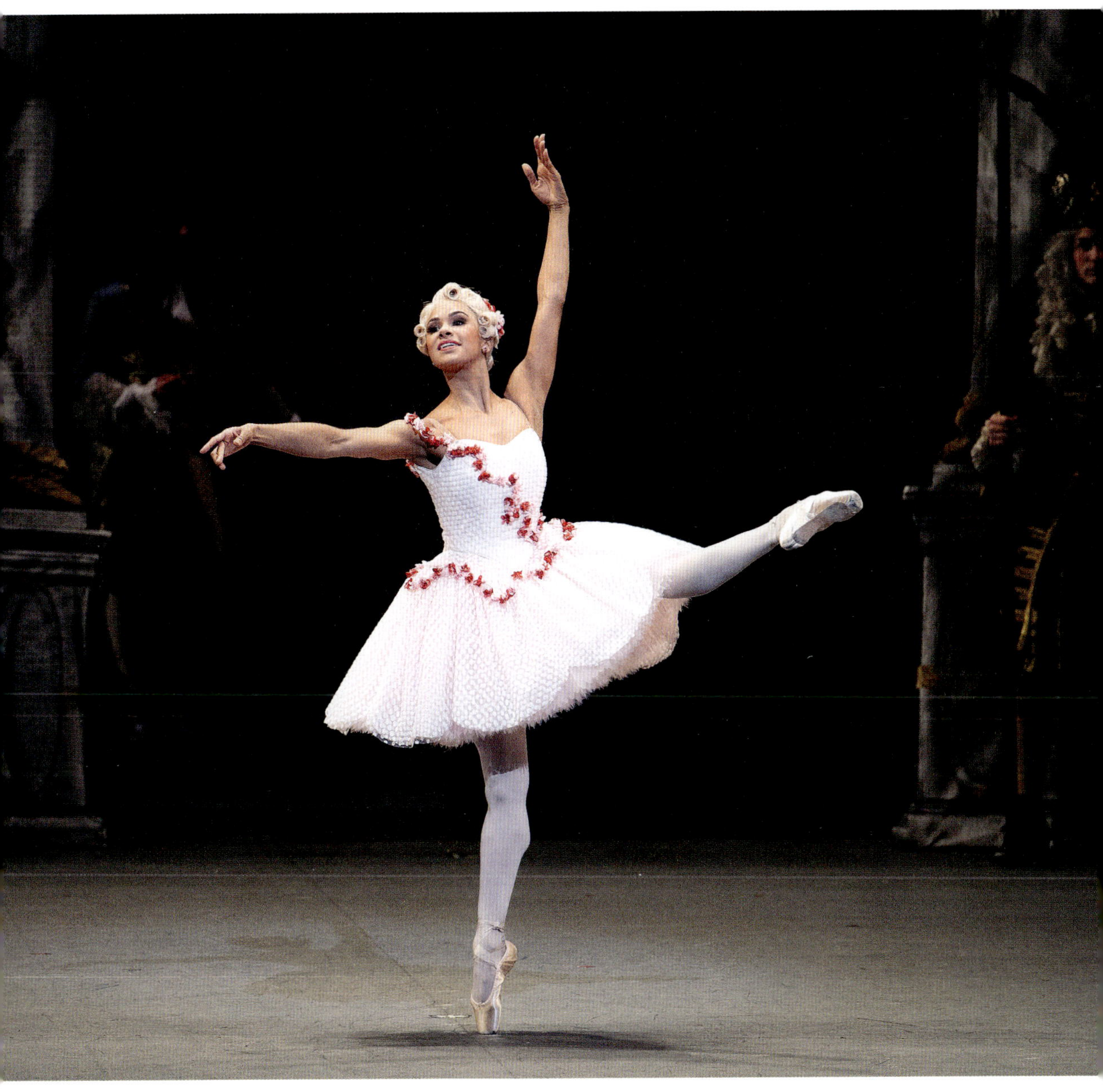

Misty Copeland in *The Sleeping Beauty*, 2015.
Photo courtesy of American Ballet Theatre.

Odile—but she never did. It felt like the passing of a torch for her to share that special moment with me. It shows Raven's impact not only on me and my career, but the ballet world."

Misty now has her own place in history as ABT's first Black principal dancer. If there's one overarching ethos to all her endeavors—she's now also an author, actor, producer, teacher, mother, and motivational speaker—it's the concept of being a role model and a guiding light, noting that the majority of her own mentors weren't dancers, but were trailblazers in a variety of different fields, women who she trusted and who she knew believed in her. Misty also learned, though, that guiding doesn't mean holding someone's hand too tightly. A mentor can provide encouragement, advice, and reinvigorate flagging energy, but can't replace the questioning that every young

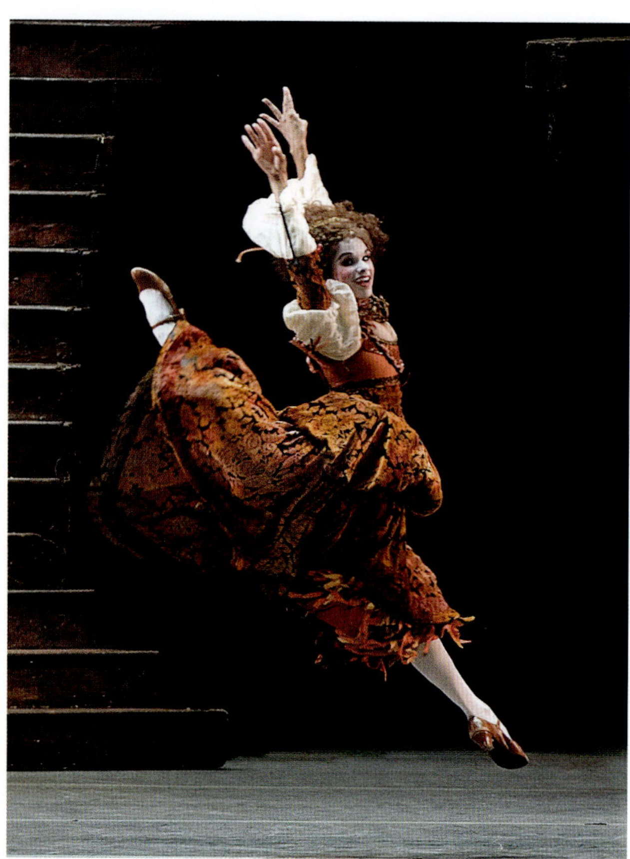

Misty Copeland in *Swan Lake,* 2009. Photo courtesy of American Ballet Theatre.

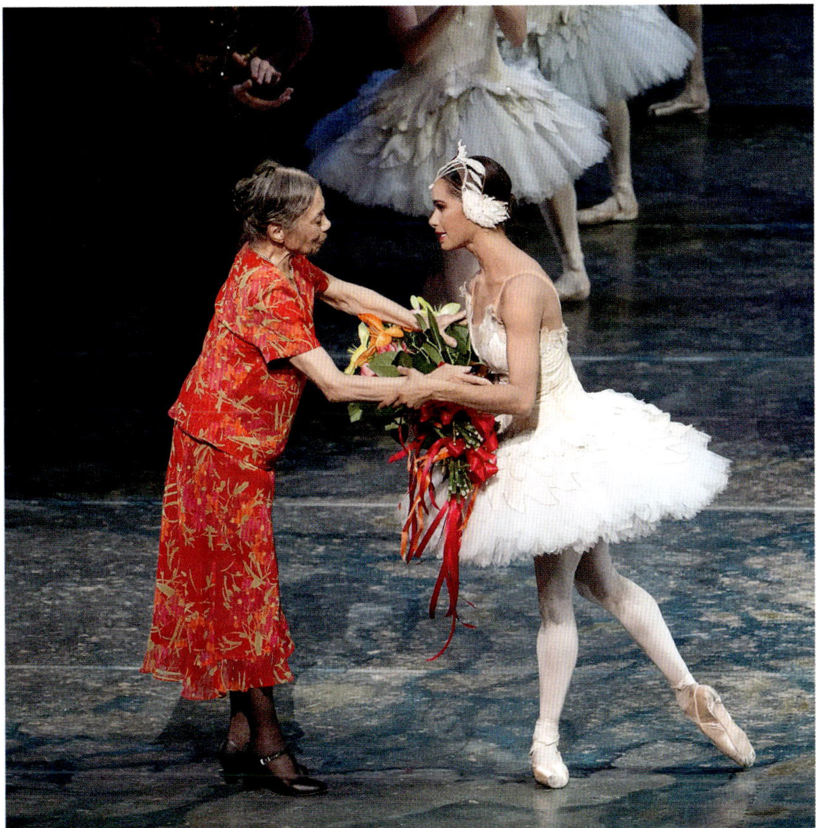

Misty Copeland and Raven Wilkinson, curtain call, 2015. Photo courtesy of American Ballet Theatre.

person and artist has to do for themselves. Misty firmly believes that the context of one generation's lives can't hold back where tomorrow's dancers aim to go. She sees the power in holding onto tradition and history while still bringing our own individuality forward.

"I'm in a position where I have a platform and people see and hear me," she said. "Everything I do is connected to this same narrative: giving voice, not only to Black and brown dancers, but to dancers, period! Dancers aren't often encouraged to have a voice and an opinion, but there is change happening. We have so much more work to do, but to me, it's not about how long it takes. It's the fact that people are paying attention in a real, genuine way. We need to think about how coming together as unique individuals makes an even more powerful collective."

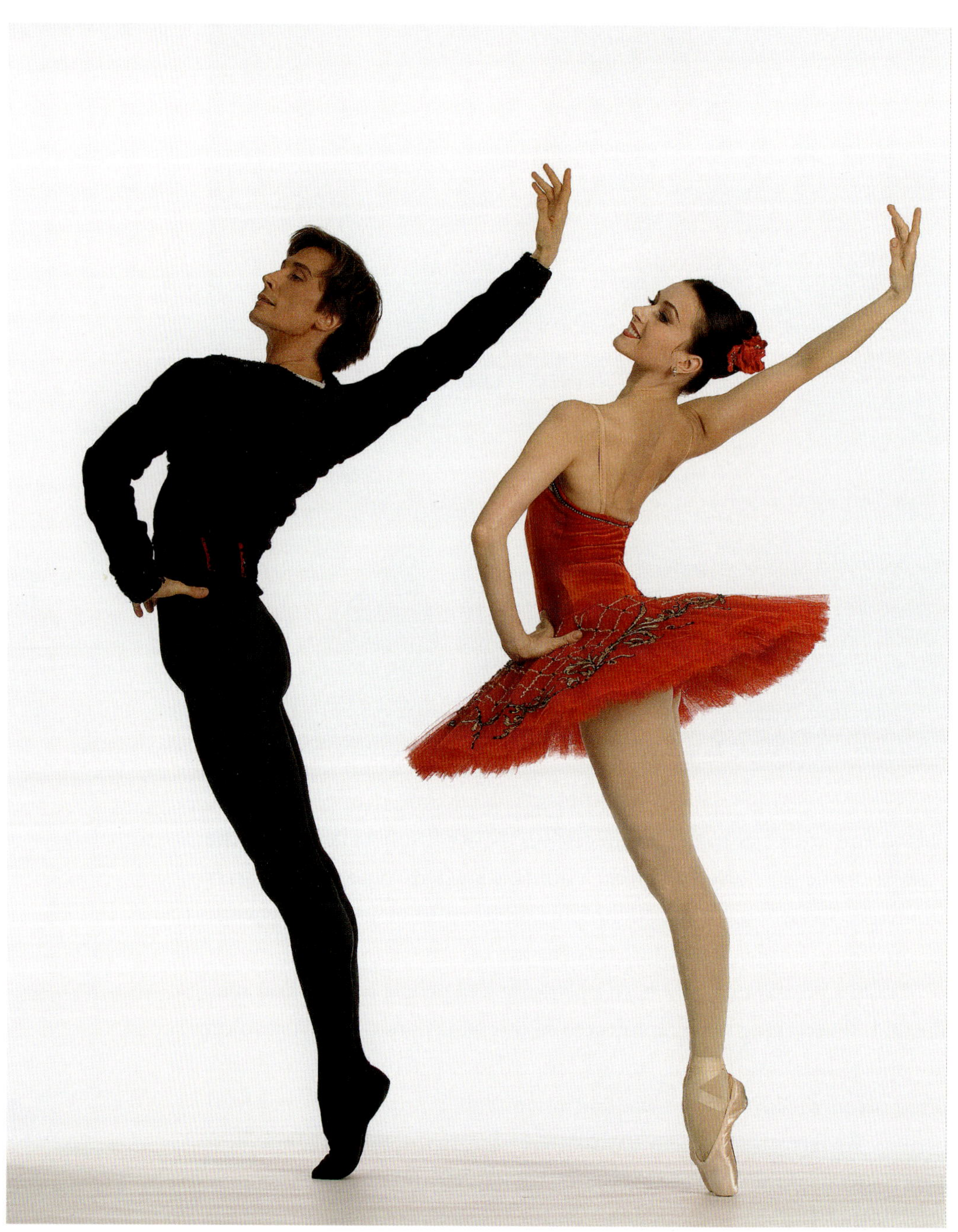

Irina Dvorovenko and Maxim Beloserkovsky, 2007.

MAXIM BELOSERKOVSKY & IRINA DVOROVENKO

Everyone has doubts, even those at the very top of the company. It's about how badly you want it. For me, I was able to push aside any negativity or downfalls because I wanted it so badly. It was a life choice.

MAXIM

The deeper side of a performance, the artistic satisfaction and fulfillment, the drama or comedy, not necessarily whether the foot is pointed or not, that is what you remember through the years. That's what stays in people's hearts.

IRINA

"MAX AND IRINA," one of the ballet world's legendary couples, were not always known as a single entity. But even long before their onstage and offstage lives grew to fit as perfectly together as interlocking pieces in a jigsaw puzzle, Maxim Beloserkovsky and Irina Dvorovenko were already running on parallel tracks.

As day students at the Kyiv National Ballet Institute, living at home with their families instead of in the school's dormitories, Max and Irina would find themselves every morning and evening at the same Kyiv train station on their commutes to and from school. Over the course of the eight-year program, the two became fast friends despite being a year apart in age and grade level, each rising to the top of their respective classes and graduating with the highest level of diploma. Their paths did separate from there briefly, but by the time they reunited, married, and moved to the United States, they were an inseparable pair in life and work.

Max and Irina are, however, strikingly distinct. Their individual views on dance, life, and career show two people bonded by independence, mutual love, commitment, passion, loyalty, and respect—for their art form and for each other.

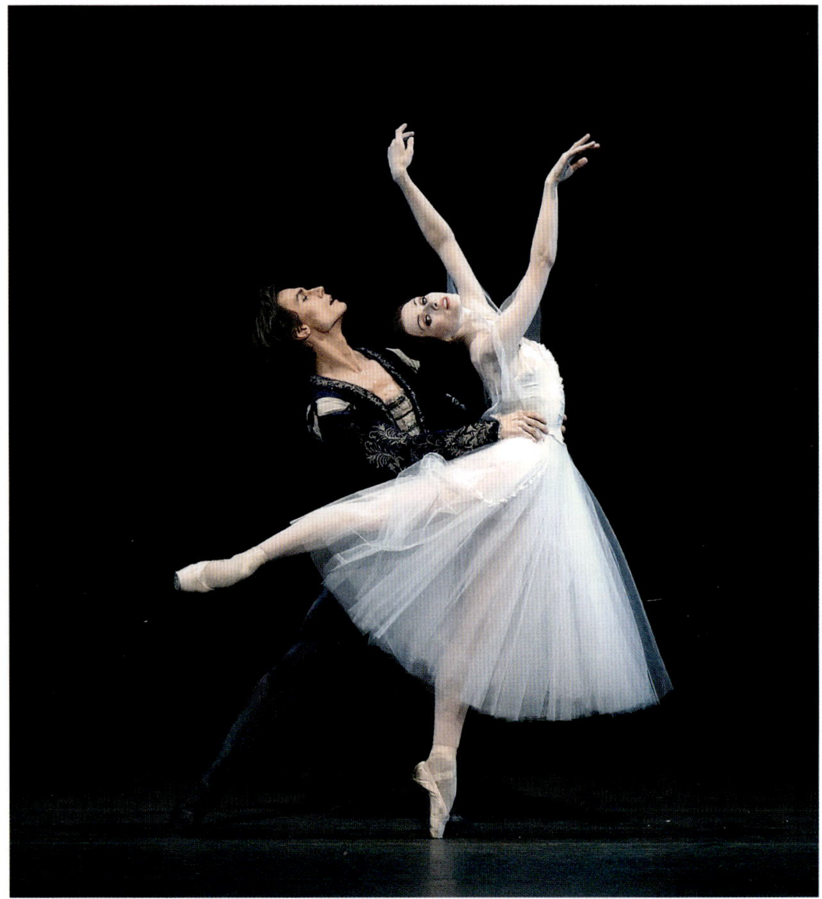

Irina Dvorovenko and Maxim Beloserkovsky in *Giselle,* 2008. Photo courtesy of American Ballet Theatre.

Irina and Max's highly visible and popular partnership at American Ballet Theatre was an integral part of the company for almost two decades, but it's interesting to remember that they did not join together, and neither was immediately a principal dancer. Although they'd wanted to partner together in school, they'd largely been kept apart. Both were exceptional students, but Irina's teacher was especially eager to show her protégé off to the world, so as a young teen Irina started entering—and winning—international ballet competitions. By the time she graduated from the ballet academy she had a collection of gold, silver, and bronze medals, a soloist contract with the Kyiv National Opera, and the ballet world's attention. While Irina stayed to perform in their home city, Max turned down an offer from the same company to follow opportunity abroad to Bulgaria, where he tasted personal independence (it was his first time away from home), toured the Mediterranean and Southeast Asia, and studied with a new teacher he calls "extraordinary." Two years later, armed with the experience and confidence from having worked as a dancer outside the only ballet world he'd ever known, Max returned to Kyiv and joined the Opera, where his childhood friend Irina was already on the rise. Very soon, the pair's wish to partner together came true when they were cast together as the leads in *Giselle.* From then on, their partnership was "like an express train," as Max put it—but not romantically, at least not at first. Irina's international successes on the competition circuit brought her frequent invitations to appear in galas outside Ukraine, and after their *Giselle* debut, she asked Max to join her at a gala in New York. Up until that point, their close relationship was limited to working together as dancers, though the concept of something more was hanging in the air. Max drew a vivid picture of how they must have appeared to others when he described their arrival at their hotel in New York, where the manager assumed their preferred accommodations and handed them a key for their shared room. "I don't know if we were too shy and didn't know what to say, or it just happened so fast, but we just went along with it. For us, it was always, 'Let's have an equal partnership in dance, and see what happens from there.' We looked for significance in dance with each other first, and then it went further and became a life partnership."

BY 1992, Max faced a difficult choice. His mother, who was fiercely proud of her son and Max's "champion in everything," passed away. Ukraine was falling into economic distress, and although the ballet company kept operating, artistically it was at a standstill. At twenty-one, Max had already done every role in the repertory and there were no new ballets or choreographers on the horizon. He knew that waiting for the country and company to revitalize would mean losing precious years of his and Irina's careers. Married by then, Max and Irina moved to the US, but not together. Max went first to ensure he could find work while Irina kept her stable job with the Ukrainian Opera. Dancing with ABT was their goal, but even for two world-class dancers, doors do not necessarily swing open. Max arrived in New York alone,

Irina Dvorovenko in *Swan Lake,* 2010. Photo courtesy of American Ballet Theatre.

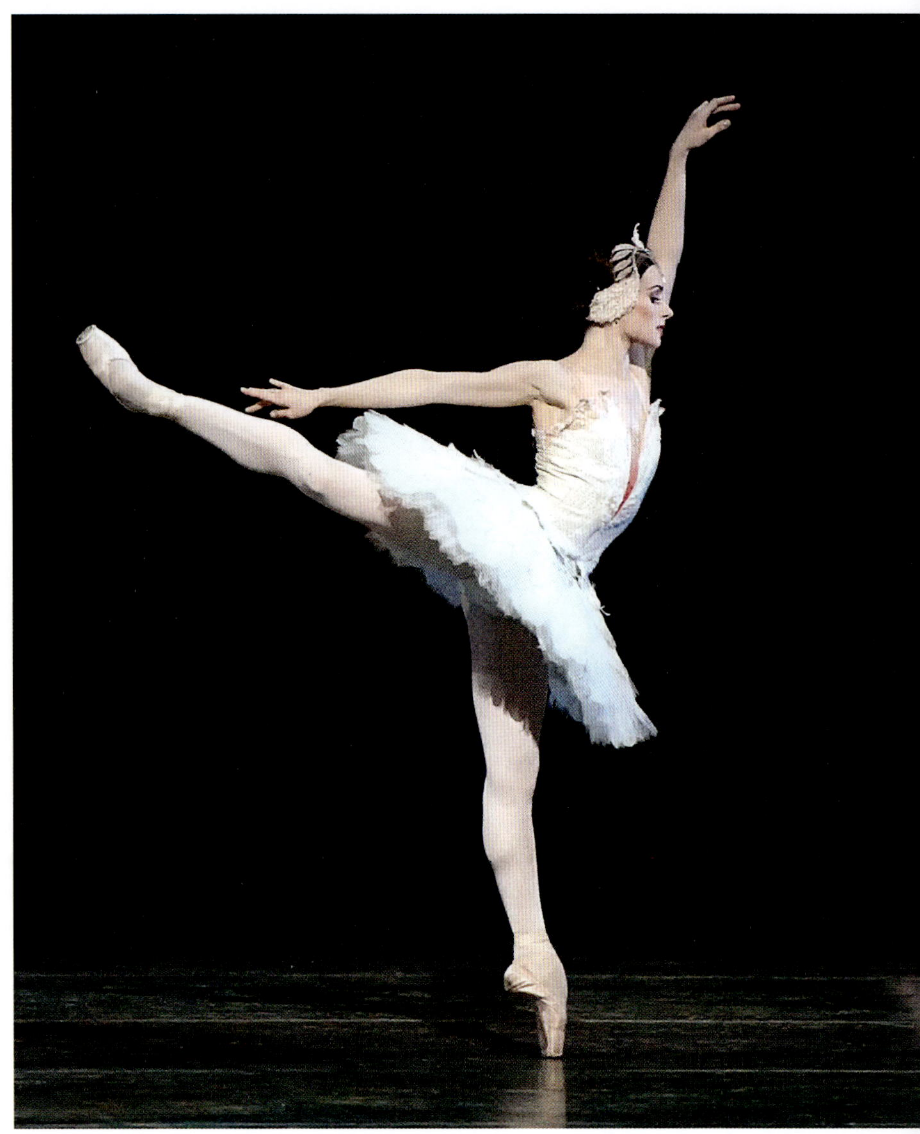

with only broken English and the phone number of the famed ABT coach Irina Kolpakova. When he called she was sympathetic, but the company's season had ended and there were no auditions. Max is still not sure whether it was fate, chance, or Kolpakova's sly assistance that brought ABT artistic director Kevin McKenzie to the studio where Max was taking an open class a few days later. "He asked my name, and to come see him in his office the next day. I still don't know why—maybe he just needed boys?—but he offered me a contract on the spot."

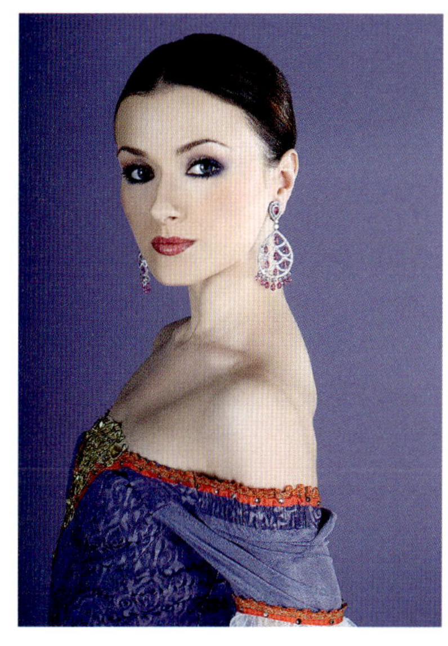

Irina Dvorovenko, 2004.

Irina joined Max in New York, though she had to freelance for two years until a position at ABT opened up for her—in the corps de ballet. She entered the company's corps but was only out of the spotlight briefly, rising to soloist and principal in a few seasons. Irina and Max quickly cemented their reputation as pillars of ABT's star lineup.

Irina and Max developed a passionate fan base devoted to their coupledom but mesmerized by their dancing as individuals, too. They each exuded charisma and star power in their own ways. When she was a child, Irina's

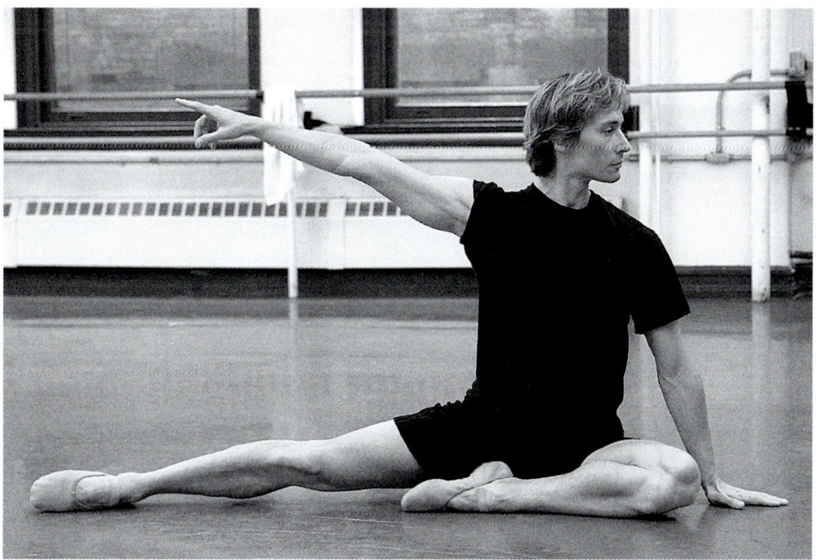

Maxim Beloserkovsky rehearsing *Apollo,* 2005. Photo courtesy of American Ballet Theatre.

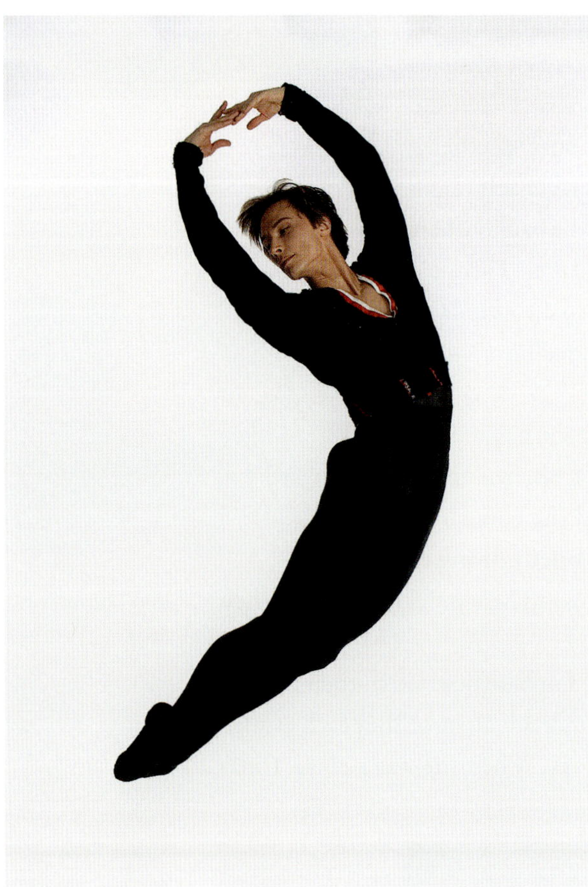

Maxim Beloserkovsky, 2007.

initial interest in dance wasn't just the physical joy of movement, even though she became renowned for her sublime lines and technique. She'd been pulled in by what legions of little girls love—beautiful costumes and fairy-tale glamour. She said she always wanted to be a star, but not just to be the center of attention. "I loved to make people feel something, to laugh or cry or put myself into someone else's skin and tell their story," Irina remembered. "That was just my personality." As a dancer, that compulsion manifested into a ballerina of unparalleled magnetism, for whom the theater was always home and where she felt fullest. "We emotionally grew up in the theater," Irina said, speaking of her and Max's youth in Kyiv and that mysterious aura that those who spend their lives in the theater are so familiar with. "There, we felt at peace. It is like a cathedral; you feel like a saint. I don't care which country or city I'm in, when I'm at the theater I am at home."

For Max, it's hard to pinpoint exactly what pulled him to dance. He definitely knows it was akin to an addiction, which is why he could never consider stopping no matter what he faced, nor settling with satisfaction when he achieved the fame his mother (who'd told him as a kid that he'd perform at the Metropolitan Opera House someday) had predicted. He never took his natural gifts or accomplishments for granted, since he, too, had doubts and insecurities. He wanted to succeed to honor his mom, and once he had, he realized that being a dancer was larger than being himself.

"Ballet gives me the ability to leave my skin and become somebody else," he said. "I'm more interesting as Basilio or Siegfried than I am in real life. And the endless drive, discipline, the core of ballet have shaped me."

Max retired from ABT in 2012, and Irina in 2013. As incredibly invested in their performing careers as they were, retiring was a clear choice for both: they'd done virtually every ballet in the classical and neoclassical repertories many times over and though they still had energy and artistic curiosity, they felt the ballet company structure wasn't fueling them anymore. And Irina wrestled with ever-increasing pain. Although she was gifted with an optimal physique for ballet, she'd dealt with inflammation, strains, and sprains, particularly in her ankles and feet, nearly all her life. Being on stage was the one place the pain disappeared. "On stage, I was the happiest person. The amount of joy was totally overpowering," she remembered. "Sometimes I would literally forget the steps because I was so excited in that moment. My mind took me to a different sphere. I was limping before and after, but I was flying onstage." But when her body started requiring her to calculate every maneuver, compensate, and be cautious in performance, Irina knew it was time to stop. "You need to deliver fully," she said. "You can't fake it. If I couldn't fully express myself, I felt trapped." For Max, the entrapment was artistic and emotional. "Leaving ABT wasn't bittersweet. I felt in every fiber of my being that I'd come full circle. It was not fresh anymore. I needed to rediscover who I could be."

Luckily, Irina continued to take risks, throw herself into roles, and fascinate audiences. She moved easily through a thrilling transition into acting, both stage and screen, and she and Max commissioned choreographers to work with them in styles beyond classical ballet, exploring types of movement not typically associated with their ABT identities. They also became sought-after teachers and coaches, emphasizing to all who take their classes (from youth to principals looking for their expert perspective) that artistry must be weighted over technical showmanship, and that commitment to the humility of being a lifelong student is essential. Versatility is, too. "The world doesn't have walls anymore," Max said. "You have to speak multiple languages, train in different styles. Working with one teacher doesn't mean you

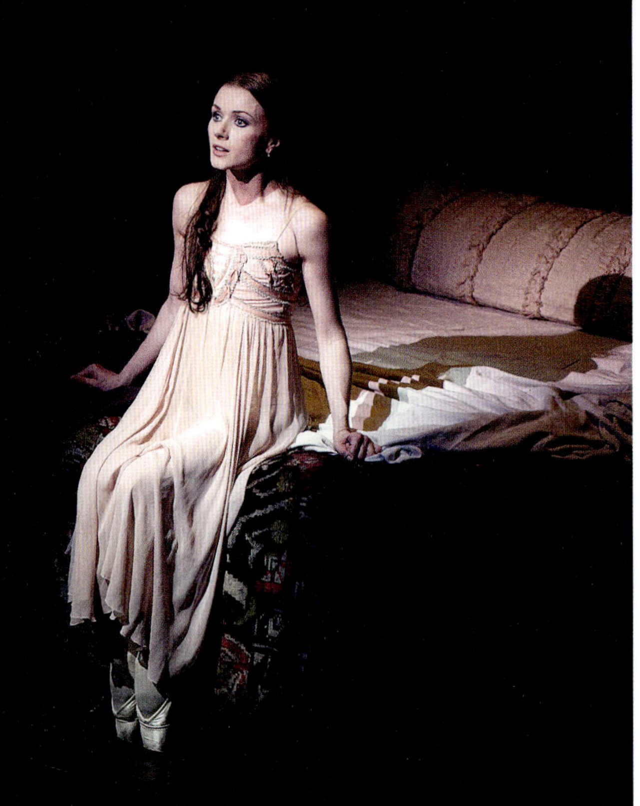

Irina Dvorovenko in *Romeo and Juliet,* 2009. Photo courtesy of American Ballet Theatre.

have to disregard what another one says. You can't just be exceptional in classical work and expect to succeed. Invest in your training."

The teaching and coaching that Max and Irina deliver to students far and wide (they launched a popular series of online classes during the COVID-19 pandemic era) are rich with their trademark fire, insight, perception, inspiration, and humor. "There's a fine line between being academically beautiful and being able to express breath and emotion through your body," Irina said. "Now, dancers are more powerful and technical, but sometimes there is a lack of emotional excitement. It looks 'perfect,' but it's forgettable. But you see, for me, there is no 'perfect.' If you are too calculated, it's boring. I was always edgy. When I look at photographs of myself now, I see the energy and excitement that I delivered. Those things overshadow any flaws. When there is depth in the performance, the picture comes alive."

IYUN ASHANI HARRISON

I'm trying to give people permission to be who they are, in all aspects of my life, not just the studio and classroom. While always working on your technique and artistry, you have to carve out a space to be what makes you authentically you, not a version of something you think you're supposed to be.

THROUGH HIS CAREERS in ballet and modern dance, professorships in university dance departments, and as a choreographer, director, and curator, Iyun acknowledges that he's had both privilege and faced challenging impediments.

Now, his mission is to give back the gifts he's had and to help others find, as he has, their most authentic, fullest lives.

Growing up in Jamaica, Iyun was always around the arts, but dance was a sideline at first. His parents were both actors—his father had gone to NYU for film and worked on Broadway; his mother acted alongside her public relations career—so he gravitated toward theater. As a young kid, Iyun joined a musical theater group where dance was, very informally, part of the drill. "It was really just 'step, touch, step, touch,'" he recalled with a laugh. One of the teachers noticed his affinity for movement, though, and suggested adding in actual ballet classes to help his budding musical theater skills. Iyun's parents agreed, and he enrolled with a local teacher. Immediately, it clicked.

"My teacher, Norma Spence, had studied at the Royal Ballet School, but back then they weren't hiring dark-skinned women," he said. "So she became a teacher, and trained us in that style. It was just the children's recreational syllabus, but she really got me ready for everything else that was to come." Iyun knows exactly what it was about ballet that suited him so well. "My brain likes rules and form. There was something about the rules of ballet that my peers did not enjoy, but I was really good at. I understood what I was supposed to do, and I did it. Other more interpretive types of dance were challenging for me, but I felt at home with the structures of ballet."

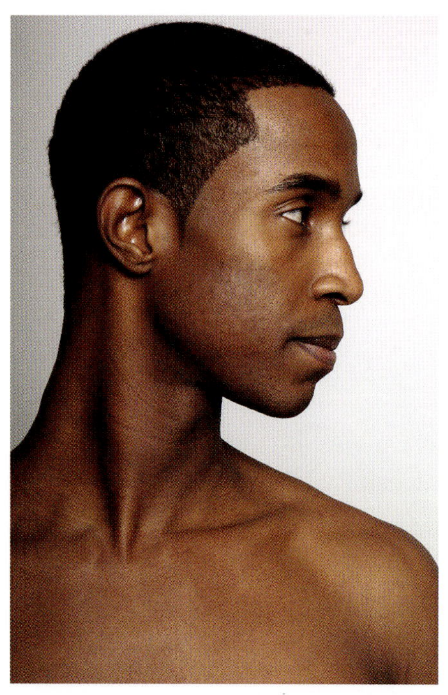

Iyun Ashani Harrison, 2005.

In addition to its satisfying form and clarity, Iyun tapped right into the aesthetic and spiritual beauty of ballet. Even at thirteen, he loved the lines, flexibility, and carriage of ballet technique, and its decorum, ritual, and formality offered a sense of escapism. The studio environment became a thing of safety and security, and also a place to dream. Mrs. Spence created a home for Iyun and the other boys in the school—"a weird home, but a dance home," he said—where they belonged and knew what was expected. "It was very defined, and I was one of those kids who thrived on that. It worked for me."

As he became more and more invested in ballet (while also keeping up with musical theater), Iyun gradually started to see how dance could be more than an activity in his life—that it could be a career. One by one, he received hints about how much possibility existed beyond the walls of his studio in Jamaica. On a trip to Washington, DC, to perform with his musical theater group, he saw a male dancer from Les Ballets Trockadero de Monte Carlo in class. "He was six feet tall, of African descent, and dancing in pointe shoes," Iyun recalled. "It was an important moment for me."

Back home, an adjudicator who'd come to his school from Australia to administer the annual Royal Academy of Dance exam took Iyun aside, telling him that with his talent, he should further his studies outside of Jamaica. She cautioned, though, that no matter where he went, very hard work would be involved. But the encouragement was all Iyun needed. He started researching dance colleges abroad.

Aiming high, Juilliard emerged as one of Iyun's top choices. He went to New York six weeks before the audition to soak up the dance scene. Taking classes at the Ailey School, meeting professional dancers from the Ailey and Martha Graham companies, and touring the Juilliard building, Iyun discovered a completely new world. He was convinced New York was where he needed to be.

Iyun was accepted to Juilliard, and the mind-opening experiences continued. He saw performances at Lincoln Center—New York City Ballet, American Ballet Theatre, the Paris Opera Ballet—including a *Swan Lake* with Susan Jaffe in the lead role that left him in tears. "It was a spiritual experience for me," he said. "It was my first year at Juilliard, and I recognized that something exceptional was happening onstage. To witness that was revelatory." In New York, Iyun was surrounded by people—onstage and off, in the studio and outside—who modeled lives he'd never known were possible. He began to realize that the disconnect between a person's inner and outer lives that was culturally and socially required in Jamaica didn't necessarily have to exist.

After graduation, Iyun spent two years as a member of Ailey II before being spotted by Arthur Mitchell and hired into Mitchell's company, Dance Theatre of Harlem. He moved on to Ballet Hispanico when a financial crisis forced DTH to suspend operations. Throughout, his concept of how dancers could live, be, and look was undergoing a radical shift.

Those years had a big impact on Iyun. Growing up in Jamaica, he'd had access and privilege that most of the population didn't: education, family social status, and talent in the arts that gave him an outlet and an escape. But he also sensed that in Jamaica, there wasn't a place for him as a gay youth. Observing the way the male dancers of the Ailey company, DTH, and Juilliard performed and inhabited their lives in New York gave Iyun a way to reimagine his own life. "I saw gay people who were well-adjusted, successful, not social pariahs," he said. "Even my teachers, although they never talked about their sexuality, showing up at events with their same-sex partner, provided me with that model."

With experience in such a wide array of styles, Iyun doesn't categorize himself as any one type of dancer. But he's always thought of himself as a storyteller. A storyteller with a strong work ethic, big stage presence, and deep musicality, which he continues to be, offstage, as a choreographer and teacher. And that's where he always knew, in his heart, that his most important work would take place. His ongoing story is to allow people to be who they are, while examining the concept of identity, whether that is racial, ethnic, sexual, or geographic. "I'm trying to show that there are more ways of being queer than people probably realize. We don't all have to be that gay stereotype. I want people to see themselves onstage. And to be themselves onstage."

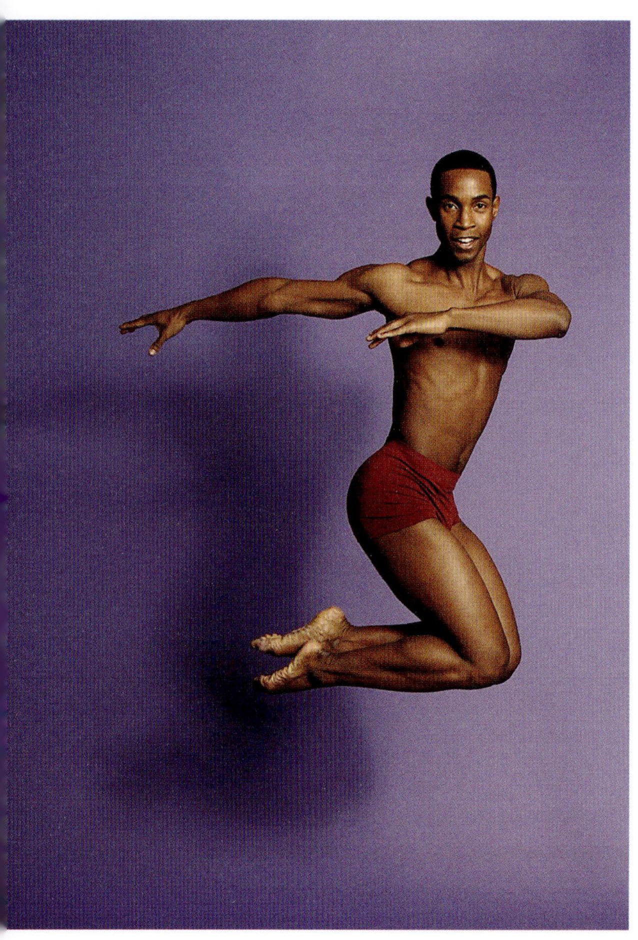

Iyun Ashani Harrison, 2005.

Iyun became a professor of dance at Duke University and set out to complete a doctorate in educational leadership and organizational innovation. He choreographs regularly for his company, Ballet Ashani, and imagines someday bringing his accumulated experience to a leadership position, perhaps at a ballet company where he could further the momentum that's already bringing the ballet business into a new era. In his position of visibility and influence, Iyun takes seriously being a model like the ones he didn't have early in his life but found in his formative college years.

"That means showing good work ethic, being transparent about knowledge I have, showing that I have done consistent research, investigation, and am continually curious. I represent a version of queerness, Blackness, being a Jamaican, intellectual artist. But I understand, and want today's young people to understand, that 'me' keeps changing, and whatever container they decide to be in needs to facilitate all their various parts."

SUSAN JAFFE

A dancer's technique is just words on a page.
Your job as a performer is to make meaning out of them.

EARLY IN HER CAREER with American Ballet Theatre, Susan realized something that usually takes a dancer years to understand and that even then, many find too daunting to address. When she was just a teenager in ABT's corps, Susan was unexpectedly chosen by the company's then-artistic director, Mikhail Baryshnikov, to replace Gelsey Kirkland in a gala performance. Suddenly, Susan was an early-blooming star—and one with an unusually curious nature and mature approach to the other major roles she soon took on. But for all the attention on the ballets' technical feats, she sensed something was often missing in performances she saw—she felt that even the most physically astonishing steps could somehow look empty, or even meaningless, and wondered why. She decided that when she danced, she would try to make the characters she portrayed seem real, dimensional, and human, even in the context of a fairy-tale ballet. "To do that, I really felt that one of the most important things, as a performer and interpreter, was to know myself on the deepest level—all the good, the bad, the dark, the light," Susan says. "And therefore, to understand humanity and to have compassion for all the things we go through as humans. The subtleties of what it means to be alive."

To that end, Susan became, and remains, committed to a meditation practice that she believes has been essential in learning to see those subtleties and bring them out in her work, both onstage and off. Since retiring from her twenty-two-year career as a dancer with ABT (nineteen of them as a principal) in 2002, she has taught students of all ages, run her own school, and been a university dance administrator and artistic director of two companies—including, as of this writing, ABT itself. In every setting, her motivation is to translate what she did as a dancer into what she does as a teacher, coach, and leader. Susan sees herself as an eager lifelong learner

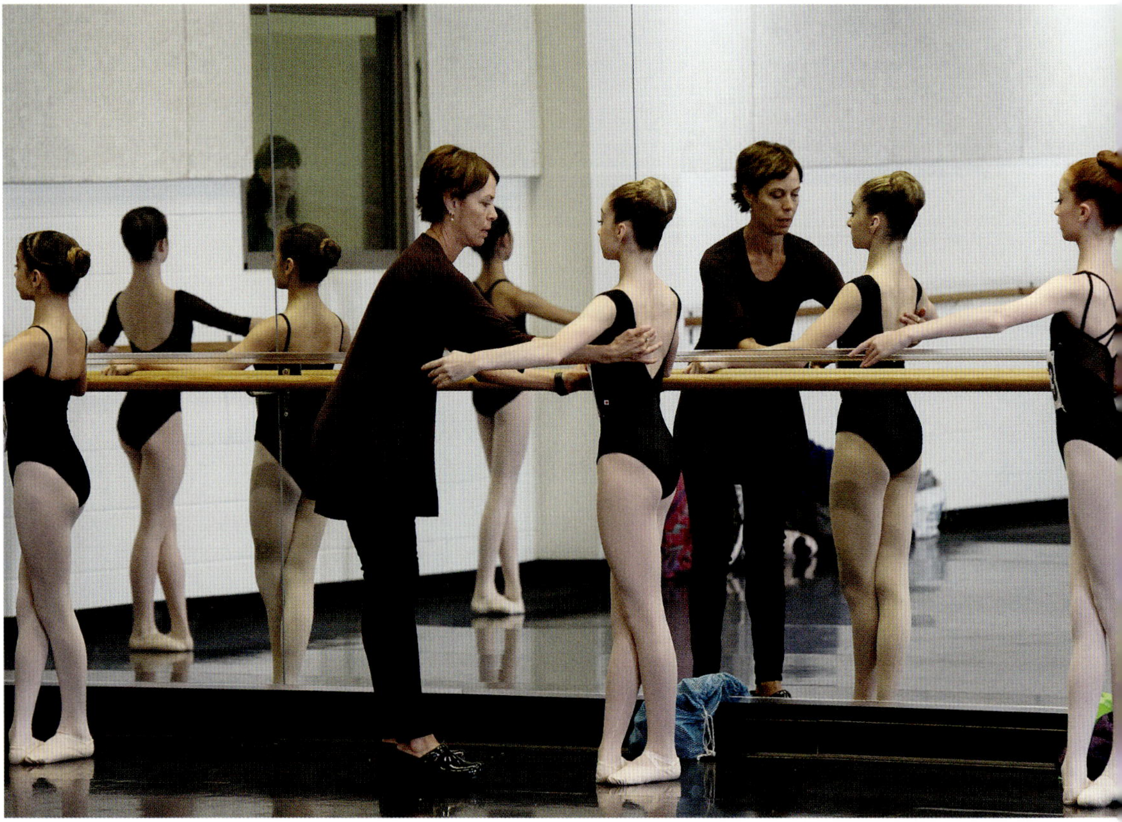

Susan Jaffe teaching class at Indianapolis City Ballet, 2015.

who's proud to now be in a position to use and spread what she's collected from years of observation and thought. She remembers being influenced by many wonderful mentors, teachers, and choreographers, but also many who were not. "Now, as the person in the front of the room, I know that everyone who's a professional has deep talent and something special to offer. What I want to do is bring out their confidence, their best, and push them in the direction that maybe even they didn't know they could go."

SUSAN IS FAR FROM ALONE in embracing the grittiness of dance—all dancers have some degree of compulsion for hard, hard work—but she sees that too often the requirement of extreme effort becomes an overwhelming psychological burden. She turns back to how she developed her own onstage characters to help her students and the professionals she coaches rein in and use their darker emotions, emphasizing that it's incumbent upon them as performers to work with the negative voice we all have, and to become larger than it. "If you can do that, then you become fully present and empowered."

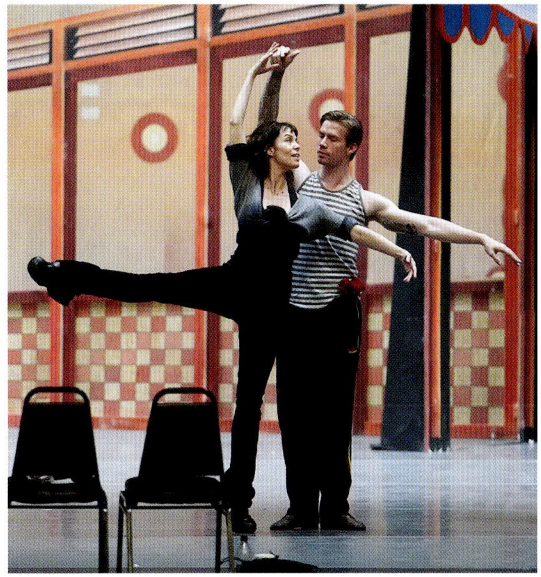

Susan Jaffe coaching ABT dancer Kenneth Easter, 2015.

Criticism can be rich fuel for that negative voice, yet it's necessary and unavoidable in the life of a performing artist. Susan's strategy is to lead by showing admiration and care for anyone she works with, from students to pros to staff and board members, instead of leveraging the power dynamic of being the one in charge. "If you don't have deep respect for the people you work with, they feel it," she said. "Being a leader doesn't mean you get to talk down to people. It means being a support and an uplift. Then, even if I have to give insight that may not be comfortable to hear, they know it's because I am their cheerleader."

Susan knows she's lucky to have a career's worth of wisdom, but for dancers at any stage, it all starts with asking the right questions—and the hard questions—even if the answers are not immediately clear. In the dancer's world, growth and work are endless, she says. "We all have a responsibility to our own heart," she said. "And that begins with knowing who you are, and then aiming for the place that's right for you. You need to be realistic and practical, but you can still aim your arrow and shoot high. I push the joy of that effort, because the rewards you get back are hundredfold."

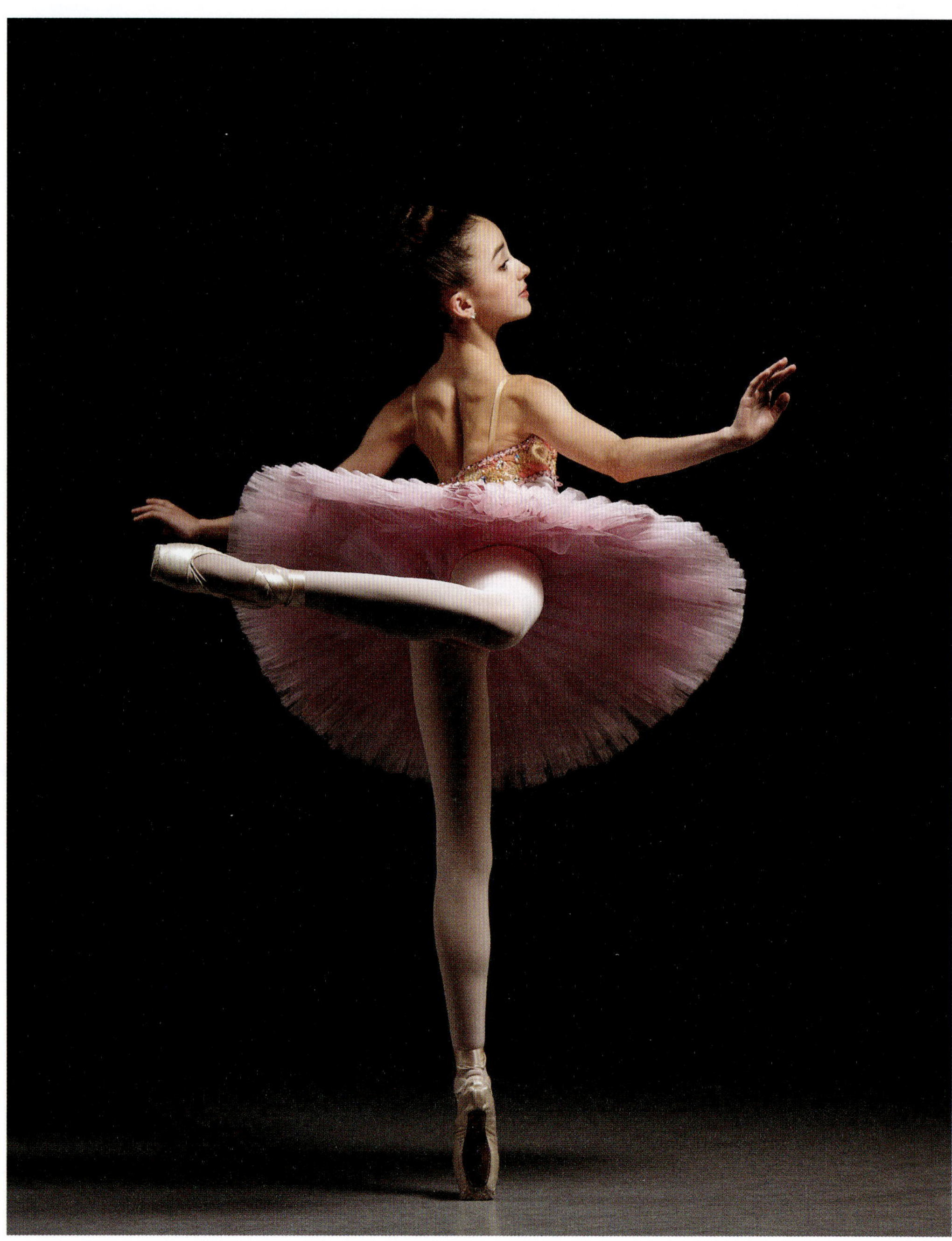

Viola Pantuso, 2015, age eleven.

VIOLA PANTUSO

When you become a professional, you have to be your own teacher, your own mentor. You have to use your voice, because there's going to be no one looking out for you.

WHEN VIOLA FEELS STRONGLY about something, she doesn't hold back. She has had many teachers and mentors along the way, but she also has an instinctive take-charge approach. When she was a fourteen-year-old student at the Royal Ballet School's White Lodge, "being her own teacher" meant waking up at 5 a.m. to sneak out of her dorm room and into the dance studio, where she'd do exercises and practice technique before breakfast. Viola had just moved to London from New York, where she'd been studying at Ellison Ballet, a school with small classes and a heavy emphasis on technical accomplishment and individual coaching. The Royal Ballet School's prioritization of the subtleties of style and artistry made Viola fear she'd lose the hard-won technical skills that weren't being challenged in her new classes—hence, her early-morning solo practice sessions.

Now a dancer in the Royal Ballet, Viola has been living away from home for almost half her life. She's from Chicago originally, where she started dancing at a local studio before switching to the Joffrey Ballet School. Viola's talent had been noticed by the time she was eleven, and she was put in a class with sixteen- and seventeen-year-olds which, as a naturally ambitious kid, she didn't find intimidating at all. In fact, being among older dancers only made her crave more challenge. Viola and her mom spent a summer in New York so she could attend the American Ballet Theatre school's summer intensive, and while there, Viola took a drop-in class with Edward Ellison on her day off. Afterward, he came over to talk. "He said he thought I had potential and he wanted me to audition for his school the very next day," Viola remembered. "I hadn't heard of him, but my mom knew his reputation for very good training. I thought there was no way I'd get in, let alone move to New York, but I went to the audition just to see what happened."

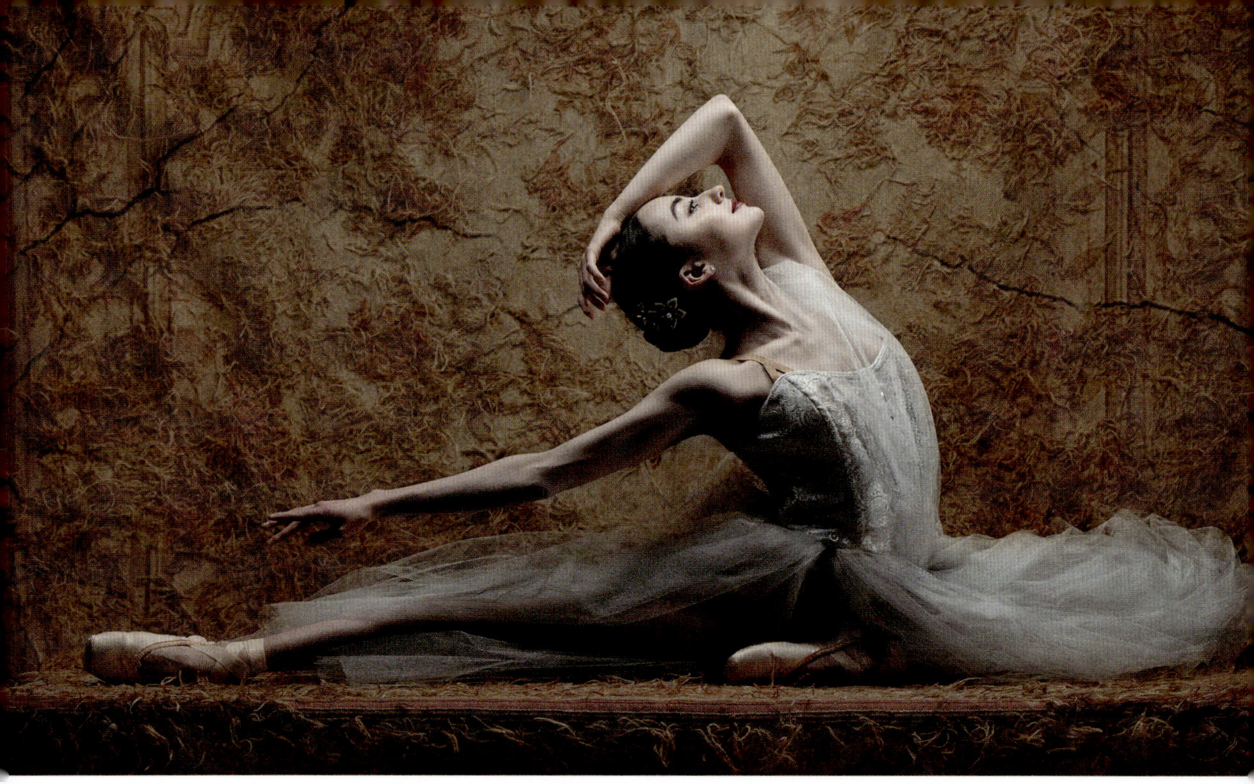

Viola Pantuso, 2019.

What happened was that out of a pool of 150 auditioners, Viola was accepted. She was very young to commit to full-day, intense ballet training, but Mr. Ellison's encouragement and the promise of receiving coaching that could help her fulfill her potential were hard to pass up. "It's what I was craving," Viola said. "I wanted to take ballet much more seriously. Of course, at that age I didn't think about money or logistics or how hard it would be, but something in me said to do it."

Viola's parents agreed to let her enroll at Ellison Ballet, despite the upheaval to their family. It was hard for them, especially for Viola's mom, who gave up her job to come with Viola to New York, where finding a place to live was only the first reality check (they stayed in a low-end hotel for several weeks until a friend's sublet miraculously came through.) Viola remembers being quite scared during her first week at Ellison Ballet, in a tiny class with only ten other girls. The businesslike teachers immediately focused on Viola's shortcomings and mistakes. Despite how startled she was by the teachers' intensity, very soon Viola knew she'd made the right choice. "They told me how to fix everything I was doing wrong, which made me really want to

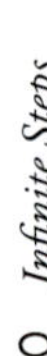

work for it," she said. "I hadn't realized ballet could be broken down into such detail—sometimes we spent an hour on plié—but I also saw how much my teacher wanted it for me and supported me."

Amazingly, while she was putting in a full day of ballet classes (and fitting in online academics afterward), Viola was also seriously training in Irish dance, getting up at 4:00 a.m. for private lessons with her Irish dance coach before running to her 9:00 a.m. ballet class. She'd been doing it since she was nine and loved it as much as ballet, but the two styles pulled her in opposite directions. She even competed in the Irish Dance World Championships—in secret from her ballet teachers—before making the decision to focus on ballet, which unlike Irish dance, offered a career path. Viola thrived on the rigor of both Irish dance and ballet training. "It made me used to working hard," she said. "I always had someone pushing me, telling me what I needed to do to progress. I learned what tough love is."

An unexpected aspect of being an Ellison Ballet student was the expectation to participate—if selected by the faculty—in competitions like Youth America Grand Prix. Being chosen to compete was an honor, and since students who did well received high visibility, the preparations were just as competitive as the event itself. Neither the high-pressure atmosphere at Ellison nor taking the competition stage rattled Viola when she participated for the first time. Although she disliked competing, she handled it with her characteristic easy-going yet headstrong style, making it through regional rounds to the very selective finals. Even after falling during her variation performance, she "kept her blinders on," as she described it, and laughed about it later. "I guess I felt I'd already proved myself."

The judges agreed, and Viola finished with the silver medal and a scholarship to the English National Ballet School's summer intensive, landing her within arm's reach of the next step toward her dream: the Royal Ballet. At the end of the intensive, fourteen-year-old Viola applied and was accepted to White Lodge, the Royal Ballet School's lower division. Since she'd already been away from home for years, living in a foreign country wasn't a big deal to her. What was harder was discovering that after having previously had multiple hours of classes on a daily basis, her schedule at RBS didn't feel like enough. She feared she'd be going backward.

Viola Pantuso,
2019.

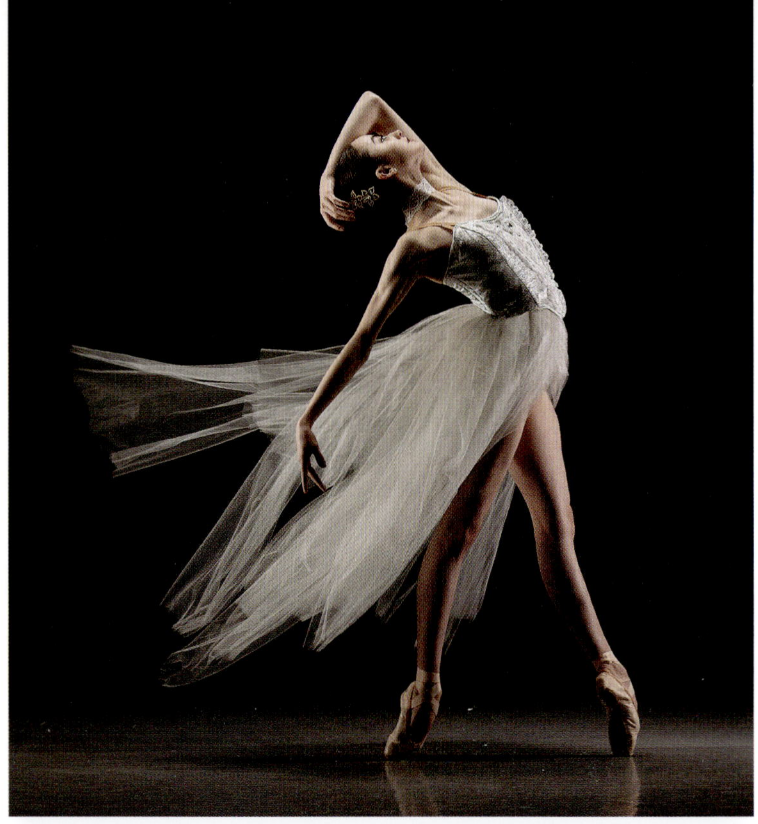

Viola Pantuso,
2019.

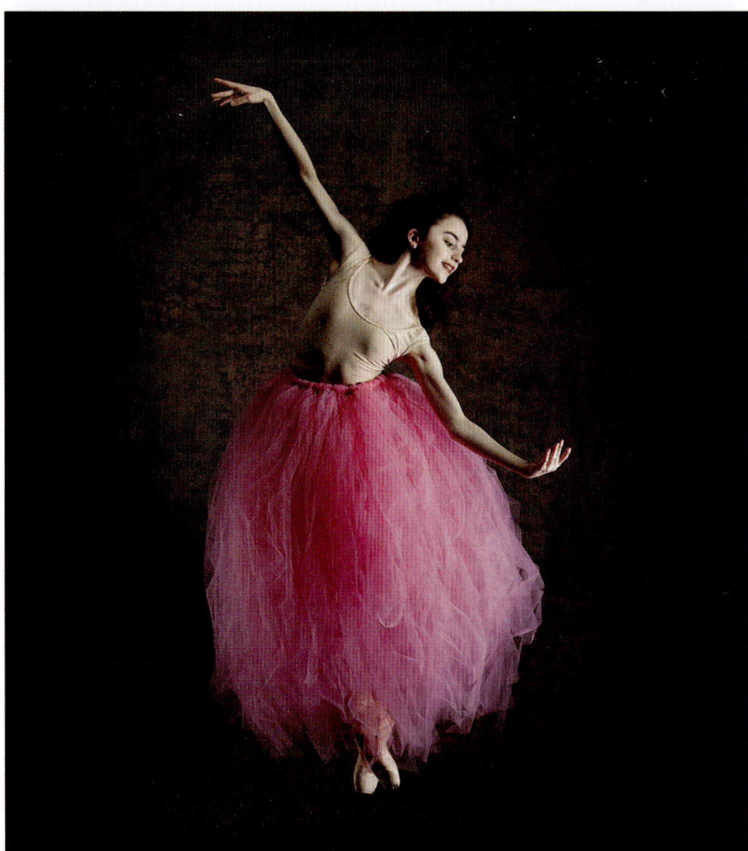

Even back then, Viola knew the importance of her hard-earned physical and technical strength, which had been so prioritized during her years at Ellison Ballet. She determined not to lose any of it, even as she adapted to the quite different British approach. She also had catching up to do academically, which meant more hours studying and less time for ballet. She panicked a little, which triggered her to put in the extra studio time on her own. "I decided to work really, really hard to take what I learned from Ellison and apply it to what I was learning at RBS," she said. "And I kept that up for every year I was at the school."

When Viola advanced to the RBS Upper School she had fewer hours of academics, more dance classes, the anticipation of graduation, and the chance of a Royal Ballet contract—but nothing was certain. Even moving to the next level each year hinged on passing an official assessment. And when Viola developed a stress fracture in her foot that was agonizingly slow to heal, she hit a major roadblock that, for the first time, hard work and determination couldn't push away. It was the most vital time of her training, as she was close to graduating and company directors frequently came to observe and offer jobs. Viola felt so much pressure that she tried to dance through pain so immense she could barely walk. During a jump combination in class one day, she heard a crack and fell to the floor. "I'd been pushing so hard, but I just couldn't do it anymore," she said. "It was terribly stressful."

That literal breaking point also woke Viola up to the futility of trying to dance full-out against her body's signals. Her characteristic mental strength *wasn't* injured, though, so she vowed to continue working, just differently. She did intense—but non–weight bearing—exercises every day to stay fit while her foot healed. Finally, after a year and half that included COVID-19 lockdowns that slowed everyone else's progress, too, she was ready to dance again. But it was almost too late—the year-end assessments had happened without her and Royal Ballet apprentice contracts had already been awarded to a few of her classmates.

Viola was given the option to repeat last year of training, but that didn't feel right. She decided to voice her concerns to her teacher and to Kevin O'Hare, the Royal Ballet's artistic director. "I was back dancing, but Kevin had not seen me before he made job offers. I really wanted a chance at dancing in front of

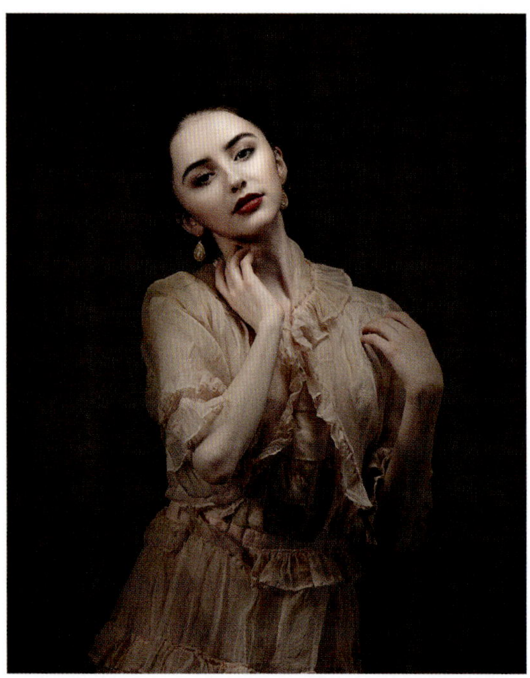

Viola Pantuso, 2019.

him. They were discouraging and said it was unlikely he would watch class again. But a few days later, he walked in during my class. And afterward, he offered me a contract."

With her natural self-assurance, Viola fit easily into company life, which she describes as family-like, where principals chat with apprentices and offer guidance, coaching and encouragement. Even taking class alongside her idols wasn't intimidating, as evidenced by her habit of taking a spot in the front line, unlike many of her more hesitant corps de ballet peers. "The professional atmosphere was freeing," she recalled. "It was the chance to be the dancer I always wanted to be."

That's not to say her dreamt-of life as a Royal Ballet dancer is always easy. The touring and performance schedule is grueling, and on many mornings her body aches so much that getting out of bed seems impossible. Not all dancers can justify their love of dance with the realities of the daily slog, but Viola tries to separate those feelings and find some reason to continue from day to day. And her future is bright. She was soon being given major featured roles and was promoted to First Artist in 2024.

Every day in the Royal Ballet is a "pinch me" moment for Viola. She still revels in sharing the studio and stage with artists she's idolized for years. Getting to watch them up close and trying to absorb the nuances they bring to their work and to audiences are what's most exciting and important to Viola. As technically gifted as she is, she knows the real value of a performance is in something deeper than impressive physical tricks. "I don't agree with people who compare us to athletes," she said. "Yes, we have that physicality, but although our bodies can do extraordinary things, I like how you can bring someone into your world with your artistic capability. How high you can get your leg or how many turns you do is exciting, but what's really special is the quality you bring to the movement."

DEVON TEUSCHER

How do I keep these ballets relevant, timeless, and interesting to audiences now, while also respecting their history and classicism? It's not easy, but when I'm able to do it, it's very rewarding.

DURING THE NINE YEARS it took for her to become a principal dancer, Devon never took her bedrock-strong technique for granted, but she also didn't want that to be all she was known for. As an established figure in American Ballet Theatre's lineup of ballerinas, the challenge she's set for herself, in an age when evidence of ballet's ever-rising standards of technical virtuosity is prominent on social media feeds and competition stages, is to show us why those steps exist in the first place. What are they for, if not to say something?

When Devon joined ABT as an apprentice in 2007, she was awestruck to find herself taking company class with dancers she'd revered since her student days, like Paloma Herrera and Julie Kent. Standing at the barre with them, she was mesmerized and inspired. She watched, copied, tried to model her own dancing after theirs.

Devon's eyes weren't focused only on her idols. She genuinely liked watching other dancers, period. When she wasn't needed at any point in a full-company rehearsal, while her peers might be sitting on the side chatting, she'd be discreetly observing the dancers working around her, taking in bits and pieces of information from everyone. It's a habit Devon kept up, and that she considers a fundamental part of being a professional dancer. "I'd be constantly listening to corrections others were getting, even if I was never going to do that role," she says. "And that's something I still do. There's so much value in being able to soak up information in that way. You don't even need to be up on your feet, moving."

Like many dancers whose ascent to the highest rank appears to have been inevitable, Devon was never sure she actually would make it there. As a teenaged apprentice, some of her peers seemed a lot more confident

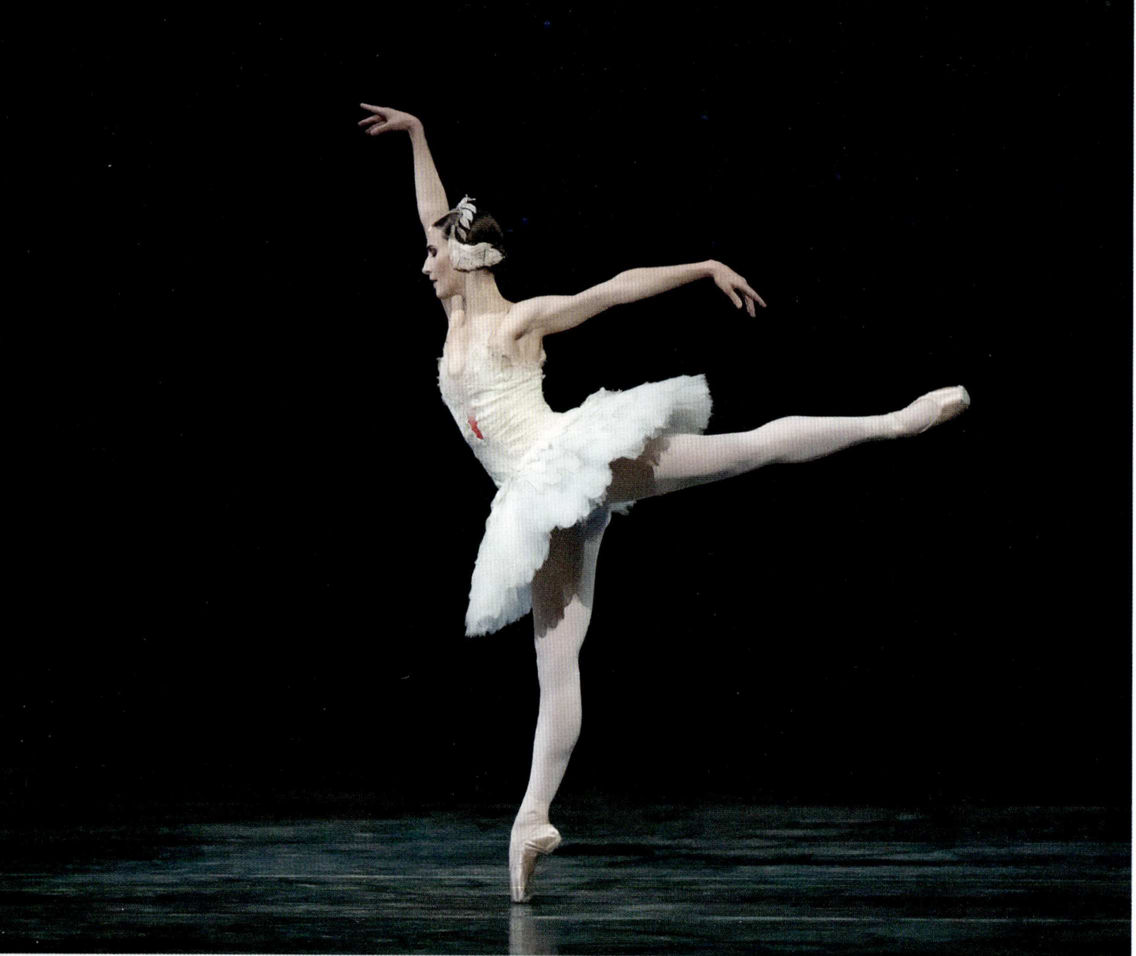

Devon Teuscher in *Swan Lake,* 2019. Photo courtesy of American Ballet Theatre.

about their futures than Devon did about hers. She remembered a fellow dancer in the Studio Company assuredly answering, "Yes!" when asked if they thought they'd be a principal dancer someday. "I just thought, 'How can you be so sure?'" Devon said. "Obviously it was a dream of mine, too, but it's out of your control. All you can do is put in your work and hope for the best."

Devon did put in her work, which meant a lot more than drilling the turns and jumps that come so naturally to her. The quiet work—the watching, listening, and thinking—is how she developed into the dancer she is today, known for so completely transforming herself into the character of any role she performs that those watching her almost lose sight of the steps. But becoming an artist takes time. Devon, like most gifted young dancers aiming for a ballet career, showed her talent early and was given scholarships to train at several selective schools, including ABT's own, from where she joined the ABT Studio Company and the main company soon thereafter. For the next six years Devon was in the corps de ballet, where she remembered being grateful for the colleagues who helped buffer her entry into the fast-paced, sometimes rough world of the ensemble. "When I joined, it was not as positive and friendly as it is now," Devon said. "I mostly stayed quiet and kept my eyes open."

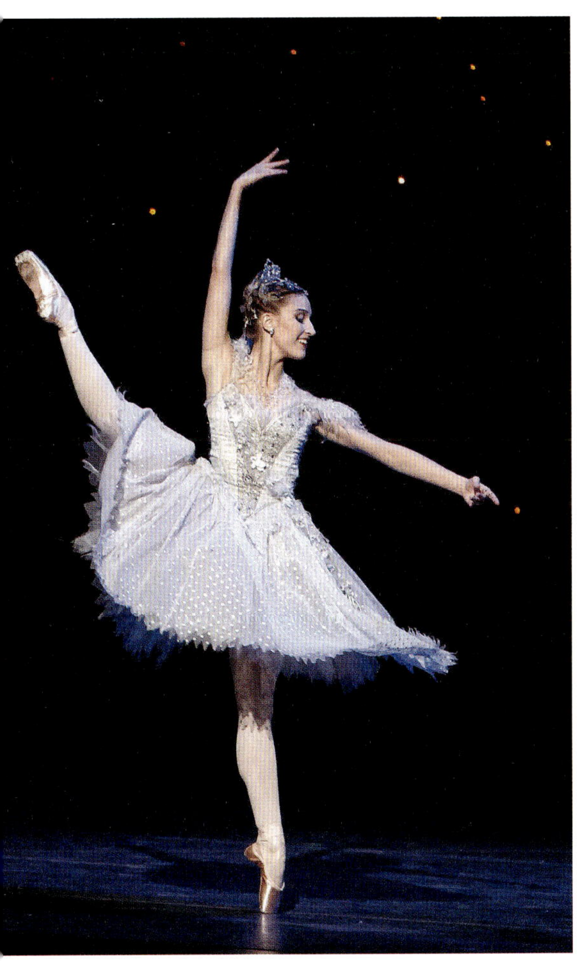

Devon Teuscher in *Cinderella,* 2014.
Photo courtesy of American Ballet Theatre.

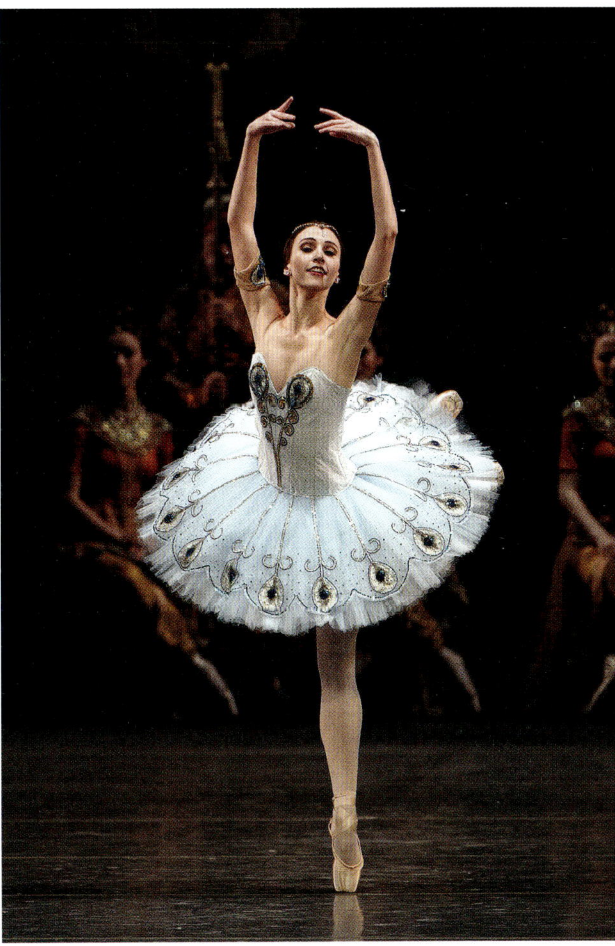

Devon Teuscher in *La Bayadère,* 2012.
Photo courtesy of American Ballet Theatre.

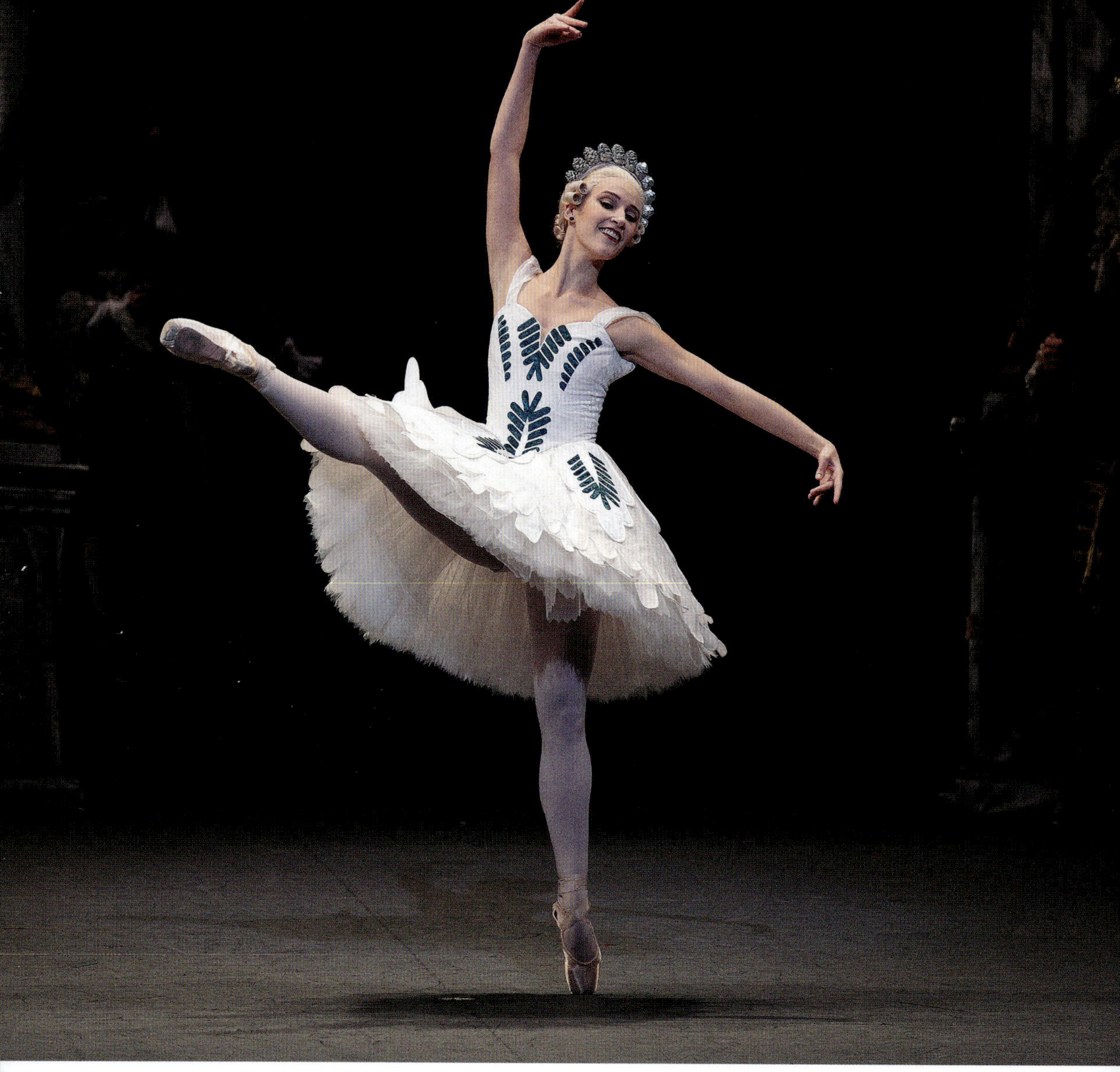

Devon Teuscher in *The Sleeping Beauty,* 2015.
Photo courtesy of American Ballet Theatre.

Devon was almost immediately cast in technically tough solo parts that would be daunting to any dancer. That was an encouraging sign for her future in ABT, but she worried about being typecast in powerhouse roles without many chances at more character-driven ones if her dreamed-of promotion ever did come, which it did when she rose to soloist in 2014. From that point on, Devon showed her ability to turn technique into language in every major role she danced, including her first Odette/Odile in *Swan Lake,* which may well have been the catalyst to her rise to principal. A reviewer in the *New York Times* called her a "poet in pointe shoes," which is exactly what Devon wants to be.[1] Devon remembered the day she was finally promoted to principal. "I had a rehearsal with David Hallberg and Alexei Ratmansky, and they both said, 'Now is when the real work starts. Now is when you get to decide who you are as a dancer, what your voice is, what your vision is. And everyone's watching you.' That was terrifying."

As a twenty-first-century ballerina in a company whose foundation is performing nineteenth-century classics, Devon is perfectly situated to maximize the opportunity to define how ballet fits into the modern world. The full-length story ballets that are sometimes thought of as relics of the past and whose relevance is questioned are instead, to Devon, exciting opportunities. "As a current dancer doing historical work, I would love to bring them into the present and push them forward, to allow people to see why they're important and timeless."

What makes these classic works timeless is a hard question. Devon thinks the answer lies in the people who perform them. She's looking for ways to convey age-old themes—love, trust, the human body—with a modern physicality. "I have to find the fine line between humanity and more modern technique while keeping the classical lines," she said. "That's something I'm really excited about and try to imbue all my dancing with."

---

1. https://www.nytimes.com/2017/06/01/arts/dance/devon-teuscher-abt-ballet-swan-lake.html

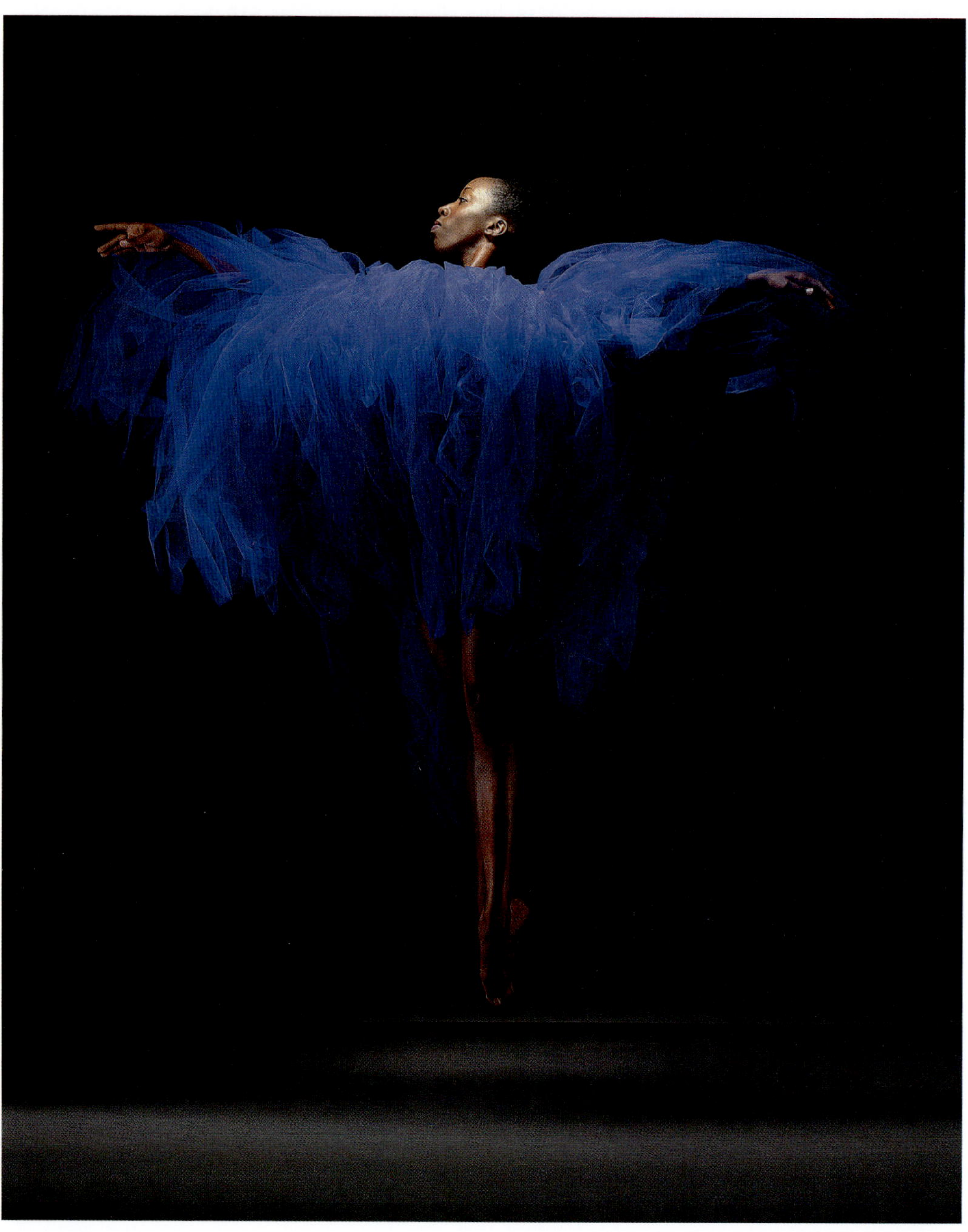

Trinity Cox, 2018.

TRINITY COX

I've always felt I had something to say. I don't want to move through my career with perspectives that were assigned to me instead of taking a step back and looking at them.

TRINITY FIRMLY BELIEVES that ballet can lift a person up and take them to heights they may never have imagined, perhaps because it happened to her.

Trinity knew she was born to dance when she was just a young girl, even though she'd never even seen as much as a photograph of a professional dancer, let alone a performance. Her early training at an arts program at her Ft. Lauderdale, Florida, middle school was a somewhat haphazard assortment of modern, jazz, and contemporary, with the merest smattering of ballet basics thrown in. She didn't have a ton of knowledge, but dance felt like a treasure that just kept offering more and more. By high school, Trinity got her first glimpses of professional dance, and those feelings exploded. "I saw an image—I don't even know where I got it from—of Linda Celeste-Sims, who was an Ailey dancer. It was that famous picture of her in a tilt jump, with her hair down and against a purple background. She is just so strong. That was the image that made me think, 'Okay, maybe I could do that, too . . .'"

Trinity was hungry to advance further in dance, but even with the very limited exposure she'd had at that point in her life, she knew she wasn't learning enough. She entered an arts-focused high school and continued training, but the ballet portion was still only rudimentary. Her innate gift was apparent when she auditioned for, and was accepted to, a Joffrey Ballet summer program, even though her formal training was lacking. She didn't go, but a subtle, almost imperceptible psychological shift must have happened that gave her a sense of possibility.

Trinity wanted to dance professionally, but without any guidance on how to do that, she set out for college. She didn't think a dance degree would help her launch a dance career and she wanted to move into sports broadcasting someday anyway, so she chose a communications major. But when

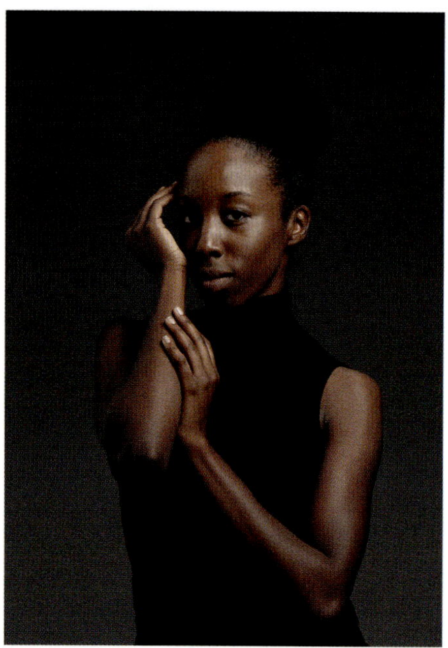

Trinity Cox,
2018.

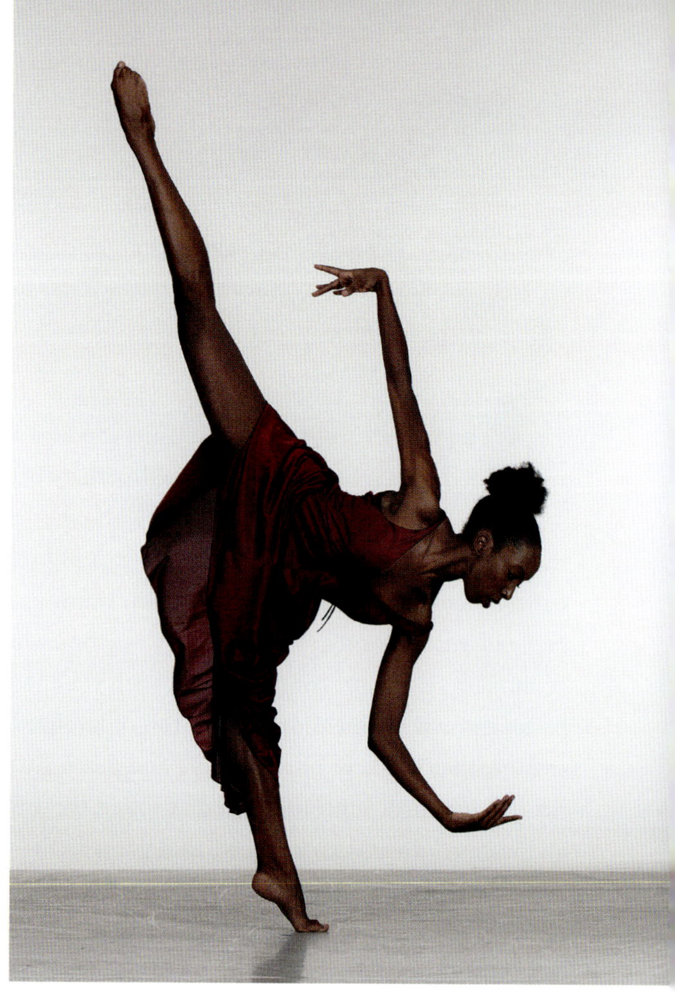

Trinity Cox, 2018.

she arrived at the University of Alabama for her first semester, a friend told her about the school's brand-new dance BFA program and urged Trinity to come along and audition for the dance department's inaugural production. Trinity confidently went, feeling secure in her contemporary technique and strong stage presence, and ended up with a soloist role. After the performance, one of the dance professors told her, "You have to be a dance major." Trinity's understanding of what it would take to dance professionally seemed to distill in an instant: she needed to train, train, and then train more, in everything—especially ballet. Trinity switched her major and, at eighteen, took her first pointe class.

"That was a steep learning curve," she said, thinking back on those heady days in college. "It was frustrating a lot of the time, because I was surrounded by people who'd grown up in dance studios and been doing ballet since they were two years old, and I was like, 'What is this? Petite allegro? Renversé? Forget it!' I had these natural abilities, but I needed more than that to do ballet."

Trinity's ballet professor saw how driven she was and set aside time to add intensive pointe classes for her. As he saw Trinity's technique strengthen, that same professor tried to help her plan for jobs after graduation. Her first post-graduation gig was Dance at the Yard, a Martha's Vineyard residency, and was followed by repeated invitations from the director of Columbia City Ballet to join that company. The pandemic disruptions of 2020 threw things off, but Trinity joined CCB anyway, completing an almost full 2020–2021 season.

By 2022, Trinity was ready to spread her wings even further and moved on from CCB. In addition to freelance performing, teaching, coaching, and continuing her ingrained habits of self-guided study and training, she publishes essays on dance and culture in regular posts on her blog, The Artist Impression. She'd been keeping track of her thoughts on the dramatically shifting ballet landscape since her college days but finally felt moved to be public with them. "We're watching dance morph into something with new layers. I realized that on some of these matters, the positions are becoming blurry. Now that I have experienced some of these things myself, I have perspective and things to say about them. And I truly do feel like I'm being heard and reaching people."

Trinity's long-term aspirations are "dynamic," as she put it, but they absolutely involve her commitment to ballet, which she loves for its "beautiful rigor." Being part of the lineage and legacy of an art form like classical ballet is important to her. "It's about being able to look back and know I have contributed my very heart and soul, to have given of myself to the art of classical ballet, because honestly . . . that is what I give every time I think about anything having to do with dance."

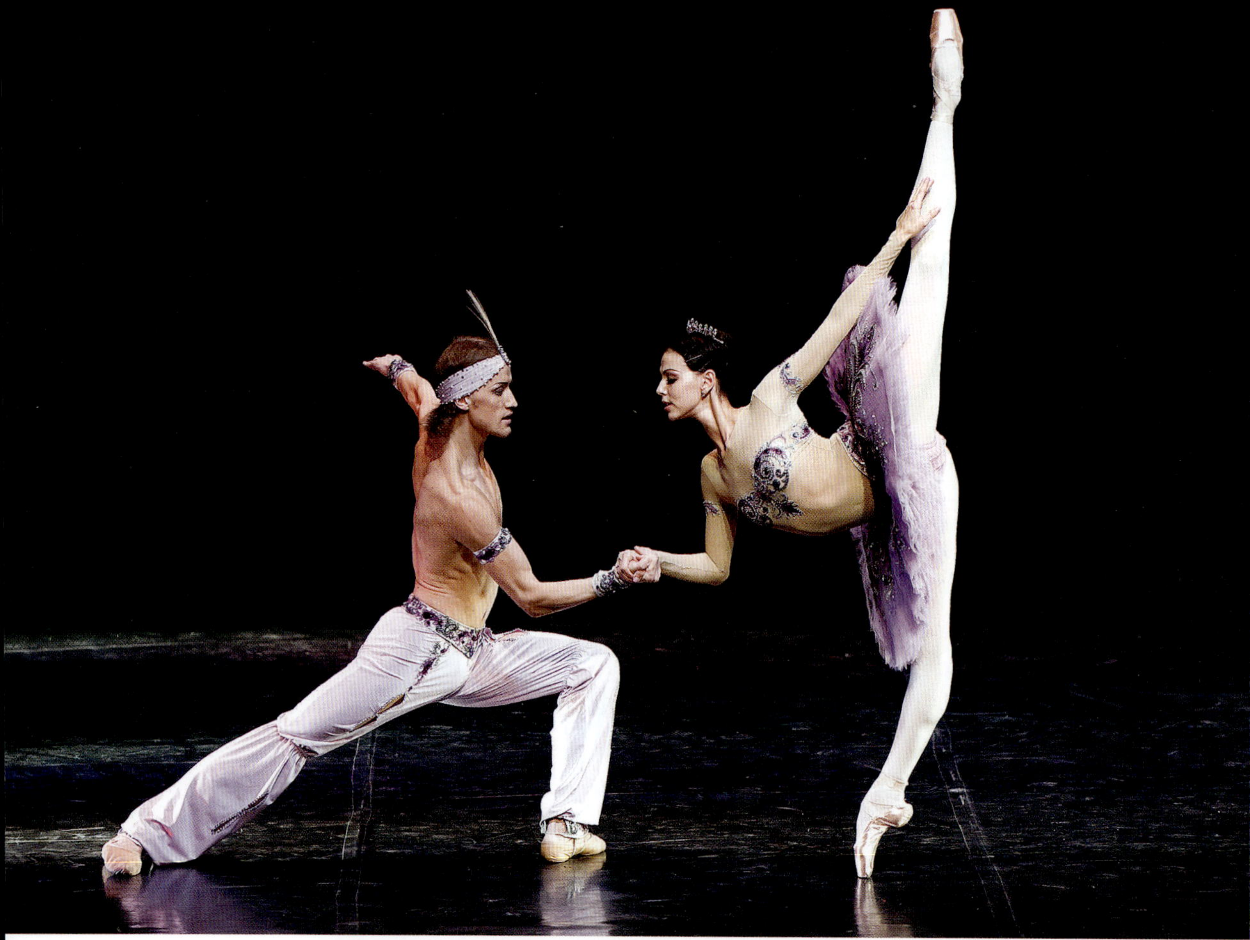

Anastasia and Denis Matvienko in *Le Corsaire,* Savcor Ballet Gala, Finland, 2008.

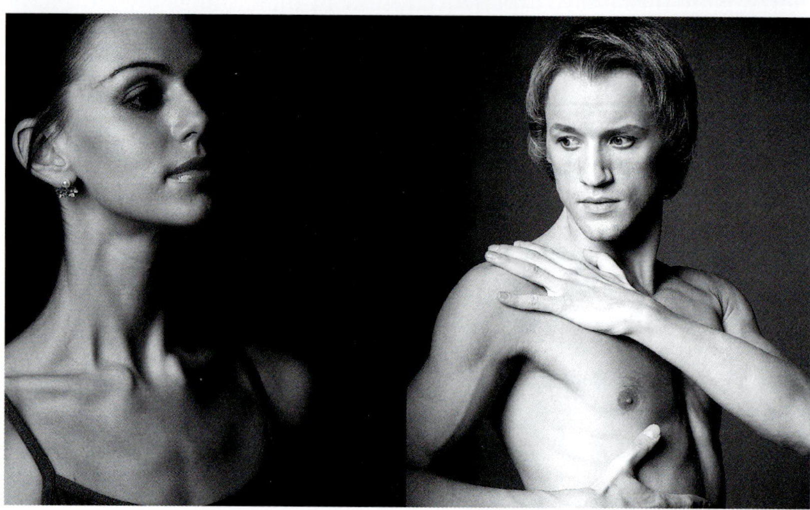

Anastasia and Denis Matvienko, 2007.

ANASTASIA & DENIS MATVIENKO

We didn't see a future . . . we were so worried about what would happen in our lives, but after doing class, we would feel motivated to take our next steps. Regimens and training are everything, whether in ballet or in life. We do everything with strong feelings. That's why we were able to move on.

ANASTASIA

When I am in the ballet studio, I am really happy. Really, truly happy. Even if nobody pays me, I have to do this.

DENIS

IN FEBRUARY 2022, Anastasia and Denis hurriedly packed as much of their and their two young children's belongings as they could fit into a few suitcases and left their St. Petersburg apartment, unsure when or if they would see it again. War had just broken out between Russia and Ukraine, and in the quickly tightening region, travel was already difficult. The family found a flight to Dubai, from where they made their way to Ljubljana, Slovenia, hoping for a relatively quiet, stable place to regroup and rebuild their lives. Leaving behind fifteen years' worth of work, friends, and memories wasn't easy, but the necessity to relocate was clear. Anastasia and Denis, who had been major dancers in the Mikhailovsky Ballet, the National Ballet of Ukraine, and Mariinsky Ballet, won medals at major ballet competitions and performed as guests around the world, are Ukrainian by birth and did not want to remain in Russia during the conflict between the two countries. Before they'd left St. Petersburg, Denis had begun to transition away from performing and had started teaching at the renowned Vaganova Ballet Academy, and Anastasia was a busy soloist in the Mariinsky Ballet, at the apex of her career.

The family's first few weeks in Ljubljana were bleak. Denis and Anastasia were reeling from their abrupt move and, for the first time, had no contracts

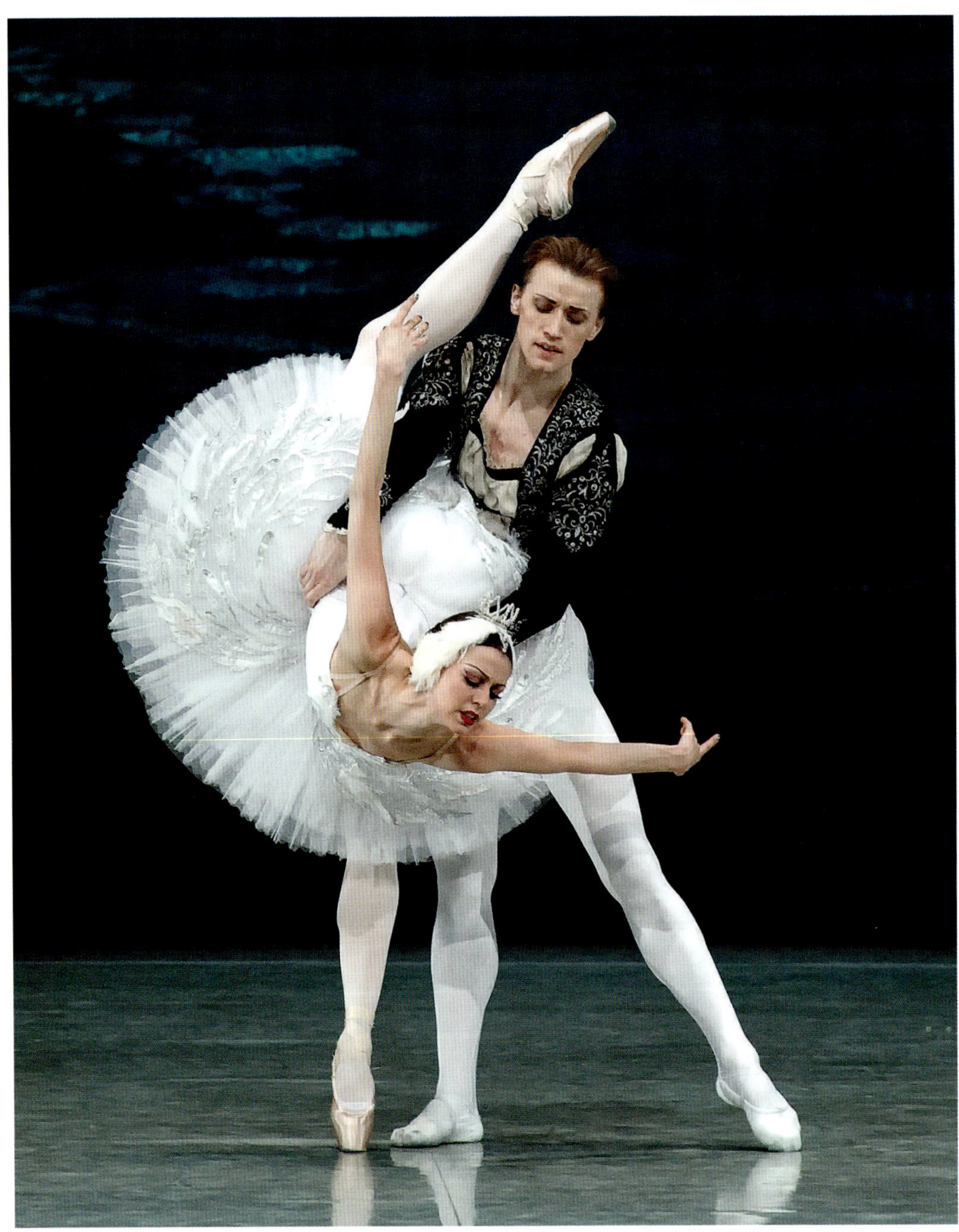

Anastasia and Denis Matvienko in *Swan Lake,* National Ballet of Ukraine, 2012.

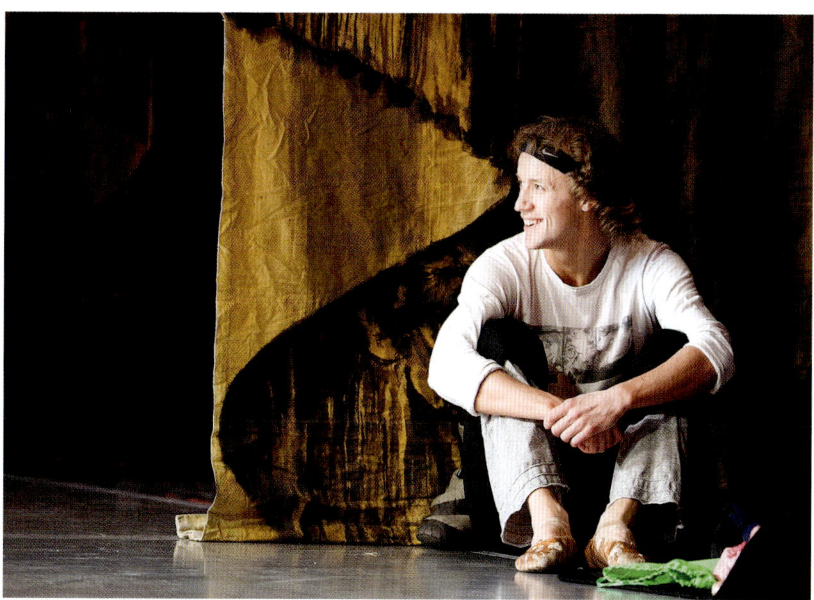

Denis Matvienko, 2008.

or possibilities for work. They were living in a cramped apartment, somewhat stunned and in disbelief about their situation. "We got to Slovenia with so many worries. We had no future. For our entire lives, we had a plan, a schedule, a regimen. But for the first time, we did not know what was happening to our lives, our careers, our children . . ." Anastasia remembered. But what they did have was the built-in strength of their ballet training, which was such an essential part of who they were that its familiarity, predictability, and repetition lent a comforting stability to their nondancing lives, too. The couple didn't know what the near or far future held, but they found a small studio where they could take class every day and started to feel their energy coming back. "We stopped worrying about what would happen to us," Anastasia continued. "Every day after taking class, we were motivated to take our next steps."

A turning point came the day that their nine-year-old daughter, Liza, bored and frustrated, demanded to know when she would be going back to school. Her insistence jolted Denis and Anastasia with the realization that it was time to take action. Denis sat down in the kitchen of their tiny apartment and wrote a letter to friends and colleagues asking for help,

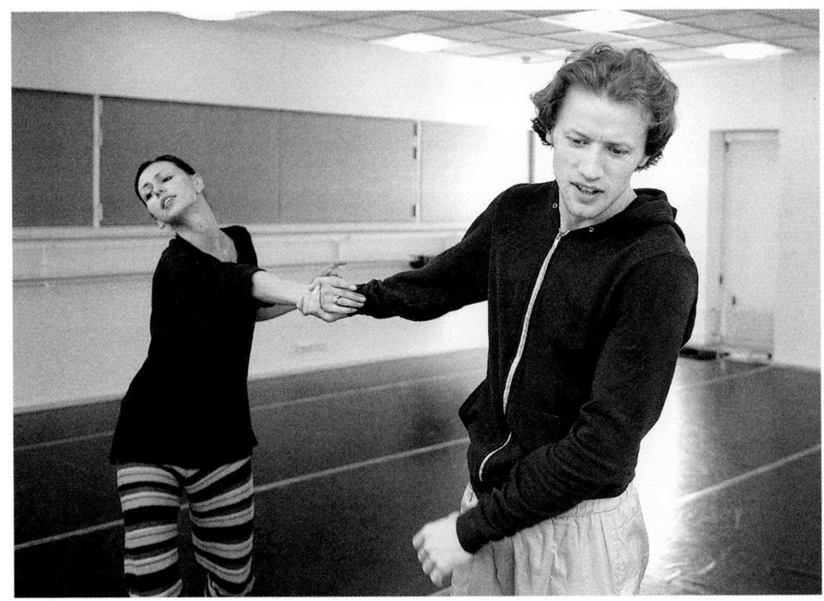

Anastasia and Denis Matvienko rehearsing *Giselle,* 2009.

many of whom didn't know the family had left Russia. He didn't ask for money, just for any opportunity to work, to dance, to teach. It was a first for someone who, for his entire life, had been on the receiving end of invitations to dance and teach.

Offers and requests started coming. Denis put off his planned retirement, despite having multiple ongoing physical issues ("I can still dance, but at forty-three, I cannot dance like at twenty-five," he laughed) to take a guest principal dancer position with Anastasia in the Slovenia National Opera Ballet, and Anastasia was asked to perform at a gala in Italy. Both began teaching and coaching in Slovenia and throughout Europe. Within a year, opportunities were so frequent that Denis and Anastasia were making regular trips for work. The family moved to a more comfortable apartment, Liza started school, and their son entered kindergarten. While their future plans remained very much unknown, they began to feel a sense of day-to-day normalcy.

Some married dancer-couples only perform together infrequently, or not at all, either because they are simply not physically compatible as dance partners or to maintain a separation between work and home life. Anastasia and

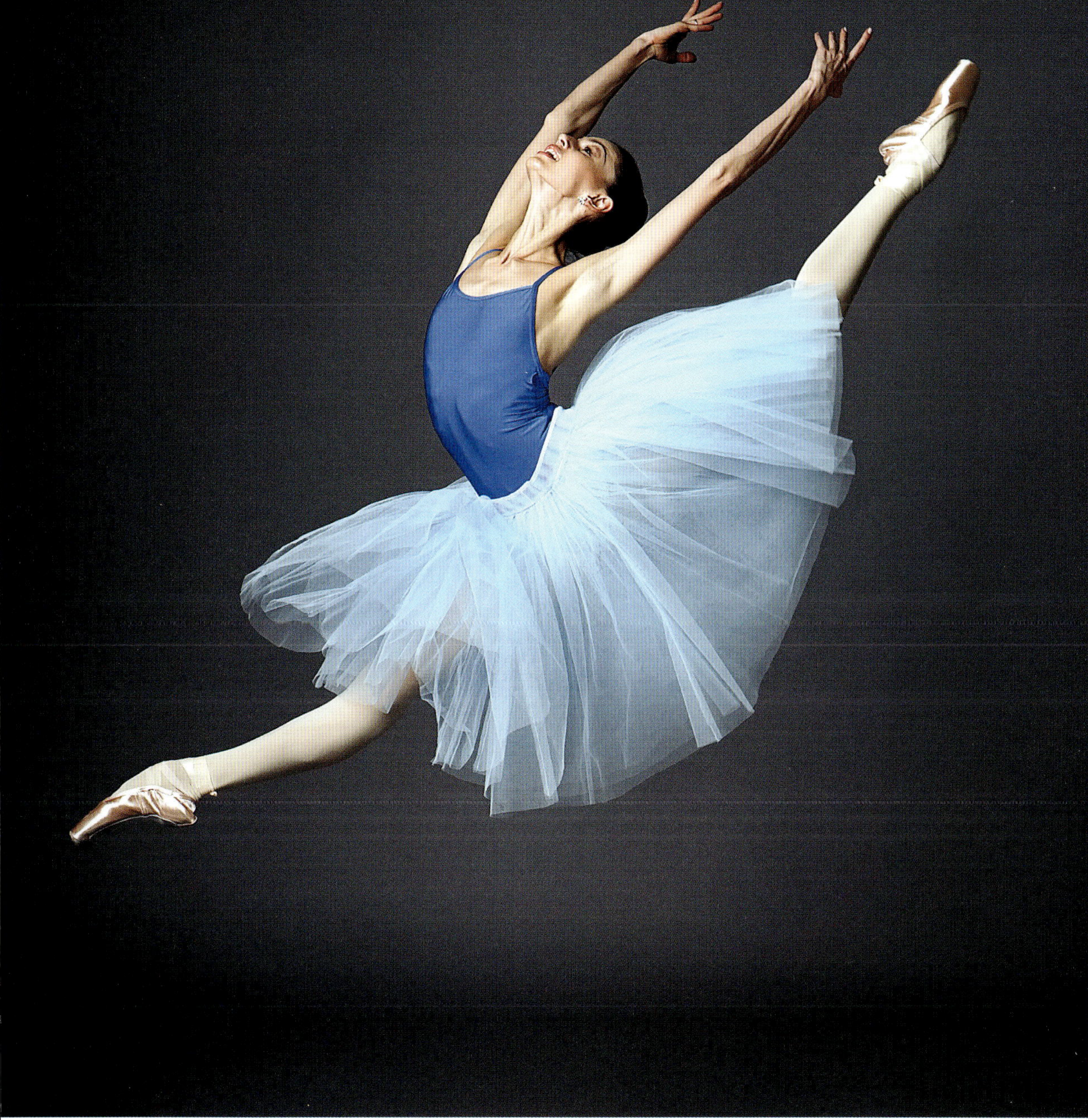

Anastasia Matvienko, 2007.

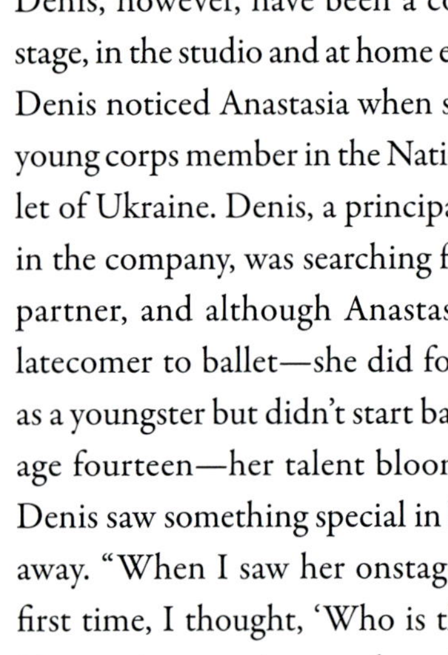

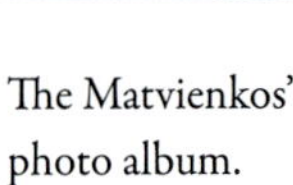

The Matvienkos' photo album.

Denis, however, have been a couple on stage, in the studio and at home ever since Denis noticed Anastasia when she was a young corps member in the National Ballet of Ukraine. Denis, a principal dancer in the company, was searching for a new partner, and although Anastasia was a latecomer to ballet—she did folk dance as a youngster but didn't start ballet until age fourteen—her talent bloomed fast. Denis saw something special in her right away. "When I saw her onstage for the first time, I thought, 'Who is that girl?' She was just starting out, but already so beautiful. I started thinking about her as a new partner, and yes, a new ballerina." The two did start working together, and not long after, they competed as a pair at the prestigious and highly visible Varna International Ballet competition. It was Anastasia's first time performing a full pas de deux, a huge leap for her. They didn't win at Varna but were invited to compete soon thereafter in the equally important Moscow International Ballet competition—where they swept the top prizes. After that, their lives changed forever. "Everyone then understood that she was a new ballerina," said Denis. "I knew it already, but sometimes people don't see."

As their dance partnership continued, their romantic relationship began. After the two married, they questioned whether to separate their dancing and domestic lives, deciding that they complemented each other too well in the studio, onstage, and at home to sacrifice one relationship for the other. The arrangement led to brilliant international careers but has also made for difficult moments. "It's not easy, because we both want each other to be better

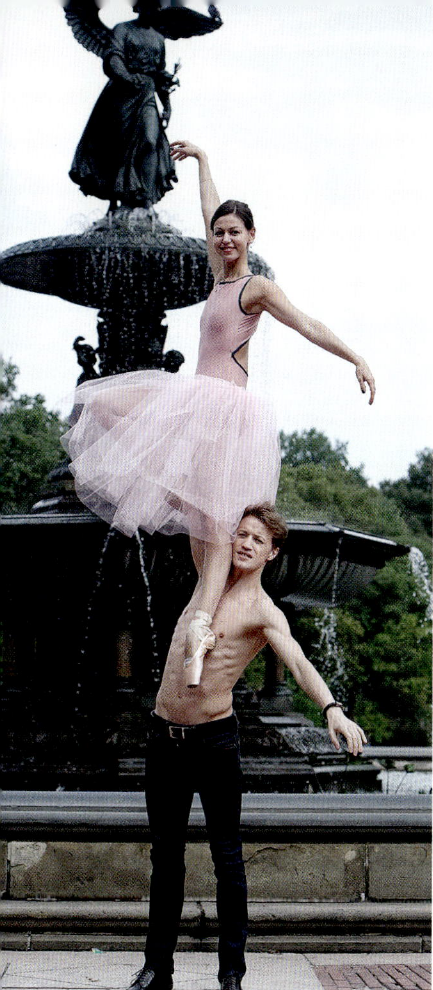

Anastasia and Denis Matvienko in Central Park, 2001.

and better all the time," Anastasia said. "If we were dancing with other people, maybe we'd not care so much, but that's not for us. We try to find perfection in each other."

Denis's calmness on stage balances Anastasia's fretful worrying beforehand, and the two are each other's biggest fans and fiercest champions. Ballet is their constant, stable, comforting companion. "I love ballet because onstage, you can have many lives," said Denis. "When I dance onstage, I forget everything. I never worry."

One treasure they brought from St. Petersburg is a gift from Gene, a small album full of photographs he'd taken of the couple over the many years he shot them on stages and studios from St. Petersburg to New York, and also several images from a happy family outing in Central Park. "He caught in his pictures exactly what we felt at each moment, not just the ballet poses," Anastasia said. "Our feelings onstage. We didn't take much when we left Russia, but we took this. It's very special."

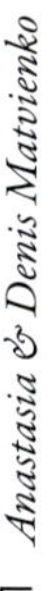

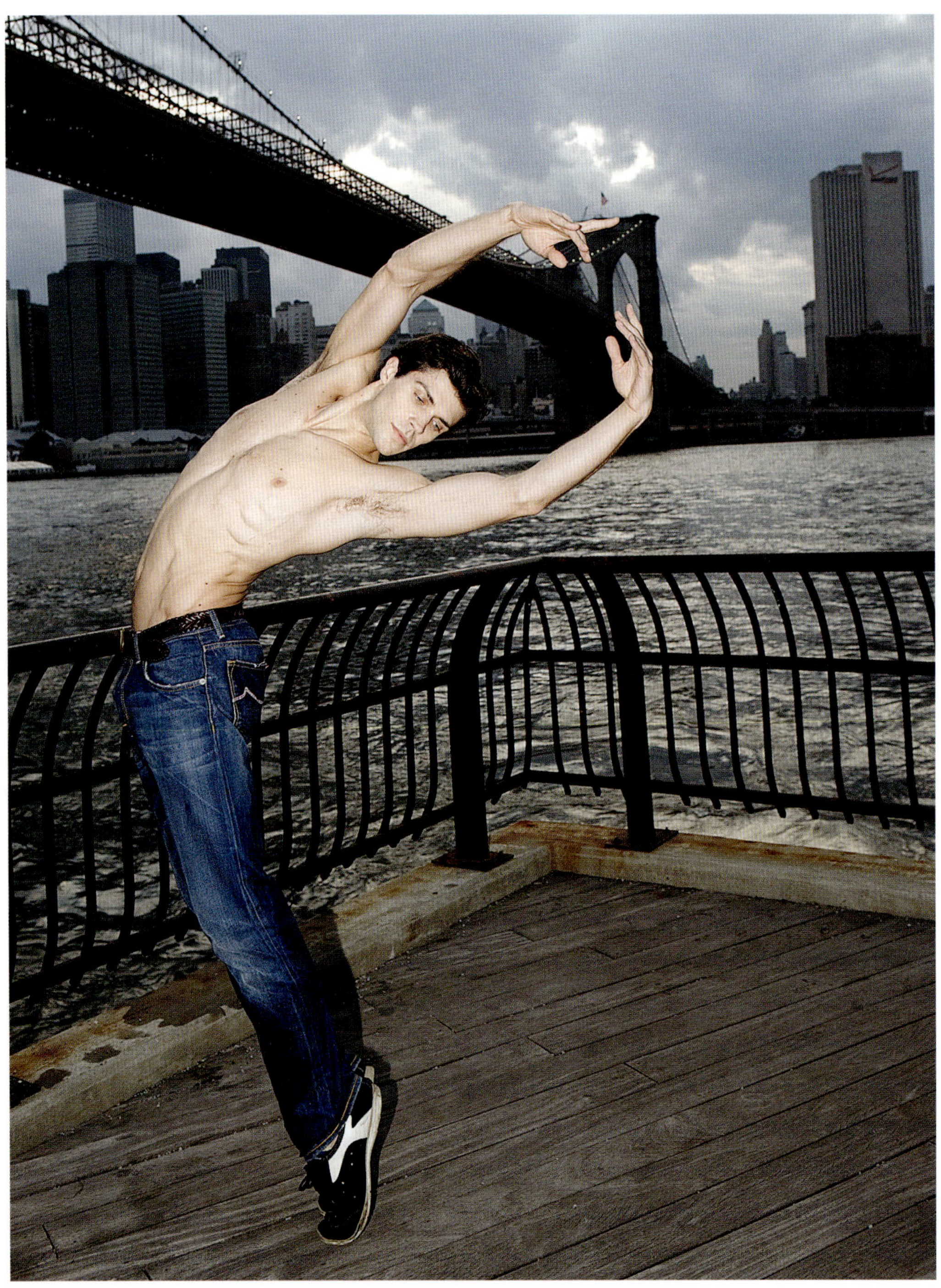

Roberto Bolle at the Brooklyn Bridge, New York City, 2009.

ROBERTO BOLLE

It's important to me to change the mentality and perspective people have about ballet, to bring it to the public, to the squares, to the big arenas. Ballet is not considered at the same level as opera, or music, or theater. I want to bring it to prime time.

IS ROBERTO BOLLE the most photographed male dancer on the planet? "Maybe, maybe!" he laughed.

Without question, Roberto is among the most well-known and popular dancers in the world today. He's also a captivating subject for many photographers, including Gene, who first photographed him in 2007, in Roberto's American Ballet Theatre debut with Alessandra Ferri in *Manon*. From then on Gene captured every one of Roberto's ABT performances, traveled to Milan to photograph him on stage with the La Scala Theatre Ballet, did several informal studio sessions, and documented the first "Bolle and Friends" gala at New York's City Center in 2013.

Soon after arriving in New York, Roberto's excitement about and love of the city prompted him to ask Gene for some photos taken outside the Metropolitan Opera House—candids, free from the costumes and makeup of onstage performances. They did two photo shoots, one in Central Park and another at the Brooklyn Bridge, attracting the attention of even jaded New Yorkers used to seeing anything and everything on their streets.

The dynamic of life in New York and at ABT was a bit shocking compared to what Roberto was used to in Europe, where he'd been living and dancing for years. The company's practice of preparing many ballets simultaneously over several weeks, and having few stage and orchestral rehearsals before performing them was especially hard, but stimulating. "You have to be very focused mentally as well as physically," he remembered. "It was a special, important time in my life."

Roberto's introduction to dance was at age seven in his small Italian hometown, where he tagged along with a friend to ballet class because he was curious about the moves she was showing off when they played together after

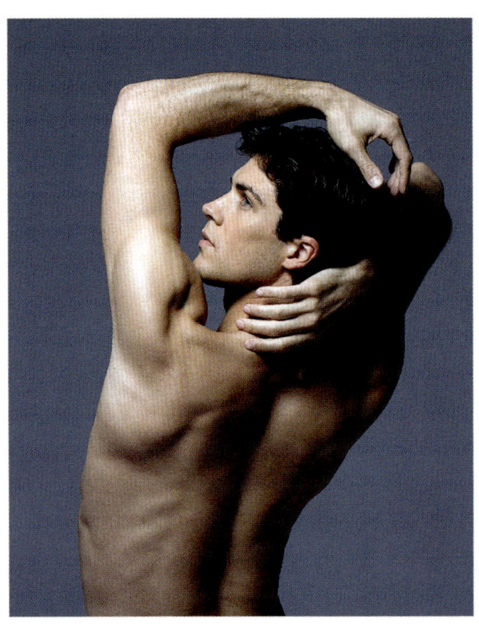

Roberto Bolle, 2008.

school. He joined the class and liked it so much that by the time he was twelve, he had moved to Milan to train at the famous La Scala Academy Ballet School. He didn't immediately take to the regimen of training. "I loved to move my body in space and just dance freely to the music," he recalled. "But by the time I was fourteen or fifteen, I started to enjoy technique. I saw ballet as my possible future."

At nineteen, he joined the La Scala Theatre Ballet and his future unfolded fast. Almost immediately, he was partnering the greatest ballerinas of the time, notably Sylvie Guillem, Darcey Bussell, and Ferri, and performing at famous theaters around the world, while maintaining principal dancer étoile status at La Scala. Thirty years later, Roberto has amassed a collection of once-in-a-lifetime experiences almost impossible to grasp: he has danced for the pope, the Queen of England, in the Roman Coliseum and at the Olympics and the Davos World Economic Forum, and been awarded medals and honors from UNESCO and the Italian government. In addition to these accolades, he's been spotlighted on film, TV, and in too many books and magazines and newspapers to count. In a life of superlatives, though, he's kept a sturdy sense of place and purpose, marveling that he's been lucky and available when historic opportunities presented themselves. Now, he wants to use his fame to direct attention to something larger and longer lasting than himself.

Roberto is simultaneously grateful to have the physique and talent to perform at the top of his game at an age past when most dancers have stopped, and also to have the resources and energy to carry his successes beyond the stage. His belief in the ability of dance to transform, brighten, and elevate lives—and not just through observation—motivates Roberto to take ballet outside the magnificent theaters where it mainly lives, particularly by using the leverage of his iconic status in Italy and his personal story. Through the many festivals he's organized that bring free classes to the public, he hopes

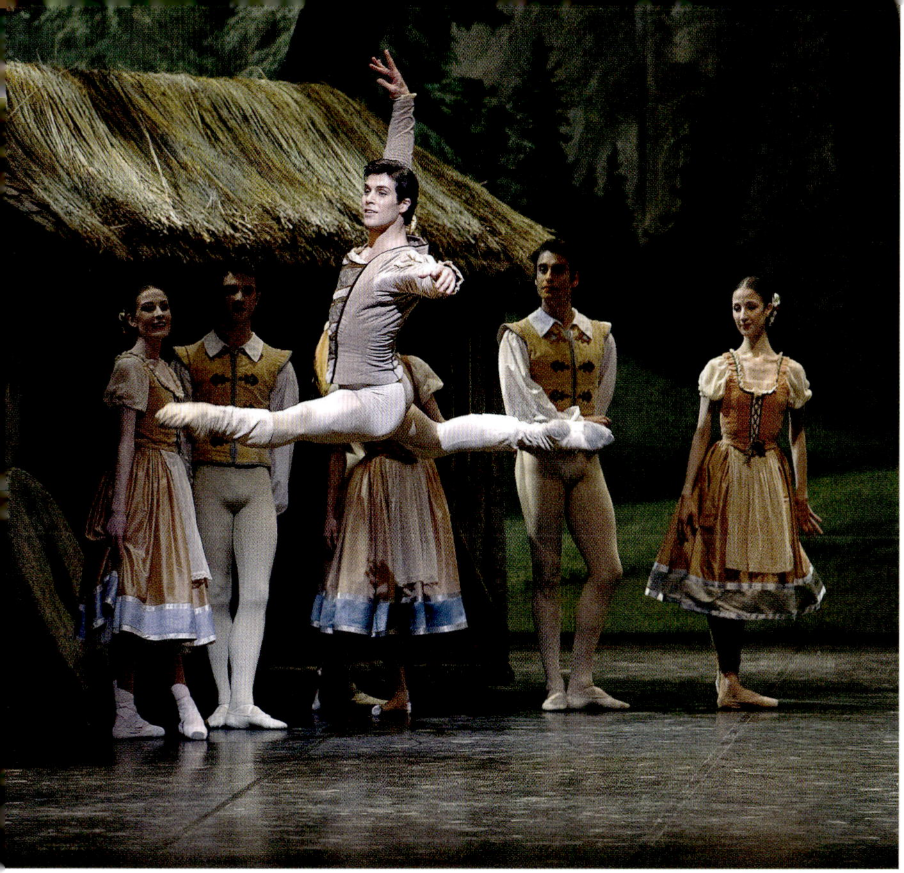

Roberto Bolle in *Giselle,* La Scala Theatre Ballet, 2012.

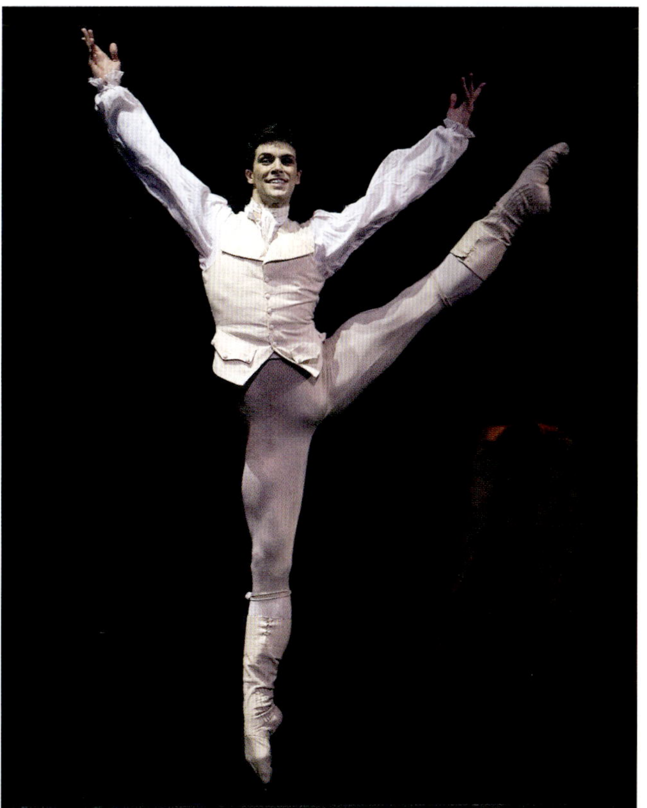

Roberto Bolle in *Manon,* 2007. Photo courtesy of American Ballet Theatre.

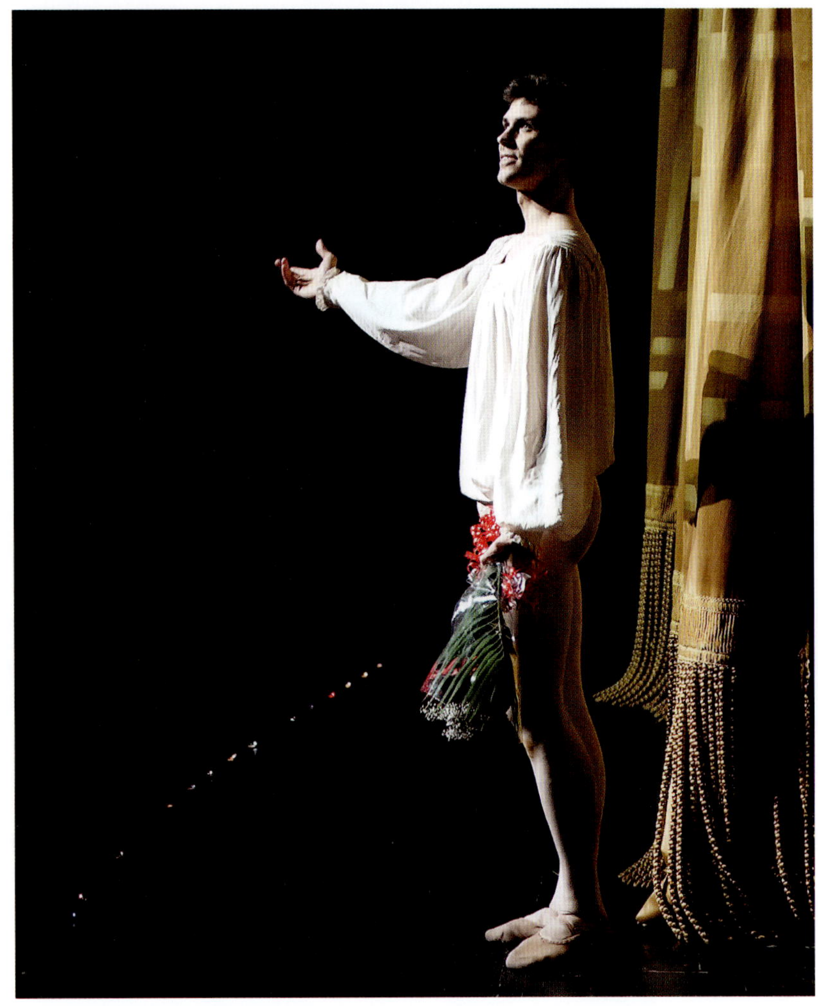

Roberto Bolle curtain call, 2009. Photo courtesy of American Ballet Theatre.

to unify the concepts of ballet as high art and dance as a universal instinct so that everyone can feel, in their own body and soul, a variation of the completeness a professional dancer knows so well and what he first felt as a young boy, moving with freedom and expression on the playground after school.

"We all move. When I see people doing it for the first time, discovering something beautiful in themselves, it opens up a different world. Inspiring people through the arts is, for me, very important. We did a class for 2,000 people in Duomo Square. There were people from all over Italy. I realized how ballet really is the school of life."

ANNALISSE VELDHUYZENVANZANTEN

Progress is so hard to see in the studio. I think if I hadn't had Gene and these photo shoots, I might have stopped dancing. Because when I looked at these photos, I thought "I might actually be good at this."

ANNALISSE KNEW HER DANCE CAREER would be short, so she made every single hour count.

She started ballet very late—at age fourteen—after an early gig as a singing, dancing, child entertainer at a dinner theater near her home in Florida. She and her siblings performed there together to make some pocket money, and besides, it was just fun. But once she got a little older, the directors of the show suggested Annalisse try ballet. "They needed me to be more than just a cute kid," she remembered. "I had to have talent in something."

Annalisse's first class, at the Gulfshore Ballet in Ft. Myers, Florida, was not a hit with her. No singing, no pop music? She was bored, and told her mother she wouldn't go back. But Annalisse's mom, who'd paid for a month of classes, wasn't letting her money go to waste. So every week Annalisse went to ballet, but being behind the other girls and not knowing as much as they did made her dislike it even more. "And I hate doing things I'm not good at," she said.

At the month's end, the school director took Annalisse aside after what she thought was her last ballet class for a surprising conversation. He told her she had a lot of talent and could actually be very good at ballet. They walked over to the studio where the advanced girls were working and the director pointed out the student who was that year's Sugarplum Fairy in *The Nutcracker* and who, like Annalisse, hadn't started ballet until age fourteen. Suddenly, her attitude about ballet changed. "When he said that I could be the Sugarplum someday too . . . it made me think that maybe I could."

The suggestion that she had untapped potential changed everything for Annalisse, who is nothing if not challenge-driven. With the tantalizing goal

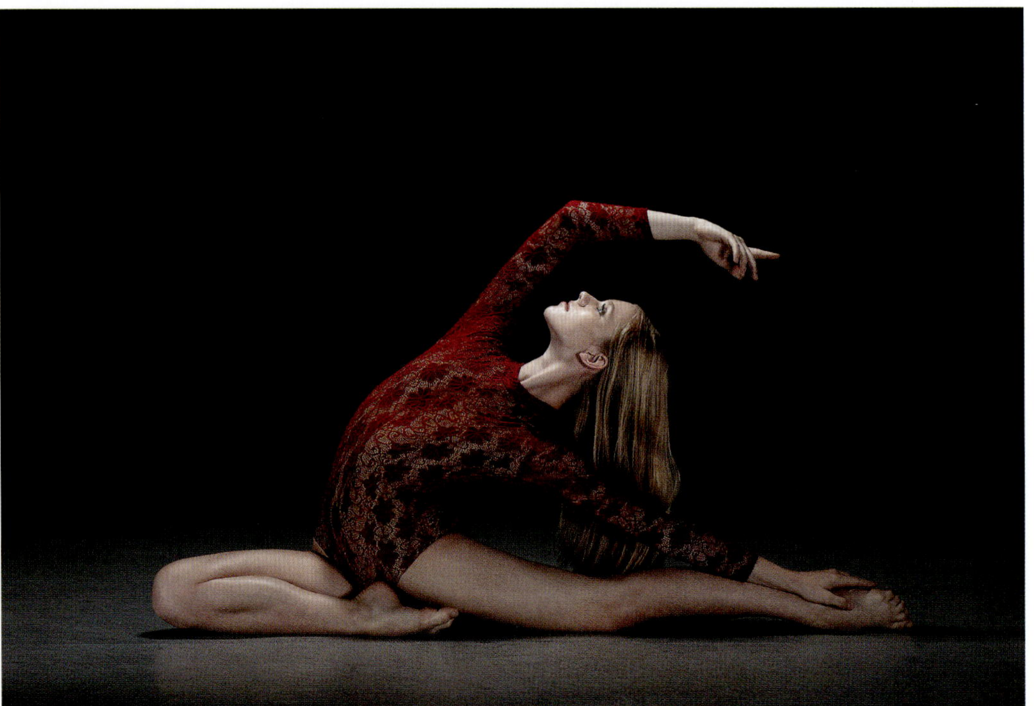

Annalisse Veldhuyzen van Zanten, 2019.

of becoming Sugarplum Fairy- quality in mind, Annalisse poured herself into her classes—there was no more dinner theater. She started to fall in love with ballet itself, especially the nitty-gritty of technique, which appealed to her detail-oriented mind. Later on, she would find that same satisfaction in a completely different setting.

After only about a year of training, Annalisse's mom saw a sign on Gulfshore Ballet's bulletin board that a local photographer was looking for a dance model. The photographer was offering a photo session for no pay but also at no cost, so that he could experiment with different ways of capturing movement. She submitted a casual snapshot of Annalisse in first arabesque ("It was absolutely terrible!" Annalisse remembered with a laugh), and a note describing her daughter's late start but intense devotion to dance. And, to Annalisse's complete surprise, her birthday gift that year was an envelope containing an invitation from Gene Schiavone to come to his studio for a shoot. Annalisse thinks back to what went through her mind the first time she and Gene worked together. "He'd asked me to come with some ideas of

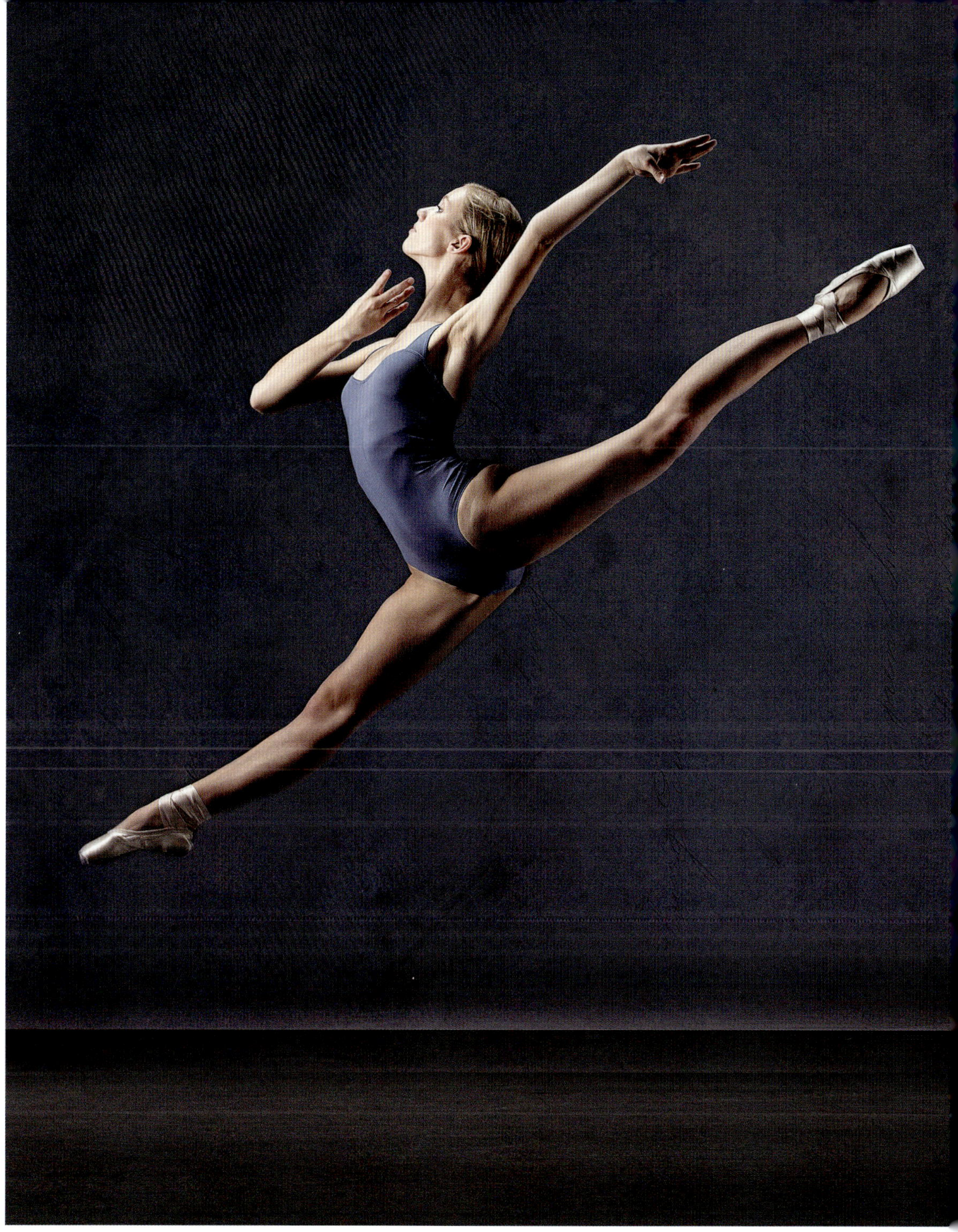

Annalisse VeldhuyzenvanZanten, 2018.

poses, so I brought a picture of an advanced dancer doing this jump that I kind of wanted to try, but I didn't think I could actually do it. He said, 'Just try and we'll see if we can catch it.' So we did, and the first shot ended up being the perfect picture. I didn't recognize myself. I had no idea that I'd come that far in my training." Just like hearing the school director's belief in her talent, seeing photographic proof that she'd made progress—and that her hard work was paying off—completely changed her sense of herself. The goal she'd set of dancing professionally had seemed so far in the future as to be potentially unreachable, but seeing that picture motivated Annalisse all over again. "I saw that I was closer than I thought I was," she said.

Now that her dream seemed possible, Annalisse doubled down. She was lucky to have world-class training at Gulfshore Ballet but knew that studying with other teachers at different schools and getting seen elsewhere would be essential in paving her career path. Summer intensives were the way to do that, but although she was accepted to two competitive programs, attending them was another matter. Annalisse's parents supported her but also urged her to be independent. If she was determined to go to a summer program, she'd have to raise the necessary money herself. And she did. Through after school jobs and fundraising, Annalisse made her way to intensives at American Ballet Theatre's affiliated school and the Boston Ballet School, where she had her first taste of Balanchine-style training, which she loved. Learning excerpts from Balanchine ballets that summer made her vow that if she ever did get into a company, it had to be one with a lot of Balanchine in its repertory.

In 2020 Annalisse graduated from high school with two years' worth of college credits already under her belt, along with a handful of college acceptances and scholarships. She had a plan: defer college for two years to dance professionally, and then begin school as a junior to pursue a biochemistry degree. Her plan did play out, with slight alterations due to the COVID-19 pandemic. Auditions that she'd lined up were canceled, and companies were only concerned with keeping the dancers they already had. It was time for Plan B.

Refusing to give up her dance career dreams entirely, Annalisse decided to give herself a little more time. She found a job at a medical clinic (aiming to

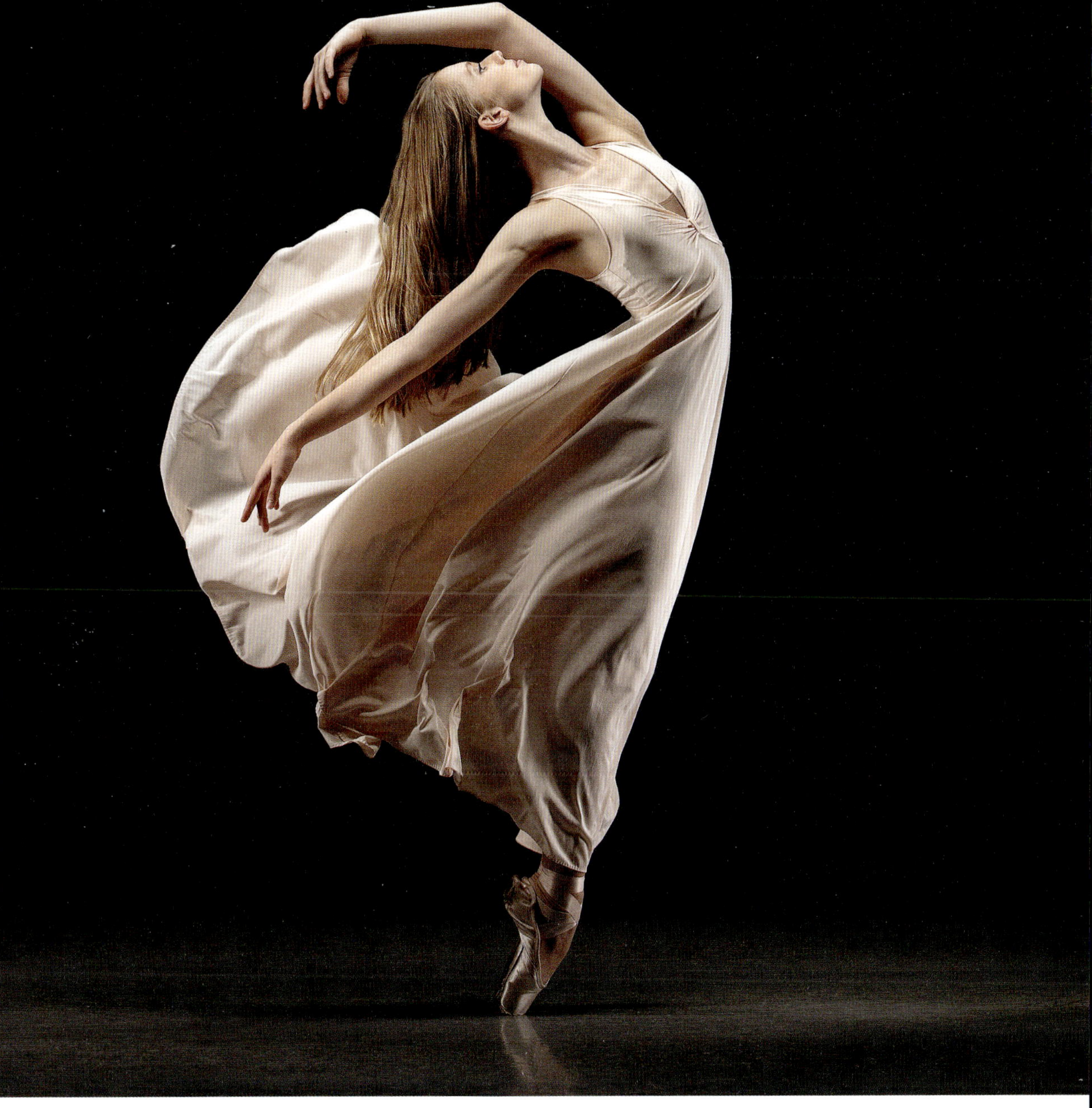

Annalisse VeldhuyzenvanZanten, 2019.

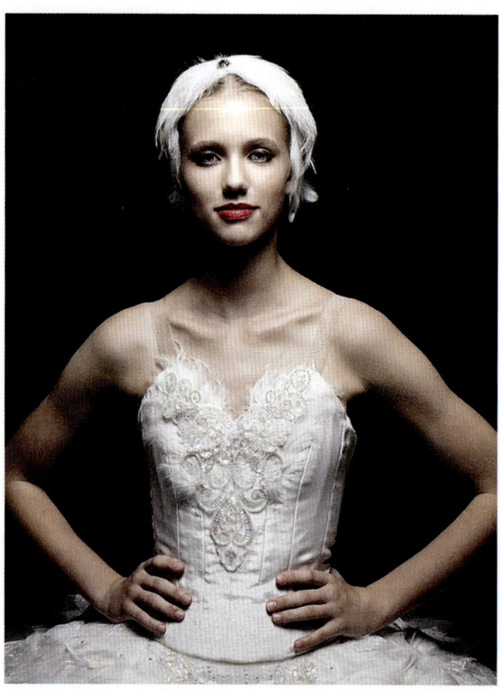

Annalisse Veld-huyzenvanZanten, 2018.

bolster her future career in the sciences) and put in additional hours cleaning the ballet studio and teaching lower-level classes to pay for her own continued training. A few months later a call came from Ballet Arizona, one of the companies she'd hoped to audition for. They needed an extra dancer who could be ready to jump into the corps de ballet for *Swan Lake*. Was Annalisse up for it? "Yes! Yes, I was!" she remembered joyously. She hurriedly packed up and drove across several states to Arizona, where she learned the entire ballet in two weeks.

Annalisse wasn't fazed by her quick induction to professional life and its intense workload. She was put in all four acts of *Swan Lake* when other dancers became injured, impressing the company director and staff with how quickly she could learn choreography and jump in whenever needed. It was stressful, but she thrived. At the end of the run, Annalisse was asked to join the company's junior ensemble. Her original plan was back on track.

Joining the Ballet Arizona Studio Company was a bit of a shock. The schedule was exhausting—Annalisse and the other Studio Company dancers were required to put in a full day of rehearsals with the main company, and then take classes with the company's affiliated school and rehearse for school shows in the evening—and although Annalisse luckily avoided injury, she saw her colleagues get worn down. And Annalisse was suddenly aware that there was no teacher watching over her anymore. If she wanted to keep improving, it was up to her.

But knowing she had only one season to dance (she'd forfeit her college scholarships if she waited too long to enroll), Annalisse cherished every day. It must have been like visiting a faraway place that you know you'll never see again. "I knew my time was running out as a dancer, so I went all-in. I wanted to be as strong as I could, take every class I could, work as hard as I possibly could. It was a lot, but I was getting the max number of hours of dancing in, which was what I wanted." She considered the impersonal company class she took every morning to be just a warm-up, and on her breaks would go into a spare studio to work on technique by herself.

The artistic staff noticed her extraordinary dedication—and talent for learning choreography quickly—and cast her in several company productions when most of her peers were simply understudies. Annalisse got to perform Balanchine ballets she adored, like *Serenade* and *Slaughter on Tenth Avenue*, and danced Princess Florine in the school's year-end performance of *The Sleeping Beauty*.

By the season's end, Annalisse was fulfilled. She'd worked hard at what she loved and gotten to call herself a professional, and it was enough. She declined the company's offer to return for another season.

Now Annalisse has moved on to academic life, with her eyes focused on her microscope and a future in genetic research. It's not hard to see how a mind that relished dissecting and refining ballet technique would also excel at analyzing samples in a science lab. She still takes class sometimes and even got to check off that very first goal she set back when she was fourteen: she was Gulfshore Ballet's Sugarplum Fairy for two years in a row. Annalisse sees the parallels between being a ballet dancer and a scientist and has a lot of gratitude to have been able to do both. "I was content because I'd checked off all the things I wanted to do," she says. "I was so fortunate to have danced so much. And I know that if I'd wanted to dance forever, I could have."

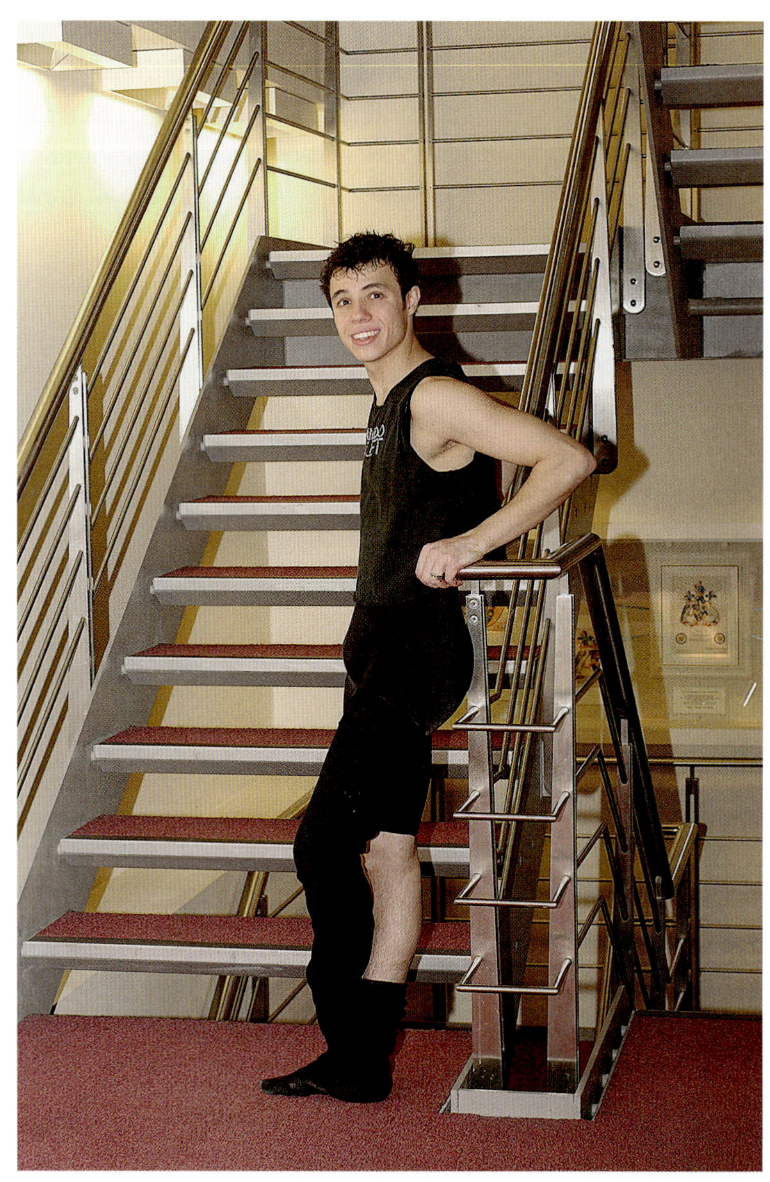

Joseph Gatti, 2005.

JOSEPH GATTI

People still don't understand just how much we use our bodies as tools. Dancers balance strength, fluidity, beauty, and expressivity, and we make it look effortless. Everything I've learned along the way is why I'm still dancing at age thirty-nine, and that's what I want to give the dancers of my company. I tell them, "Listen to your body."

IN 2004, Joseph Gatti was a teenaged member of the American Ballet Theatre Studio Company, known for his boundless energy, excitement, and passion. Poised on the cusp of a brilliant career and tantalized by the possibility of entering ABT's main company someday, Joseph had been (and still is) all-in since his first exposure to dance, around eight or nine, when he became fascinated with videos of Baryshnikov, Fred Astaire, and Michael Jackson (though it took a $20 bribe from his mother, a dance studio owner herself, to get him to actually try a ballet class.) But he suddenly found himself having to make a major, unexpected decision that would shape the rest of his life.

Joseph competed in the New York International Ballet competition, becoming the first American male to win the gold medal. It was beyond exciting and led to job offers from several companies, pushing Joseph to have to choose between the lure of ABT and the enticement of a more wide-ranging career outside of New York. "I saw friends get stuck in the corps at ABT," Joseph said. "They told me that at the end of the day, they wished they'd gone somewhere else to get more experience. And I wanted to do the roles I was hungry for." So he took a soloist contract with Cincinnati Ballet.

That hunger and curiosity propelled Joseph throughout the dance world and around the globe, giving him firsthand experience with both the thrilling highs and deeply crushing lows of life in the ballet business. After three years in Cincinnati, he joined the startup company Corella Ballet in Spain, working with major dance figures like Natalia Makarova, Angel Corella, and Christopher Wheeldon and at the same time, getting to see what went into building a company from the ground up. Unfortunately, that also meant watching it fold. Next stop was Boston Ballet, but by then he was starting to

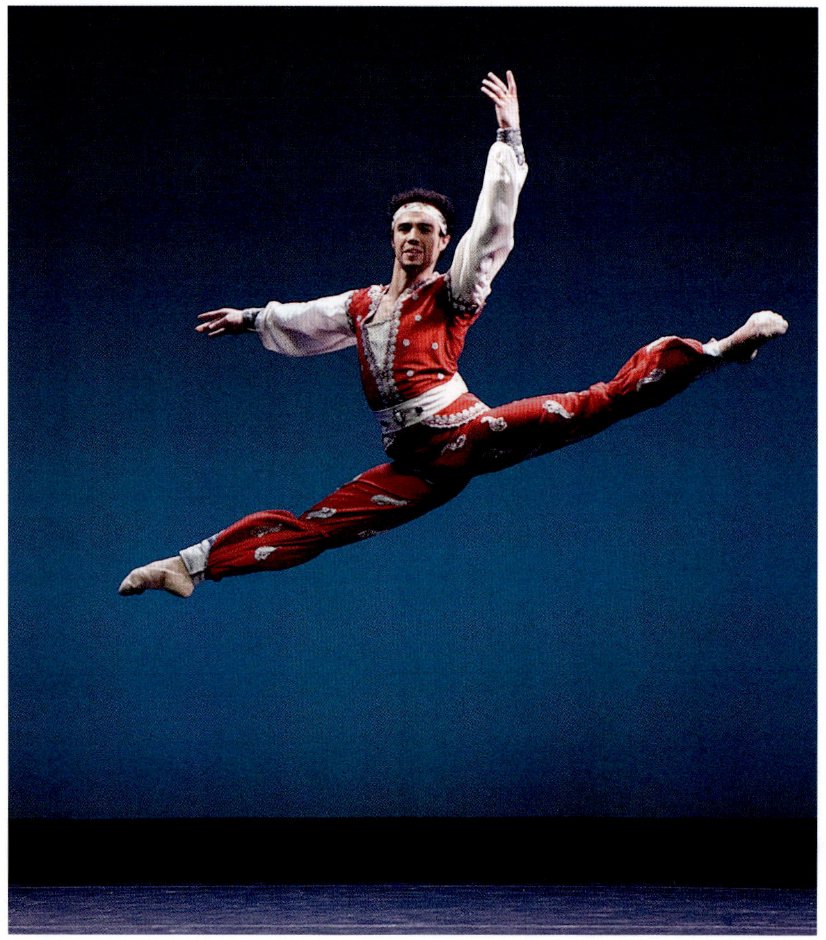

Joseph Gatti in *Le Corsaire,* Youth America Grand Prix gala, 2009.

feel the years of wear and tear on his body. It was dispiriting to realize that the way the relentless grind of rehearsals and performances affected dancers was, he felt, underappreciated. "It wears you down, physically and mentally," Joseph said, thinking back on his accumulated years in different dance jobs. "You do run-through after run-through to the point where it's not healthy. I didn't want to dance like that anymore." He felt so disillusioned that he considered leaving the profession. Instead, he decided to try a freelance career, trading the security of a company contract for the autonomy of being an independent performer. It was empowering, but came with a new kind of pressure. "As a freelancer, if you don't dance well, they don't ask you back,"

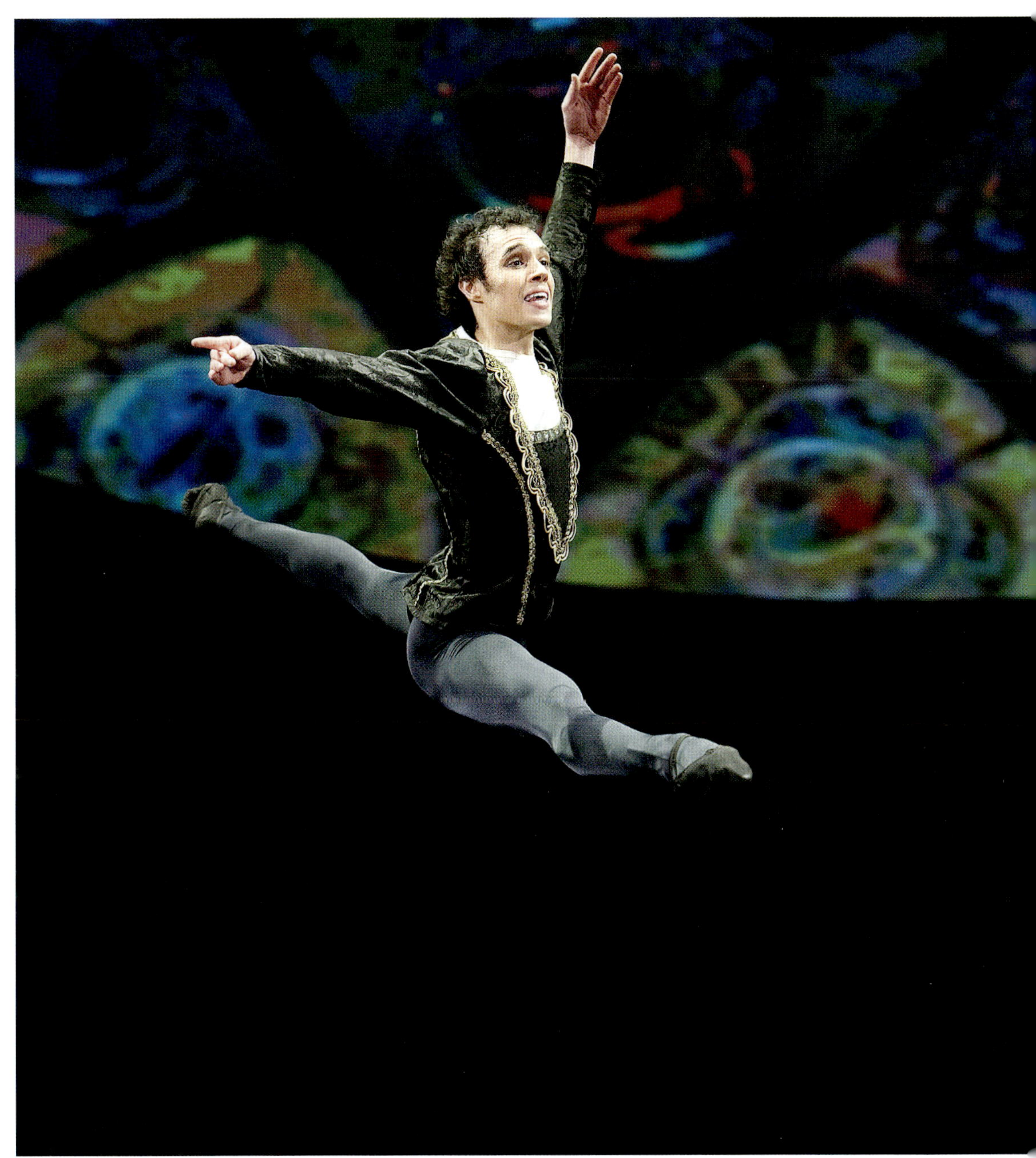

Joseph Gatti in *Santanella,* Dance Open Festival, 2010.

Joseph said. "My mentality was to do the best I could, every single show, because that's where my money was coming from."

Joseph balanced his self-imposed mandate with the knowledge that he was dancing on his own terms and could train and care for his body in the ways he knew were best. Dancing in three different companies had left him embittered about how the typical company life could be disadvantageous, even destructive, to dancers' bodies. He started to think about why it had to be that way and, more importantly, why dancers so often felt unable or afraid to advocate for themselves, to the point of pushing through injury. An incident of his own, when he'd agreed to perform on a knee injury and ended up breaking his foot because of pain-induced weakness, was always on his mind. "You should never feel that way," he said. "You should never feel afraid to ask for help. Why is it always the same vicious cycle?"

He decided to break the cycle. In 2018 Joseph founded United Ballet Theatre, a ballet company with a mission to focus on dancer health, well-being, and longevity. He devised The Gatti Method, a conditioning protocol that balances traditional classical ballet practices with cross training specifically designed to minimize overuse injuries, maximize dancers' strength and resilience, and encourage and support their agency in the daily process. Five days a week, UBT's dancers take a typical ballet class and rehearse, but two of those days are "Gatti Method days," when the focus is less technically oriented and incorporates more cardiovascular work, pointe shoes are optional, and rehearsals don't include run-throughs. Instead, the dancers take Pilates or VertiMax resistance training, and a sports medicine doctor is on-site to assess and treat injuries (or potential ones) as early as possible.

"I've personally witnessed the impact that injuries had on my friends and myself," Joseph said. "Now, as a director myself, it's part of my job to understand each dancer's athletic ability and utilize their wisdom to balance their load in the company. We're bringing high-quality, classical works to our audiences while educating them on how athletic and beautiful ballet is."

"MARIE"

In hindsight, I'd say to younger dancers that if you feel like a square peg in a round hole, you don't have to force it. You don't have to make it work because you think life without dance is unlivable. You can find other things to love, other places to be. Hold your dance dream with an open hand instead of a death grip. I wish I could tell my younger self that.

MARIE (NOT HER REAL NAME) was a professional dancer for several years in the early 2000s. In many ways, her story is not unusual: teachers spotted her talent early, directed her toward a professional career, and she joined a large company while still a teenager.

But despite the outward appearances of a ballet dancer's dream life, Marie was battling demons. A complicated, intense family dynamic compounded her self-perception of inferiority, particularly about her body, leading to a severe eating disorder that ultimately caused her to leave the profession.

Even then, Marie's mental and physical health struggles continued. As you will read, today she has found relative peace, but the effects of her wounds remain.

Marie's work to heal herself has been very hard and very painful, but it has also given her insight into her own life and circumstances as well as the workings of the ballet world. Pressures from every direction became, as she put it, "gasoline on the fire" of her eating disorder. Her perspective, now that she stands apart from ballet and has analyzed what happens inside it, is important.

When we first approached Marie about being included in this book, she was reluctant. The memories, she said, still hurt too much. But the possibility of helping others by telling her story overrode that pain, and she agreed to go deep, deep into the how and why of her distinctly tragic yet highly possible life in ballet.

Marie relayed her story over the course of two interviews. "This has caused

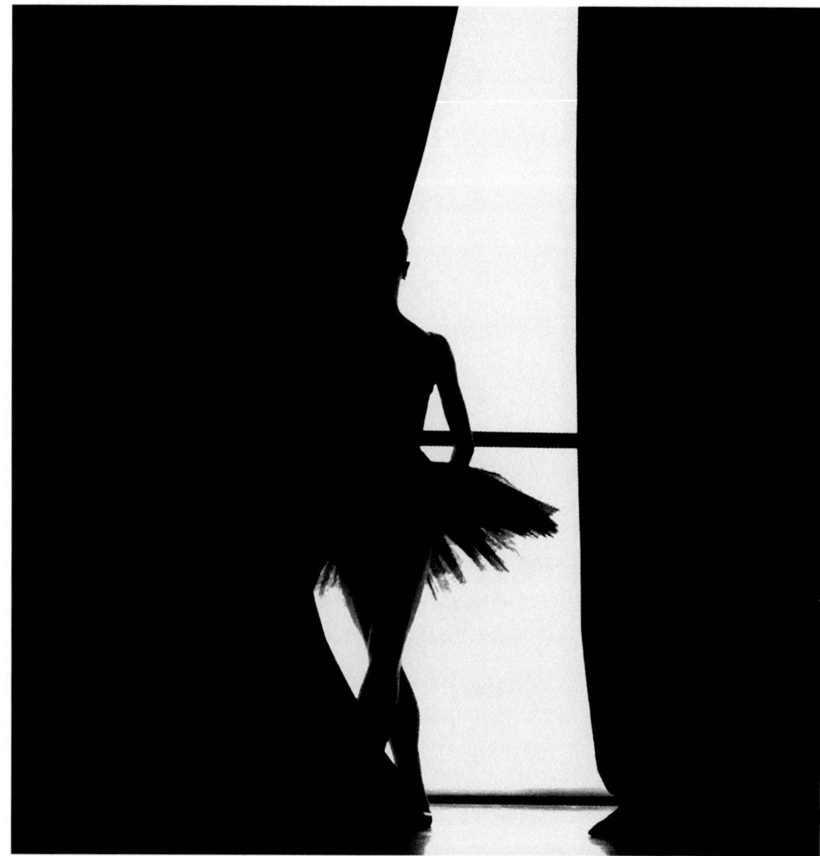

A dancer looks out from behind a curtain.

me to take a bird's-eye view," she said at the conclusion of our second conversation. "It has meant a lot to me to look at this all and express it. The lesson that I think I will keep re-learning for decades to come is that whatever you do or don't do, you have worth. Ballet isn't everything; beauty isn't everything. It makes me think of Apollo 13, which they called a 'successful failure.' Well, I do have gratitude for what I experienced. It almost killed me, and I'm really glad to be alive now."

"It's taken a lot of time to undo my frame of reference that ballet is everything."

Twenty years after her ballet career ended, Marie is still reckoning with the toll it took on her life.

Like most high-level dancers, she was a child ballet prodigy. As soon as she followed her older sister into dance class at age seven, teachers noticed her natural facility and affinity for ballet technique. At first Marie found ballet boring—she wanted to be outside, climbing trees—but performing in her first year-end recital changed her mind. "I was a ham onstage," she remembered. It was so fun that from then on, she decided to focus on ballet.

Marie's trajectory to professional life sounds familiar, too: she became the star at her school, getting lead roles in productions, praise, and encouraging, exciting comments from her teachers about how far she could go—if only she worked hard enough. Being labeled as different and special from a young age subtly but firmly tied her identity to her talent. "It became a foreshadowing of my downfall," she said, thinking back.

Marie did work hard. Almost too hard.

BY THE TIME SHE WAS TEN OR ELEVEN, Marie was dieting. Not because she was overweight, but because the only caveats whispered about her potential for a brilliant ballet career had to do with the shape of her body: one teacher told her to spend more time stretching her thighs to "lengthen" her muscles, and others would make comments about "pulling in" her rib-cage. The fear that her body's silhouette, if she wasn't able to shape it the way everyone seemed to want it to look, could make her natural turning, jumping, and acting abilities worthless, wasn't just worrisome—it compelled her to go to extremes. Eventually, the suggestions to stretch became outright instructions to lose weight.

"I'm a perfectionist and competitive by nature," Marie said about why she became so easily obsessed with her body's shape and size. "It's not something I'm proud of, but I would look around and think, 'I can be better at this than anyone else. How far can I go?' But it was never enough."

The pressure to do the impossible—change the genetically determined structure of her legs and torso—wasn't only at the dance studio. Marie's mother, whose own upbringing had ingrained in her that a woman's ultimate worth lay in her beauty, was more than a ballet mom who helicopter-parented her talented daughter. In Marie's family, nothing really mattered, in the end, except being beautiful. And being beautiful meant being thin. When it became evident that Marie's potential to achieve stardom in ballet was tied to becoming physically smaller . . . her mother was on a mission to help her get there.

"My mom and I had this really close relationship, to the point of dysfunction," Marie said. "She was, I think, wowed by the ballet world and very excited to have a talented daughter who made her feel like she was becoming somebody because I was becoming somebody. So in the dance studio, there was pressure to be the best, but that didn't let up when I got home. It was actually doubled down on. A core value for my mother, which she carried forward to me and my sisters, was that thinness and beauty were the number one most important thing. Not education or even just being a decent human. So my mom has her own sickness."

AT FIRST, Marie felt lucky that her mom was in her corner, helping her do what they both thought needed to be done for Marie's budding career. If a teacher told Marie to lose five pounds, Marie's mom would rid the house of junk food and the whole family went on a diet. But the hyper-focus on Marie's dancing made for a lopsided life. It ingrained in her that her sole purpose was to be the best.

When she was just sixteen, in what should have been a thrilling event, Marie was offered an entry-level spot in a well-known company. She would be replacing a dancer who'd unexpectedly dropped out at the last minute. Landing a job without having to audition for it, though, made her feel like an impostor who didn't get in "the right way," a mentality that would haunt her for years.

Up to that point, Marie's sense of her body being wrong all the time kept her doggedly on an endless string of diets. She was obsessed with food, what kind, and how much she ate. One afternoon, chatting after class with a friend about what they'd eaten that day, Marie heard about her friend's latest discovery: how to erase a food "mistake" by throwing up. A couple of days later, she tried it herself. "I was like, 'Yippee!' I had the secret," she said. "I knew how to undo my bad decisions."

Things picked up fast. Marie thought she'd found a way to control what was actually uncontrollable. Her tendency to want to compete for the win was magnified by pride, overwhelming self-discipline, the deep belief that she was only as valuable as her appearance, and that she alone was responsible for succeeding in ballet. And since success meant getting and staying thinner so as to be closer to a physical ideal, she had to win at the food game, too. Over and over she heard—from teachers, coaches, her mother, even the director of the company—that unless she controlled her body, she would be throwing away her career.

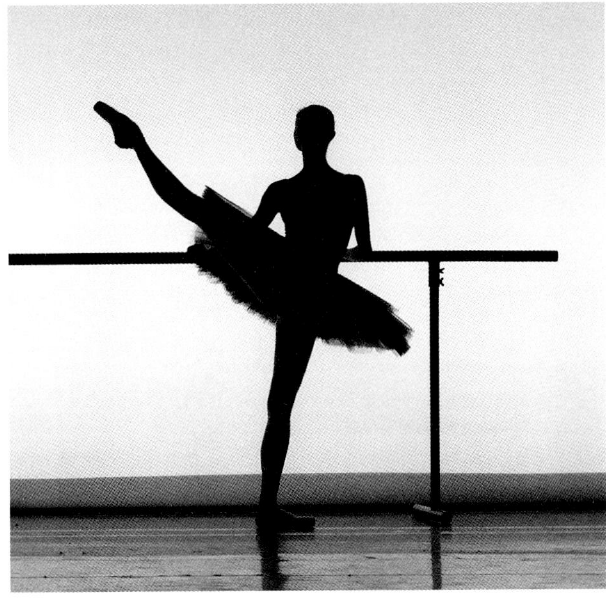

A dancer at the barre.

"I got really good at my bulimia when I was about eighteen," Marie said. "I found all the bathrooms where I could throw up in relative privacy, in the train station, at the studio . . . I had this weird double life. Nobody really knew me. They thought I was this good, disciplined person, but I felt so disgusting. It was like a rubber band pulled really tight all the time. Just pulled tighter and tighter. And eventually, it snapped."

BALLET WASN'T THE FOCUS of Marie's life anymore. Bulimia had overtaken everything. The vicious cycle of bingeing, purging, and hiding it overshadowed every hour of every day. Understandably, the pressure to both keep it up and keep it secret became unbearable. Yet throughout those years Marie maintained the charade of being a diligent, hard-working corps de ballet dancer, rehearsing, performing, going on tour. But then she'd come home to her apartment at night to be alone with this monstrous thing that had, ironically, taken an ironclad grip on her life.

Despite feeling imprisoned within herself, Marie retained a close relationship with her parents, especially her mother. She had confided in them about what she was doing, but even seeing their daughter nearing the breaking point, risking her physical health and life, didn't sway her parents from telling her to keep dancing, to stay in the company. Even though Marie was having desperate thoughts, her parents seemed to be in denial of how dangerous or how bad her bulimia was. Instead of urging her to get professional help, they reminded Marie that ballet was her currency: both literally, for the income, insurance, and security; and figuratively, because that was her identity: Marie, the ballerina. While Marie increasingly yearned for a way out, her parents only wanted her to stay in.

As desperately as she needed relief, Marie could not see any way to get it. On occasion her mind slipped to a very scary place. She recounted one of the lowest moments, when she came home after a performance late one night. After several rounds of bingeing and purging, she looked out the window. "I thought, 'I can't live like this anymore,'" she recalled. "I wanted the misery to be over."

The conflict between her pride and sense of responsibility to do the right thing—whatever that was—trapped Marie. She thought quitting ballet would be selfish and a sign of weakness, but finally, she saw that the alternative would ruin her life—or worse. She went to the artistic director of the company and told him that she had bulimia and needed to leave and go to an eating disorder clinic.

Marie's director, surprisingly to her, was supportive. He seemed to somehow understand what she was going through. He said the type of affliction Marie had was like a sprained ankle that would just keep getting re-injured without time off and treatment. He told her to go away and take care of herself and that her place in the company was secure when she was ready to come back.

But she never did.

MARIE'S RESEARCH led her to an in-patient eating disorder treatment center in another state. Hoping her stay there would be temporary and that she'd soon come back fully cured, she didn't tell anyone in the company where she was going.

The clinic was a small facility with just a few patients. Treatment involved both group and individual therapy, with residents spending evenings and nights in their individual apartments to practice being alone with food again. But the focus on re-learning to eat normally uncovered what for Marie were even bigger problems. She lacked a sense of self or purpose aside from being a ballet dancer, and her mother's influence overshadowed her own judgment. She couldn't accept that she had intrinsic worth that would not fluctuate with her weight. "These were the things I had to address before I could look in the mirror and like myself," she said. "Therapy was the beginning of my house of cards falling apart. The food issues quiet down once you do the hard work."

After a month at the treatment center, Marie went to live with her parents. She didn't avoid ballet entirely, but she also didn't take up her director's offer to resume her position in the company. She needed busyness and structure that wasn't centered around being a dancer. She needed to disprove to her brain the lie that she'd lived before—that she was likable, lovable, had knowledge and value only because she was a professional dancer.

Marie kept very busy indeed. On a whim, she took up salsa dancing, which sparked a significant shift in perspective. Seeing other people—of all shapes and sizes—dancing for pure joy, and doing it alongside them, was like a spiritual reset. Among people whose standards of beauty were completely opposite from those in the ballet world, Marie felt her spirit starting to heal.

She also took courses at community college and taught ballet to children at a nearby studio. Going into a ballet studio again might have seemed like a bad idea, but giving back—inspiring young kids, teaching them what she knew—was an important piece of her recovery. She felt proud and purposeful in the ballet realm again, and for once, it wasn't because of how she looked.

As Marie stepped toward a cleaner relationship with herself and with dance, her other relationships remained complicated. She dated and got engaged—twice—neither time to men that her mother approved of. The disputed boundary line between mother and daughter, Marie realized, was something she would never be capable of setting. Her mother's problems were too big and deep-rooted for Marie to take on. When Marie married the man who is now her husband, she and her mother became, and remain, estranged.

"I learned that I cannot change her," Marie said about her mom. "No amount of conversation or crying will do it. The problem was more than that I was with the wrong guy. I was taught at home to never have a backbone, to be a good girl, a people pleaser. And even when I grew up, she still needed me to be that good little girl. It's a big heartbreak in my life, but I don't regret leaving and getting married. I hope one day we'll reconcile, but if we don't, I still have peace about the choice I made."

BULIMIA DID NOT LET GO of Marie completely even after she left the eating disorder clinic and strove to move on with her life. She did start dancing again, and even joined another ballet company for a season, hoping for a "geographical cure" that would create physical and emotional space between her, her mother, and her eating disorder. It didn't work. She was afflicted just as badly as ever. Being on her own again, alone with the expectations to fit into a certain mold, to look a certain way, allowed the old demons of bingeing, purging, hiding and shame to come rushing back.

IT ULTIMATELY TOOK YEARS of hard work in a twelve-step program, but today Marie can look at food and "take it or leave it," as she said. Now in her thirties and a mother herself, she has largely left ballet behind and lives what she describes as a "quiet, un-flashy life." In a remarkable testament to her resiliency and emotional intelligence, Marie can look at her past with an analytical eye even after so many years of being at war with herself. She sees clearly what was so muddled before. She understands how and why something that all dancers face and accept on a daily basis—their image in a mirror and the critique of others—was, for her, impossibly hard.

Asked to consider what she might tell herself if she was the sensitive, objective mentor that young Marie didn't have, she confessed that to this day, and likely forever, she'll be making a concerted effort to prevent herself from sliding backward. She'll always be re-learning the lesson her twenty-one-year-old self couldn't: that she doesn't have to prove her worth.

Marie's self-acceptance today is not without pain. She has scars that may only fade with time, not fully disappear.

Because for so long she framed leaving ballet as a failure, Marie still feels shame about the fact that she had what so many others want—talent and opportunity—and let those things go. It hurts her so much that even now to watch ballet would take her back to a "failure" mindset, so she's hidden herself from the dance world. While she wrestles down that demon with one arm, Marie can also see her past life through a different lens that filters out the disappointment and brings forward her efforts, her triumph, and her purpose.

Marie has even turned her thoughts to what would make the ballet world a place where she'd like her own children to visit, or even live. The training should relate to what everyone needs to know as they make their way through life in or out of a dance studio, she said, and develop a spirit of common humanity. Young dancers should be shown how to handle disappointment, take pride in what they do, no matter how large or small their role, and handle themselves without self-pity or shame. "Teachers and parents should help kids find practical, real ways to serve the community instead of just themselves, to be ambitious and earnest in supporting their fellow dancers instead of seeing them as a barrier to their own ascent," she said. "Instead of having a tunnel vision for dance, get their eyes off themselves and open up their worlds. Ballet is not the end-all, be-all."

Marie thinks that if she'd had that kind of training, she might not have felt so desperate about ballet and would have been able to relax the "death grip" that paralyzed her for so long. "I wish I'd known to accept what I had and to say, 'it's enough,'" she said. "Today, I know I am useful. I can do so much good for the world and those around me. I can have light in my eyes, have joy and pride and feel, 'I belong here.'"

Karine Seneca, 2006, Museum of Fine Arts. Photo courtesy of Boston Ballet, Mikko Nissinen, artistic director.

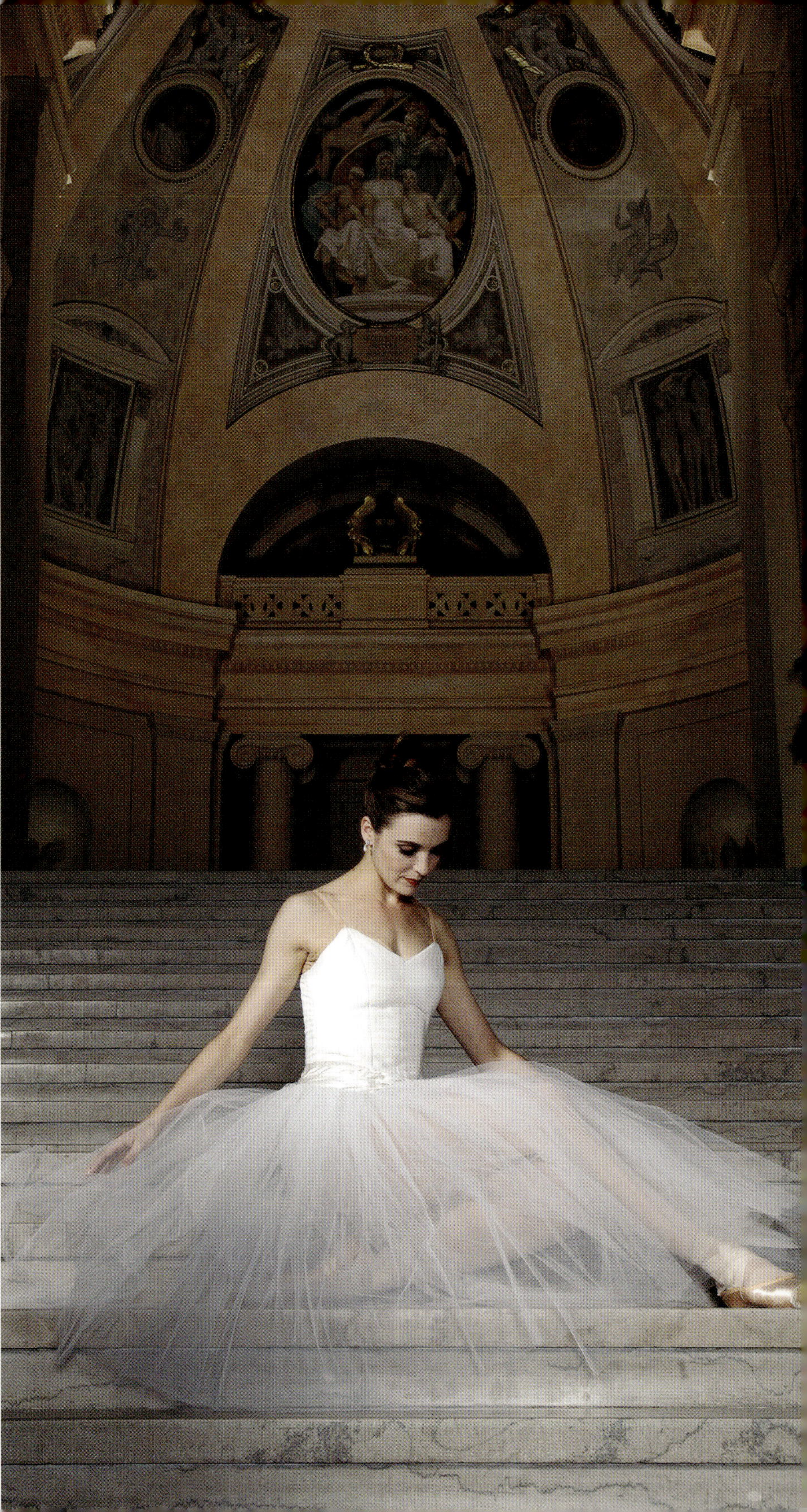

KARINE SENECA

There were times when it was very difficult. When I felt disappointed or was injured, it was easy to ask, "Why am I doing this?" But I still loved it, even when I was tired. I have no regrets.

KARINE NEVER LIKED DOING PHOTO SHOOTS. They made her uncomfortable, maybe because posing for photographs seemed artificial compared to the flow of live performance, when her natural shyness fell away. On stage, the buffer zone between her and the audience made her feel free, safe, able to relax and made room for spontaneity. But in the setting of a photo shoot, the camera's closeness and the inherent expectation to produce an image of beauty on the spot made Karine freeze up.

The day this photograph was taken was high-pressure for both Karine and Gene. It was one of Gene's first jobs for a company other than American Ballet Theatre, and his assignment was to turn out a publicity image for Boston Ballet's 2006–2007 season. The shoot was on location at Boston's Museum of Fine Arts, a spectacular, majestic setting that could make even a casual visitor hold themself a little straighter, but the cavernous spaces were not easy for photographic lighting. Gene, Karine and the crew had been working all day, trying various poses and movements in different parts of the museum, before Gene had the idea to catch Karine in a flowing sequence coming down a grand staircase. Everyone was tired by that point, and Karine struggled to re-create Gene's concept. She doesn't remember who suggested it, but they decided to take a short break and regroup. "I was getting so stressed," Karine said, thinking back to that day. "I needed a moment to breathe and pull myself together. I had almost given up, but told myself we were almost done and I could do it. And somehow, he took the picture without my being aware of it. That's why it's so good—because I was relaxed. And now I think it's one of the best pictures from my entire career."

Karine dealt with insecurity and anxiety throughout her professional life, but when she first started ballet in her hometown of Cannes, France, she was a carefree little girl who danced purely for the fun of it. Ballet was easy, casual, and she didn't think much about it. But when she became a teenager and hit the throes of adolescence, her body changed, ballet classes got harder and more structured, and suddenly, she felt unsure about everything. Before, dancing had felt like a playground, but when the physical and mental difficulties conflicted with that relaxed joy, Karine's confidence plummeted. She took a few months off.

Being away from ballet, however, made Karine realize that it actually had been more to her than a fun pastime. When dance started to grow bigger and more serious—but also more intriguing and satisfying—she'd just needed to give herself a moment to catch up. When Karine came back to the studio, classes were even harder than before, but now she was ready. She graduated from the Centre de Danse Rosella Hightower at seventeen and got her first job in the corps de ballet of Basel Ballet under the directorship of Heinz Spoerli, with whom she continued to dance in the three different European companies he led over the next fifteen years. By then, Karine was a principal dancer with a huge repertory of major roles and ballets, but she was still energetic and curious to explore. She had met and worked with Boston Ballet's artistic director, Mikko Nissenen, when he was briefly with her company in Zurich, and thought, "Why not?" She gave him a call, and at Mikko's invitation Karine spent the next four seasons with Boston Ballet before coming back to Europe to join a smaller, more contemporary company. Her last years on stage started to get painful—she'd had hip surgery in Boston and had an ongoing foot injury—so she loved finishing her career with more theatrical, less-classical pieces that weren't in pointe shoes. By then in her early forties, she was ready to retire. Her father's death around that time made her sharply reassess some big life questions. "I realized that life was not all about ballet," Karine said. "In the beginning of my career, it was all about me—it was egocentric. When my father died, I felt I had to build something else in life. It brought me back to reality. Dancing was still important, but my direction was different."

Karine's feelings about why she danced and what life as a ballerina was like for her are vivid, poignant, and frank. She understands the conflicting qualities dancers need to have in equal measure: strength and softness, confidence and humility, drive and acceptance. She looks back at the arc of her career and clearly sees places where her mentality had more influence on its course than her dancing. And now that she's a teacher of ballet to young children, she wants them to know that strength and bravery are essential to a dance career but should be balanced with perspective and trust.

"What I did not have were patience and confidence in myself," she said. "A dancer can be calm and open without being scared of not being good enough, but I never had that. The ego in me wanted more roles, always to feel the best, to be important. But if you are so focused on good feedback, you are not present enough to actually take it—to really look, to think, listen and learn. And to trust."

Work—steady, hard, committed work—was Karine's foundation, no matter her emotional state. Consistent, persistent focus on learning about and refining her technique were her lifelines at the lowest moments of uncertainty and fear. One such time was in her early twenties, when she was still a corps dancer and was offered a major chance: a principal dancer was sick; could Karine replace her in the next night's performance?

Karine knew the role but was overcome with self-doubt. She said no, in an emotional decision that she regretted for a long time. "I think I could have done it, but I did not feel ready," Karine remembered. "I was so scared, so insecure. I wanted to only do my best and was afraid I couldn't." When another opportunity came a year later, Karine grabbed it in what marked a turning point in her career. Her performance had the assurance of a principal dancer, something she'd dreamt of becoming. "Being alone on stage, free to express what I want and dance the way I want, was always my motivation," she said. "But I had to go through all the steps to grow into that position and be comfortable enough to take it."

Even once she'd become a principal dancer, Karine's personality trended toward doubt, anxiety, and stress. She had to actively work on being positive—to like herself. The more she did that, the more relaxed she felt and the more she could genuinely enjoy the work of dancing.

Ultimately, Karine found serenity and contentment in her life as a dancer, despite being torn by its inherent contradictions. Her innate tendency to hesitate and hold back made her wonder, sometimes, if she could or would

Thank you note from Boston Ballet to Gene after the 2006–07 photo shoot.

Gene,

All of us here at Boston Ballet would like to thank you for all your hard work and determination during the photo shoot. The photos are absolutely gorgeous – everyone is very happy with the results and we all look forward to seeing the photos represent our 06-07 season! It was a LONG 2 days but you and your team were fantastic and we appreciate all your hard work and talent.

Thank you!
Sheryl

have a hard enough shell to persevere. But maybe the demons of self-doubt and questioning made being an artist even more precious.

"Ballet was so much more to me than just dancing," she said. "Some people love the career just for the dancing, but I cannot say that. I loved the people, the connections we had, the atmosphere of the theater, traveling. My favorite thing was to be an actress onstage. I loved to perform not for the dancing, but for the acting. And now . . . I have not found anything else like that. I can't say that I feel complete."

That stressful day in 2006 turned out to be a successful one. Gene's candid image of Karine shows a dancer's strength in a moment of softness and conveys the humanity of an art form many see as illusory. The photo was chosen as Boston Ballet's defining image and appeared across its posters, brochures, and advertisements in the 2006–2007 season.

XIOMARA REYES

I want to teach my students that there is amazing opportunity for freedom in ballet. For me, that's what success means.

THOSE WORDS have even deeper meaning when you consider they come from a woman who grew up in a Communist country, and for whom ballet was the ticket to actual freedom. Xiomara's mother put her in music and ballet lessons very early on, strategically planning a way for her daughter to escape the rigors of mandatory labor that all teenagers in their native Cuba were required to do. The hope was that Xiomara would have enough skill to pass the entrance exam to the state-run ballet academy when she turned nine, since enrollment in a vocational school freed children from the physical labor service. Although Xiomara doesn't think she was physically perfect for ballet, her natural turnout and movement quality were, luckily, enough to get her a spot in the Cuban National Ballet School. Xiomara's dream, though, was to be an actress. She saw dancing as just something that would help achieve her fantasized-about acting career.

Even though the training at the academy was tough, it was also inspiring, and by twelve or thirteen Xiomara had fallen in love with ballet itself. She began to see it as a way to tell stories and embody characters, fulfilling her acting dreams. As a teenager, she was chosen to be part of a youth company directed by Laura Alonso, daughter of the famed Alicia Alonso. She danced her first full-length ballet, *The Three Musketeers*, at fifteen, followed by *Don Quixote* and *Coppelia*. Those experiences fueled her—and further developed her natural acting ability—when future opportunities seemed very, very far away. "At that time, even once you got into the main company, you would not get a principal role until you were maybe thirty," she recalled. "But with these performances in the youth company, Laura gave us the gift of keeping the fire going. I remember sometimes we'd rehearse very little and then go onstage, but when you're young, you don't care. You just want to dance."

Another gift from Laura Alonso was her push to send the young Cuban

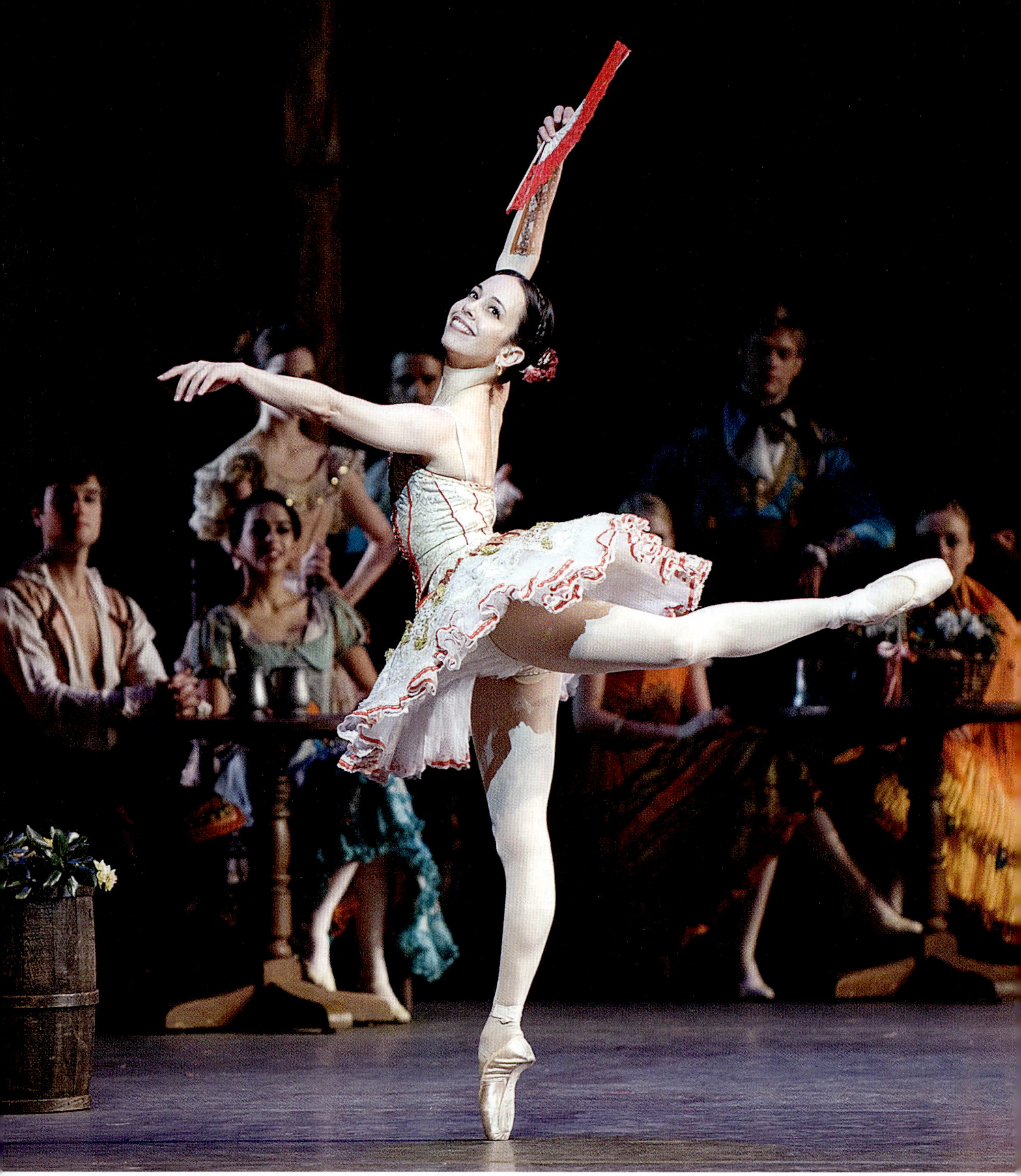

Xiomara Reyes in *Don Quixote,* 2009. Photo courtesy American Ballet Theatre.

dancers to competitions overseas, which was the only way they could see and understand the ballet world they largely were cut off from—and for the ballet world to see them. Up to that point, Xiomara's only view of ballet outside Cuba was from bootleg videos sent by her grandmother, who lived in the US. Watching ballerinas like Cynthia Harvey and Natalia Makarova captured her imagination and planted a seed of possibility.

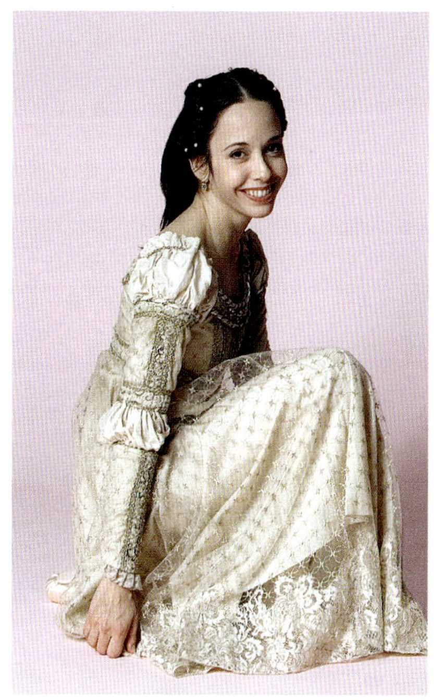

Xiomara Reyes, 2005.

Xiomara competed in Europe, South America, and Japan, where she met the director of the Royal Ballet of Flanders, who invited her to join his company as a soloist. But accepting his offer, which she desperately wanted to do, was not easy, requiring months of negotiation and tricky maneuvers before she secured a passport and could leave Cuba permanently. And when she did, the doors opened. "I was not scared to leave Cuba; I was excited," she said. "That's been the story of my life. I've always just been like, 'What's next?'"

Xiomara spent eight productive years in Belgium. She danced many principal roles, and met the man who would become her husband, fellow dancer Rinat Imaev. But internal politics seemed to dictate the artists' career trajectories, and even though she was in her prime as a dancer, she could tell that her future there was limited. Xiomara's fearless spirit took over again. She contacted other companies in Europe, asking about jobs, along with the two North American companies she idolized: the National Ballet of Canada and American Ballet Theatre. Both were interested in her, but she decided to go to New York.

With Belgian citizenship that allowed her to seek work anywhere, Xiomara went to ABT for a month-long audition. She took classes, rehearsed and performed with the company, and immediately loved it. When ABT offered her a permanent contract, she knew she'd finally found her place.

"From the beginning, it felt like home," Xiomara said. "This kind of movement was what I had been training for, what I wanted to do. I got very lucky in that I started dancing beautiful roles immediately." Xiomara grew

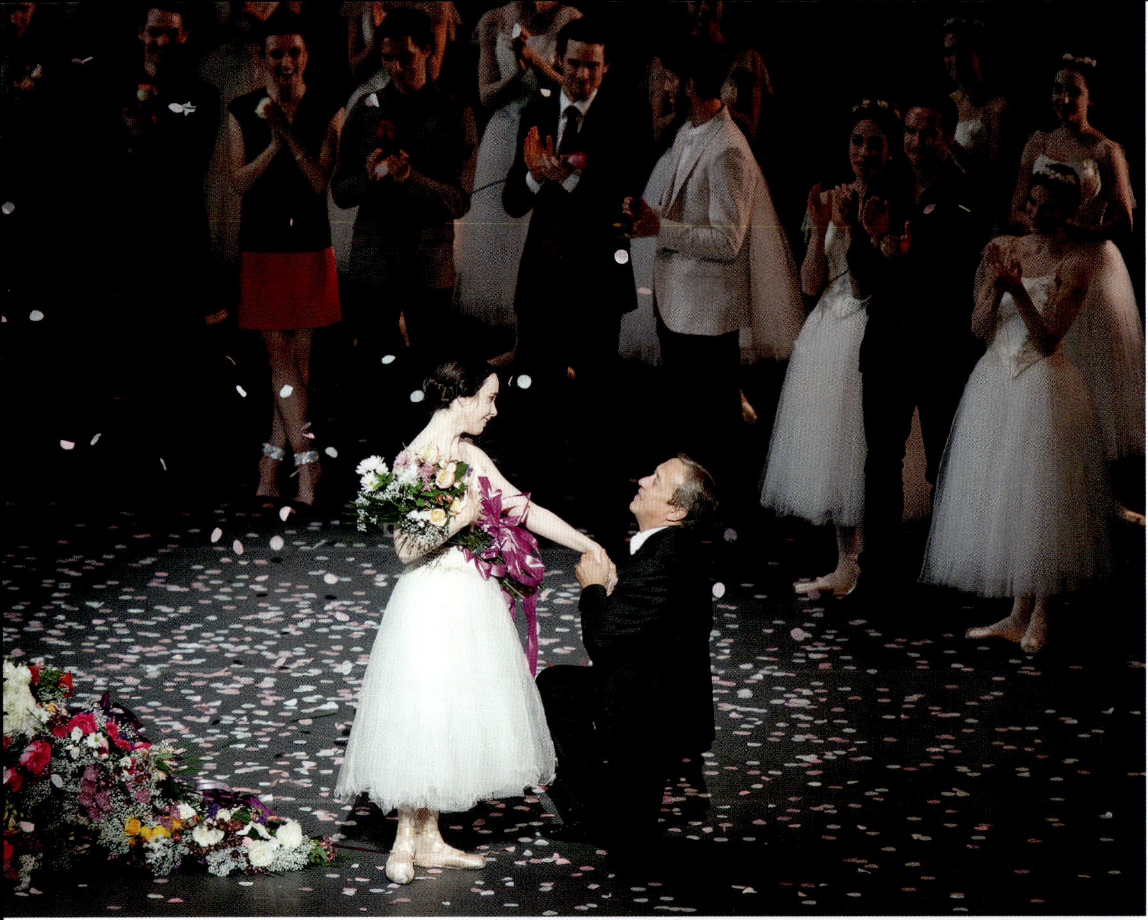

Xiomara Reyes and Renat Imaev at Reyes's American Ballet Theatre farewell performance, 2011. Photo courtesy of American Ballet Theatre.

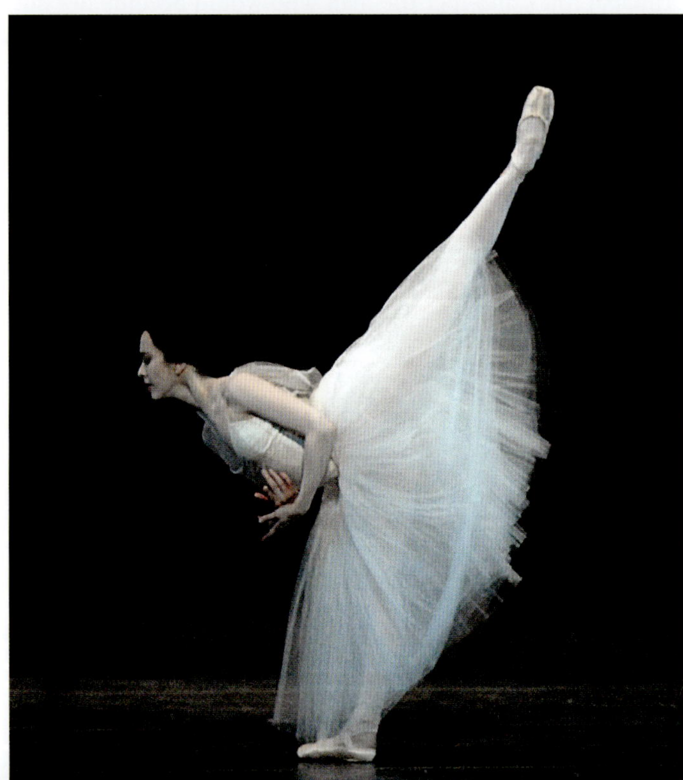

Xiomara Reyes in *Giselle,* 2013. Photo courtesy of American Ballet Theatre.

a devoted fan base and was promoted to principal in 2003. After a lauded career with an incredibly wide-ranging repertoire, she retired in 2015.

After her retirement, invitations to teach came rolling in. Teaching was never her plan, but looking back, she thinks that it was almost inevitable. Students in Cuba were trained to be teachers as well as dancers, learning pedagogy along with performance technique, so for them, offering constructive criticism is instinctive. "We grew up like that," she said. "After class we'd try to help each other. It was just normal." As she started working with students more formally, Xiomara realized she'd found a new passion that life had already prepared her for. "I think it's like that for everyone. I'm very conscious of it, and very grateful."

Xiomara sees herself as much more than a teacher of ballet to ambitious and talented dancers. She knows all too well how emotionally and mentally stressful pursuing a professional career can be, and that youth today are contending with forces she didn't face. Her own lifelong interest in self-development and mindfulness comes out in her classes and, since her first dream of being an actress never fully evaporated, she likes to add in courses in acting, mime, and even meditation. "Creating a connection with the imagination is so important when you are an actor or a dancer," she said. "So it's not just your body. It's a mind-body connection."

Ultimately, Xiomara wants her students to feel the freedom of ballet as she did. She knows the release that ballet can produce inside oneself and now, as ever, works to help others unleash it. "It's about sharing the glory, that feeling inside you. Are you able to connect to that joy every day? I am so blessed to have felt it and I know others can, too."

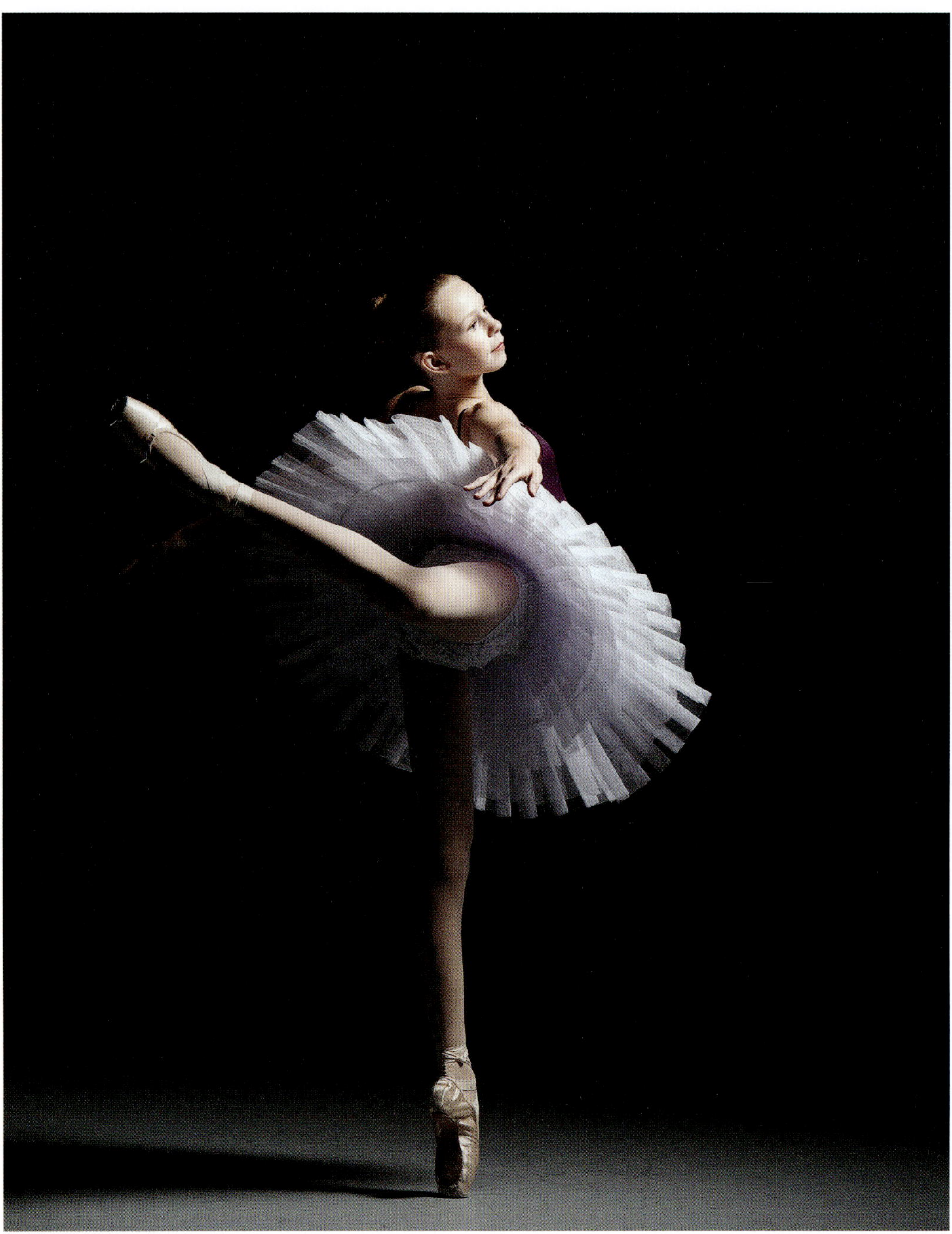

Hailey Fairhurst, 2014.

HAILEY FAIRHURST

It's such a cliché, but when I was about two years old, I told my parents I wanted to be a ballerina.

SO HAILEY'S PARENTS, not knowing anything about ballet or even much about dance in general, enrolled their very young daughter at the local studio near their home in Massachusetts. For several years she took classes in every style of dance offered, but by the time she was thirteen she was ready to narrow her focus on ballet and aim for a career. Hailey convinced her parents to let her leave home for the Nutmeg Conservatory, an arts boarding school that was only the first stop of many along the road of Hailey's training and career.

Moving around so much as a teenager—she switched schools every couple of years—was rough, exhausting, and being away from her close-knit family was painful. But everywhere she went—Cary, North Carolina; Boston, London, Philadelphia, Orlando—Hailey got stronger, more skilled, more confident. Even so, the "not knowingness" of the ballet world, as she put it, was hard. "Never knowing if I'd get a job, if a contract would come or fall through, and being away from my family were the hardest things for me," she said. "But I found good people everywhere I went, and my parents were always making sure I'd thrive. It was so important to have them in my corner."

After several years of short term positions with junior companies and traineeships, Hailey found her spot in an unexpected place, the small Delaware company First State Ballet. Even as a very young professional, having danced in so many different environments, Hailey already has a smart perspective on the ballet business. A summer at the Royal Ballet School, just after she turned eighteen, showed her a very different public view of the arts, and of ballet in particular. Largely because of that, one of her long-term goals is to perform in a place where dance is not only in the margins of most people's lives. "The love for ballet in London—by people who dance and those who don't—is so much bigger," she said. "They love dancers. They stop us on the street and want to talk about it. I'm happy here for now, and I'm

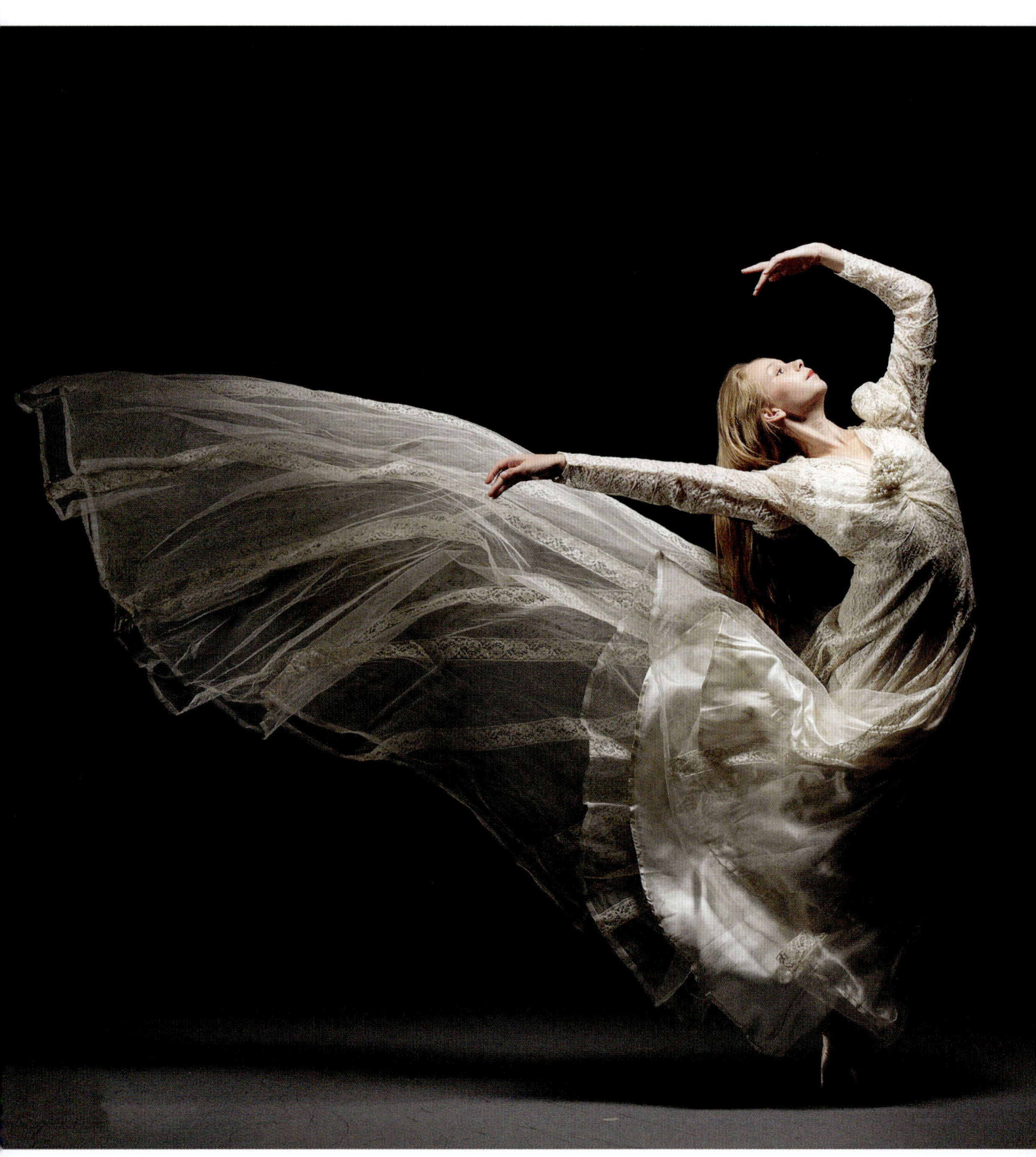

Hailey Fairhurst, 2015.

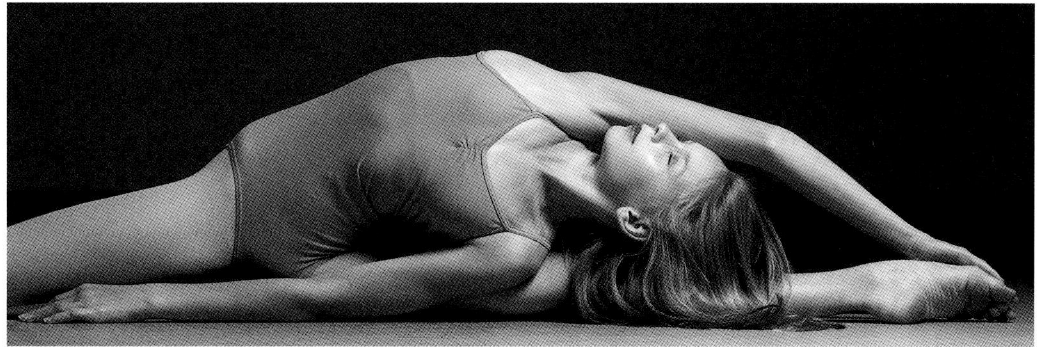

Hailey Fairhurst, 2014.

not trying to rush it, but my dream is to be in the Royal Ballet or American Ballet Theatre."

Hailey is not unaware of the negativity trap that many in the ballet world—students, pros, and also teachers and directors—can fall into, but she's determined not to let that happen to her.

"I have been surrounded by a lot of good people," she said. "But I've also seen a lot of people who let anger, fear, and frustration tear them down. And I've seen some of them not continue to dance. So I'm focusing on the things that bring me actual happiness instead of pushing against things that frustrate me. If a step doesn't work, I'll stop practicing it and tell myself that I can come in again tomorrow with a fresh mind, fresh body, and try again."

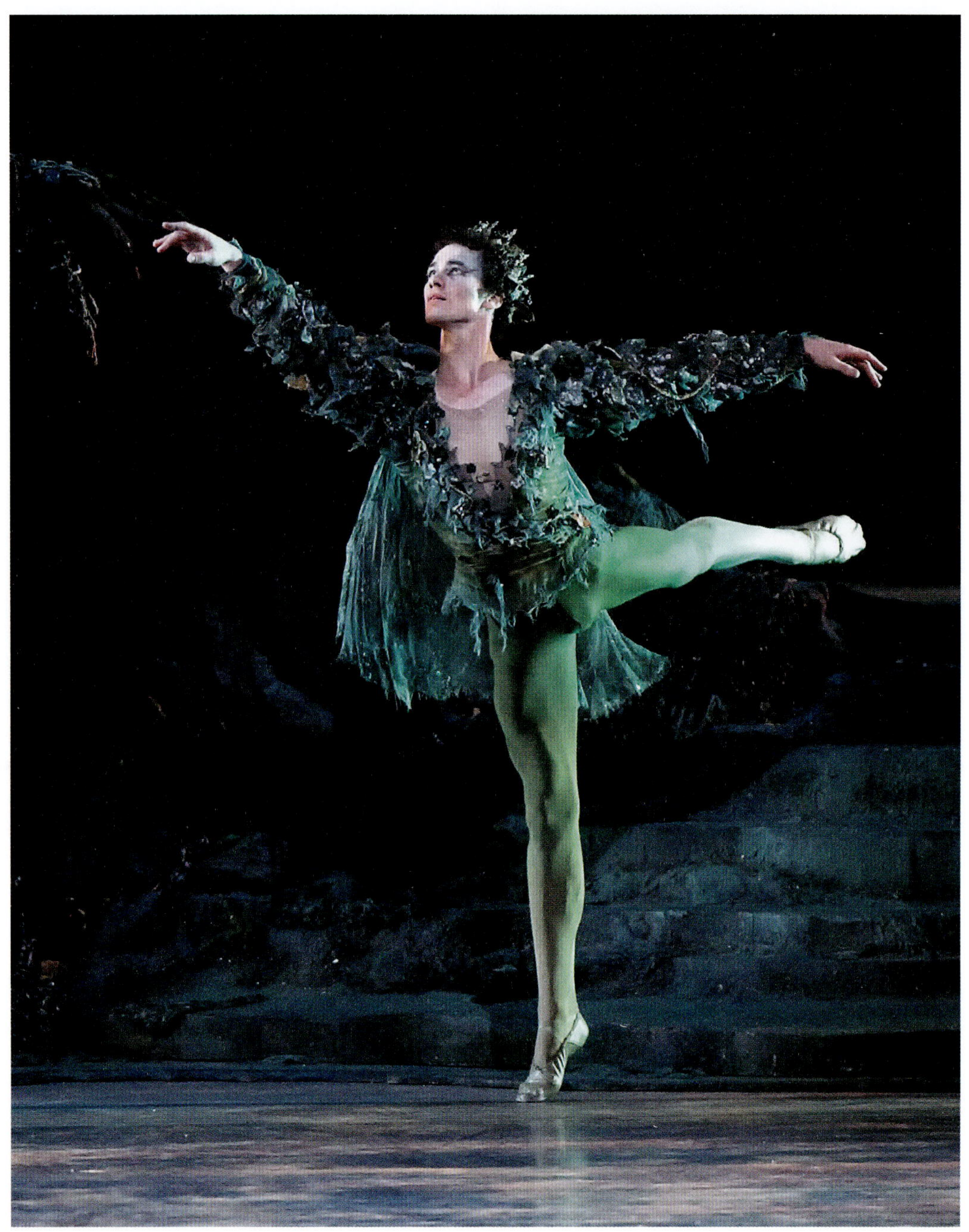

Cory Stearns in *The Dream,* 2010. Photo courtesy of American Ballet Theatre.

CORY STEARNS

I see younger dancers coming into the company now with a sense of confidence that I just did not have. I wasn't conscious of how capable I might be. I had set a goal from a young age that I wanted to be a principal dancer, but I was aware that much of it is timing and luck . . . that it wasn't wholly in my control.

WHEN CORY JOINED AMERICAN BALLET THEATRE as an apprentice in 2005, barely out of his teens, it was not a particularly welcoming place. The environment was so intense, in fact, that "I almost felt like I was being hazed," he remembered. Large, esteemed companies are notoriously intimidating for young dancers just starting out, but the structure of unspoken rules Cory entered into—including a strict separation between ranks that new corps de ballet members were not encouraged to broach—made it seem like the hierarchy was being policed. The stark disconnect between newer and senior dancers seemed to permeate every aspect of their work, causing insecurity and tension all around.

As a young and talented dancer, Cory was soon given solo roles, but the enormous pressure only added to his nerves. "There was a heightened sense of needing to prove myself because there were all these people wanting me to fail," he said.

Despite the fear factor and aura of untouchability surrounding the leading dancers (most of whom were guest artists, in contrast to the corps members and soloists on the company's full-time roster), Cory watched them closely, looking for artistic and personal qualities that intrigued him as a way to stay inspired and motivated. He found something in each dancer that he could grasp and emulate, which surely helped propel his own swift rise through the ranks of ABT—he was promoted from corps to soloist and then principal by age twenty-five, during a major shift away from ABT's tradition of infrequently promoting from within. But it took years for him to shake the uncertainty that weighed him down from the beginning. "When I started

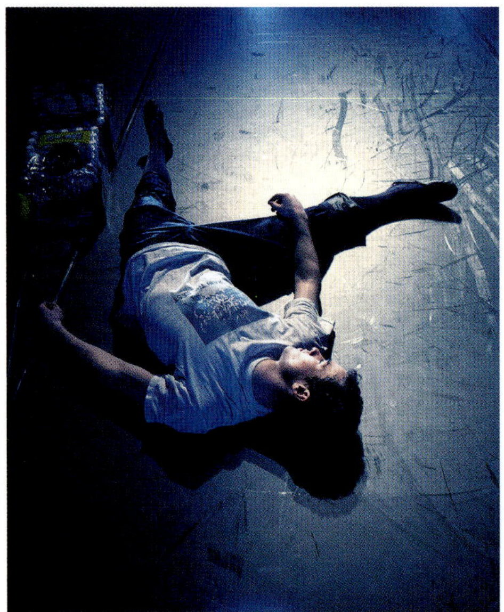

Taking a breather.

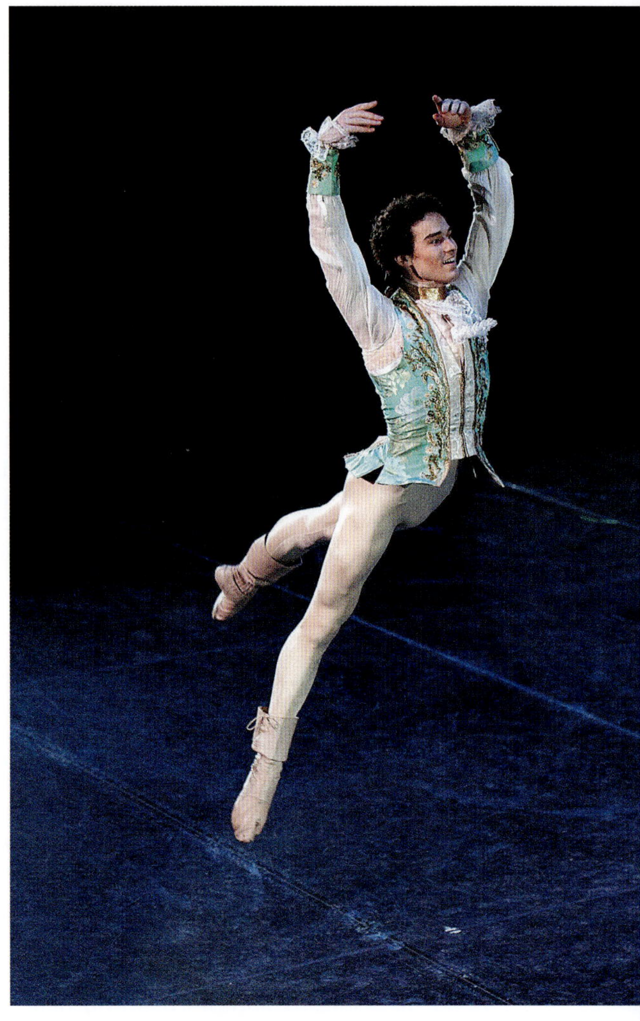

Cory Stearns in *The Sleeping Beauty,* 2010. Photo courtesy of American Ballet Theatre.

getting some important roles, I still didn't feel grounded," Cory remembered. "People might have perceived that I felt assured, but I didn't. Because of my lack of security and confidence as the 'new principal,' it often felt like even as I was doing these roles, I was trying to prove to myself that I was capable. It actually affected my performances a lot. It was always, 'Can I do this? Am I actually worthy of this responsibility?'"

It took Cory a few years to get used to the fact that he was, indeed, worthy of the title "principal dancer," but finally, with many years' experience and artistic achievements, he developed into a proud leader in a company that looks and acts very different from the one he joined. He's seen ABT's evolution from a place with entrenched patterns that tended to stifle dancers' ambition to one where the norms are openness, communication, and sincere support among the dancers. "When I was younger, I said to myself that when I was a senior dancer, if I saw things like what I went through I would not let it slide—I would correct it. But I have to say that I've not seen any circumstances where I'd need to do that. Because the company culture seemed to just naturally shift." Cory credits the most recent generations of new dancers for that shift, noting that what he sees happening within ABT reflects what's expected and accepted outside the company, too. There's an understanding that everyone will be treated with respect instead of judgment. "Now, when we perform, it just feels different," Cory said. "Your colleagues really want you to do well. It's been a wonderful change."

As the atmosphere around him lightened, Cory finally felt a freedom and excitement about his work that had been suppressed by the self-consciousness of his first several years as a principal. As he watched the interpersonal dynamic in ABT change, he also noticed artistic differences creeping in. This is where his new mission lies: he feels very strongly that the rigidity of the old days should be left behind, but not the artistic richness of decades past. Cory thinks something's been lost in the ebbs and flows of the ballet world that have brought amazing technical advances. "When you watch videos of dancers from the 1970s, you see that their priority was communication, expression. Technique was a tool for interpretation. And that's something I'd really like to see return to the art form."

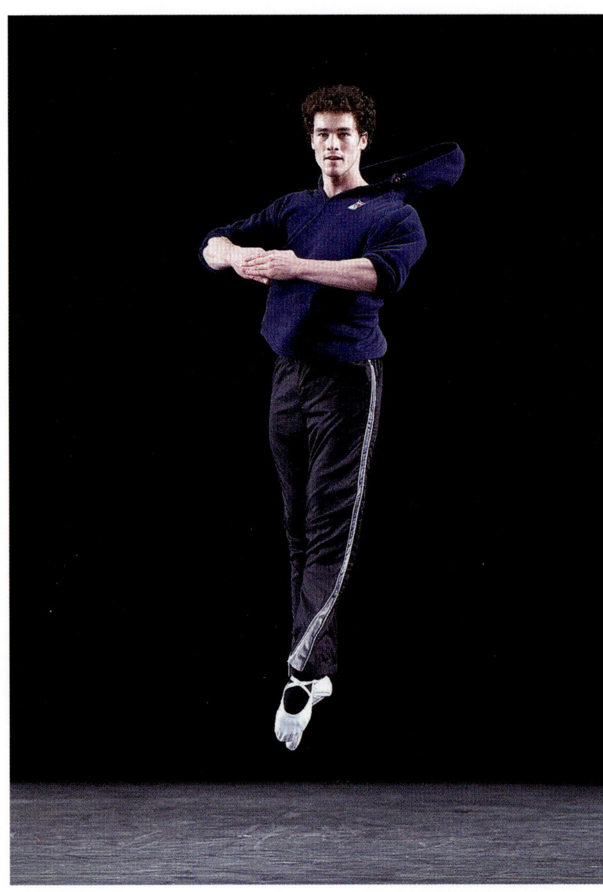

Cory Stearns rehearsing *Theme and Variations,* 2008. Photo courtesy of American Ballet Theatre.

One of the dancers Cory looks to as the most stellar example of someone who puts artistry first, without sacrificing technique, is Mikhail Baryshnikov, who coached Cory in Giselle. He remembered spending an entire rehearsal working on entrances—not the technical steps. "It was reassuring. It validated this idea I had that when you see a dancer come onstage who is engaging, or captures you without even doing a step, it's because they are immersing themselves in the role. To me, that is art."

One of Cory's first principal roles was the lead in Balanchine's *Theme and Variations,* which is widely recognized as supremely challenging and is often given to promising dancers early in their careers. In an illustration of the emotional turmoil he felt as an up-and-coming dancer, Cory remembered grappling with the weight of what he was about to do. "This photo is from the spacing rehearsal on the afternoon of my debut in the role. The experience was invaluable, but also incredibly intimidating and eye-opening in terms of the recognition of the responsibilities of being a lead dancer with ABT. Luckily, the show went pretty well."

MARIA KOCHETKOVA

For me, it's quite simple. Dance is my voice. I do not have this voice as a human being, but as a dancer I have this power that is way beyond something I could imagine. That is the most important thing for me.

"BACK IN THOSE DAYS, it was a hard system," Maria said, remembering the Bolshoi Ballet Academy's opaque machinations in the 1990s. "Students weren't treated based on their talent. Instead, those with wealth and connections were given special support. My family wasn't well-connected or wealthy, so it was a hard life."

Maria grew up in Moscow, where she first took gymnastics. A coach noticed her unusually good coordination and suggested she try ballet, but amazingly, the little girl who would go on to be a star of twenty-first-century ballet was initially rejected by the famous Bolshoi Ballet Academy. A year later, at just ten years old, she was accepted—and was thrown into the adult world of social and political dynamics that dominated Russian life at the time. Even as a child, she could tell she'd have to be her own advocate if she wanted to go where her heart led her.

As soon as she could, Maria started entering major international ballet competitions as a way to gain exposure and visibility outside of Russia, where she knew that her career would be limited by both her height (she's just five feet) and social standing, despite her undeniable talent. Without the internet (it was the early 1990s) or speaking any other languages, the notice she gained by winning the prestigious Prix de Lausanne at eighteen was crucial: it brought her an apprentice contract with the Royal Ballet, followed by a corps position with the English National Ballet, where she did some major roles but was largely kept in the background. Frustrated that she wasn't getting opportunities that she felt matched her technical level and artistic maturity—plus being typecast due to her height—Maria knew she needed a fresh start.

So, being innately courageous, ambitious, and determined, Maria took

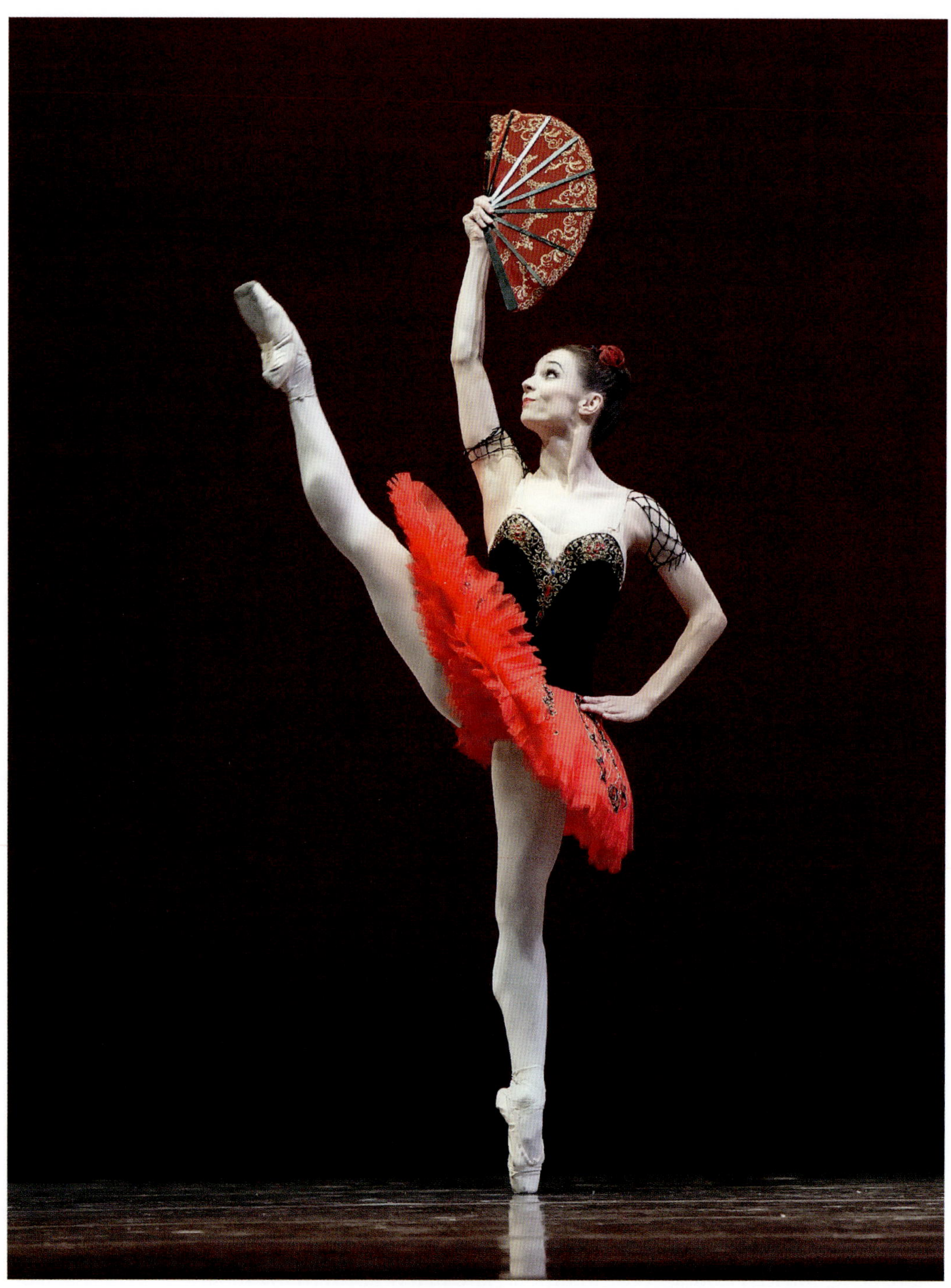

Maria Kochetkova in *Don Quixote,* Ballet Royalty Gala, Havana, 2014.

a chance and auditioned for San Francisco Ballet. And when then-artistic director Helgi Tomasson offered her a principal dancer contract, she didn't hesitate to accept.

Despite having to leave her family even further behind than she already had and knowing almost no one in the US, Maria moved to San Francisco with excitement. Her high hopes for this new chapter in her career and life were fulfilled many times over, and in ways she hadn't considered. "I had been held back for so long and not allowed to do anything," she said. "As soon as I got to San Francisco, everything felt so right . . . it just clicked. Helgi, the city, the freer approach to dancing. Everyone was so happy and friendly. I had no fears or regrets or worries whatsoever."

Over the next eleven years Maria became known as one of the most versatile, creatively ambitious, and sought-after dancers on the worldwide ballet landscape. Along with every major classical role, she performed countless neoclassical and contemporary pieces, seeming equally at home in any movement language. Tireless, and aware of the brevity of even a superstar's career, in 2015 she worked out an arrangement for dual principal dancer positions in both San Francisco Ballet and American Ballet Theatre while also adding guest artist appearances at galas and with companies around the world. But in 2018, wise to the autonomy and options she had as a once-in-a-generation ballerina, Maria made the unexpected announcement that she would leave the rosters of both companies to dance independently. Again, she'd come to a crossroads: to stay the course or take a side road and map her own route, designing her own life rather than waiting to see what happened. She'd become more interested in contemporary dance, where she felt the US lagged behind Europe, and in working with choreographers less likely to create for large classical ballet companies. "I had reached the point in my career where I had done everything," Maria said. "I looked at the upcoming season and there wasn't anything worth staying for."

A home base closer to Russia, where her extended family still lived, was another draw. As a freelancer, Maria danced with companies in Finland, Norway, Germany, and the UK, produced solo shows with specially commissioned choreography, and actively sought out unique, innovative collaborations with multifaceted artists. In 2023 she added another premiere to her repertoire, when she gave birth to a daughter.

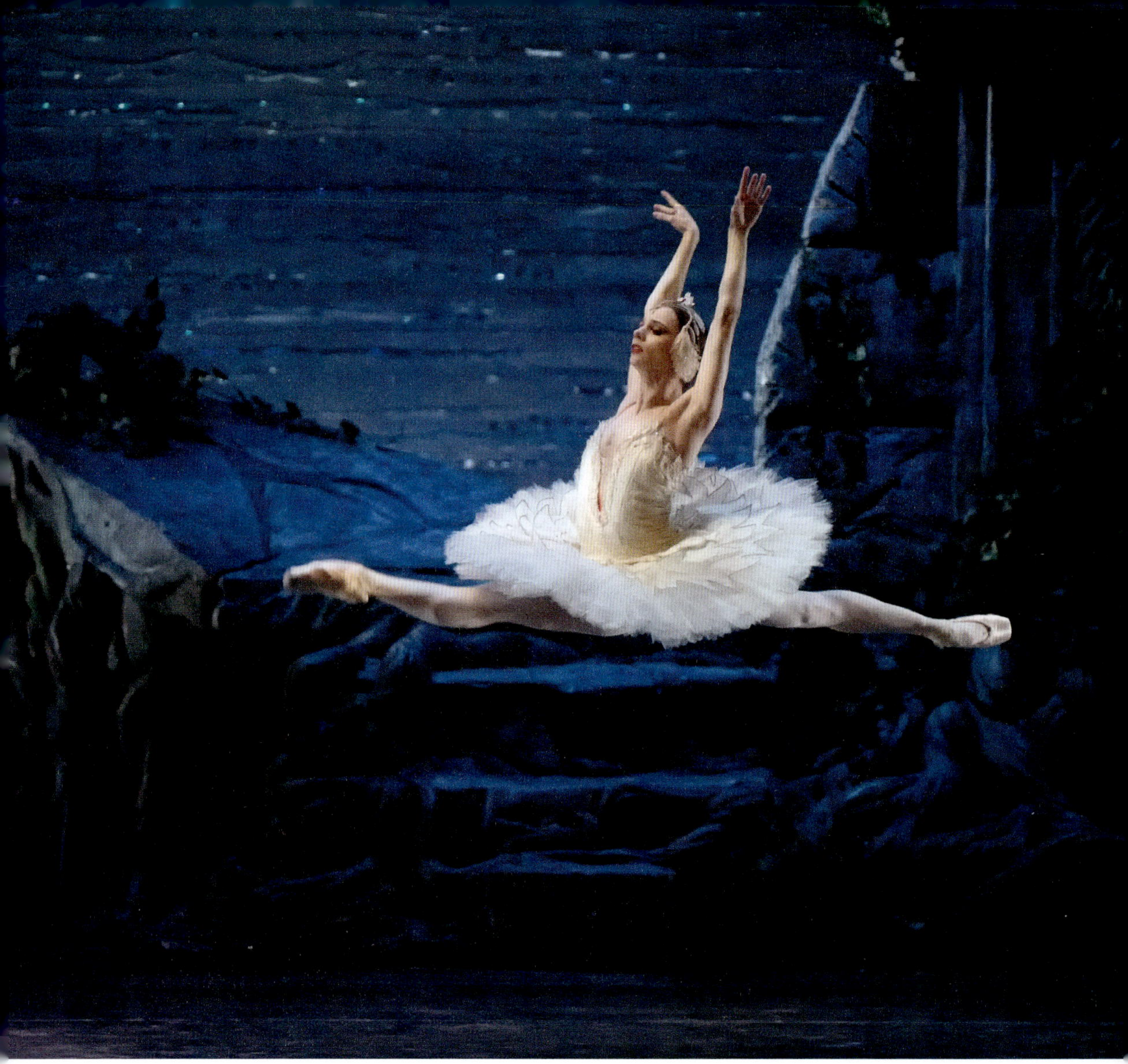

Maria Kochetkova in *Swan Lake,* 2015. Photo courtesy of American Ballet Theatre.

It would be easy to look at a dancer like Maria and think that her talent and facility are what have given her longevity and opportunity. That may be true, but Maria frankly acknowledges the realities of decades in the ballet business: it's a race between one's body and the inevitable effects of time, and a continual balancing act between mental and physical energy. Dance is a job, and therefore something you have to do whether you feel like it or

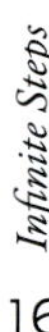

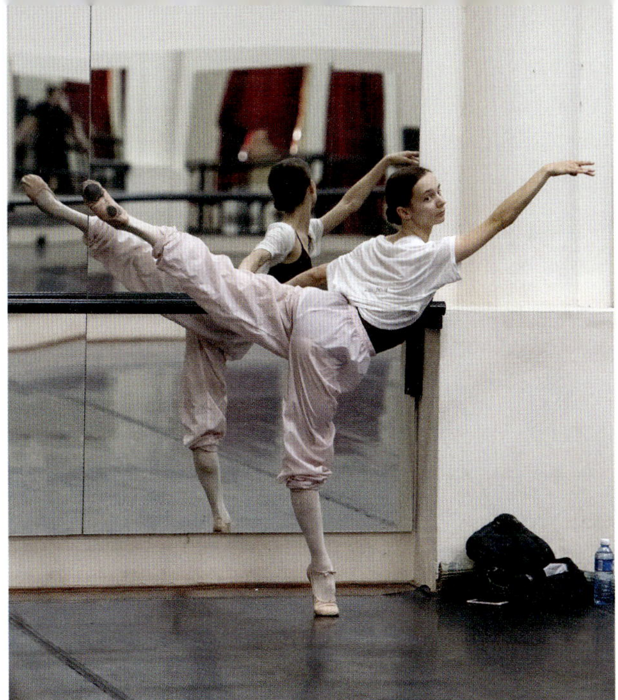

Maria Kochetkova taking class, Havana, 2014.

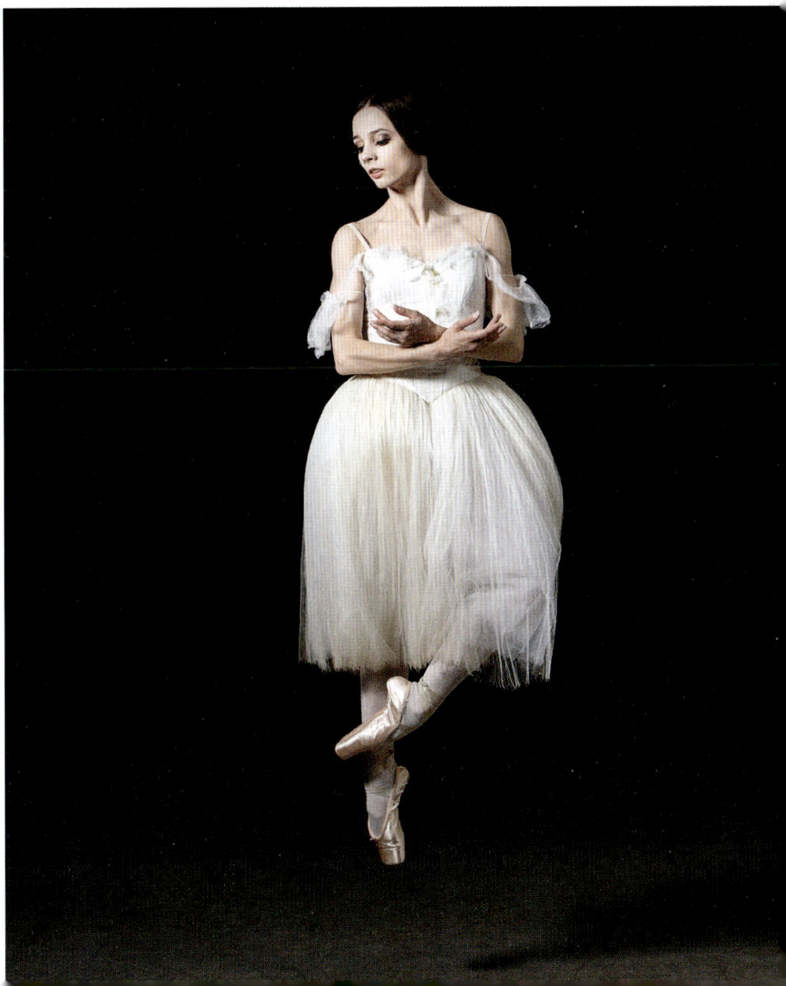

Maria Kochetkova, 2013.

not, and to have a long career a dancer has to honor their one irreplaceable instrument. “You have to take class every day. I’ve never done a rehearsal without doing class first,” Maria said.

Maria has always listened to her body to gauge when to push or rest so as to minimize injury, but just as importantly, she’s also always listened to her heart. The choices she’s made have all been driven by both practicality and passion, and the awareness of how short and precious a career is. “I don’t want to spend months on something I don’t like, believe in, or enjoy, or with someone who is toxic or not a nice person,” she said. “When I was younger, I did it and it was the right thing to do. But as your art form and dance changes, you have responsibilities as someone who has the power to do something. At some point, compromises are not good enough.”

HERMAN CORNEJO

I don't go on stage thinking about the turns and jumps. It's more about acting, being with your partner, and making the whole evening believable.

HERMAN DANCED with American Ballet Theatre for over twenty-five years, most of them as a principal. With decades of experience, he knows that while dancers love to set and work toward big future goals, sometimes the significance of the present gets overlooked. Herman's own intentions were lofty from the very beginning—he was determined to be a principal dancer—but now he thinks that being so fixated on one thing may have somewhat diminished his ability to savor the time he spent getting there. Maybe it's human nature to keep our eyes focused forward, always seeking something more, but while Herman doesn't regret any of his efforts, he does think dancers should cherish the process of building their careers instead of waiting for an ultimate moment of arrival. "When I was in my twenties and thirties, I took time for granted," he said. "Now I look back and think . . . wow, [look at] what I've accomplished, but how stressed I was in getting there. The beauty is in the work we do to produce a show, but the show itself is not the final achievement. It goes beyond."

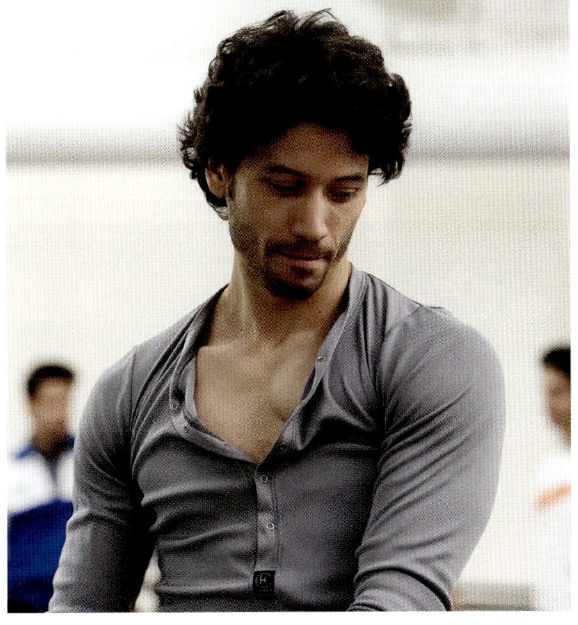
Herman Cornejo, 2012.

Despite his one-of-a-kind talent—he's considered among the best technicians in the world—Herman's smaller than average height was a significant factor that threatened to come between him and his principal dancer dreams. He grew up and got his early training in Buenos Aires, attracted worldwide attention as a teenager by winning major ballet

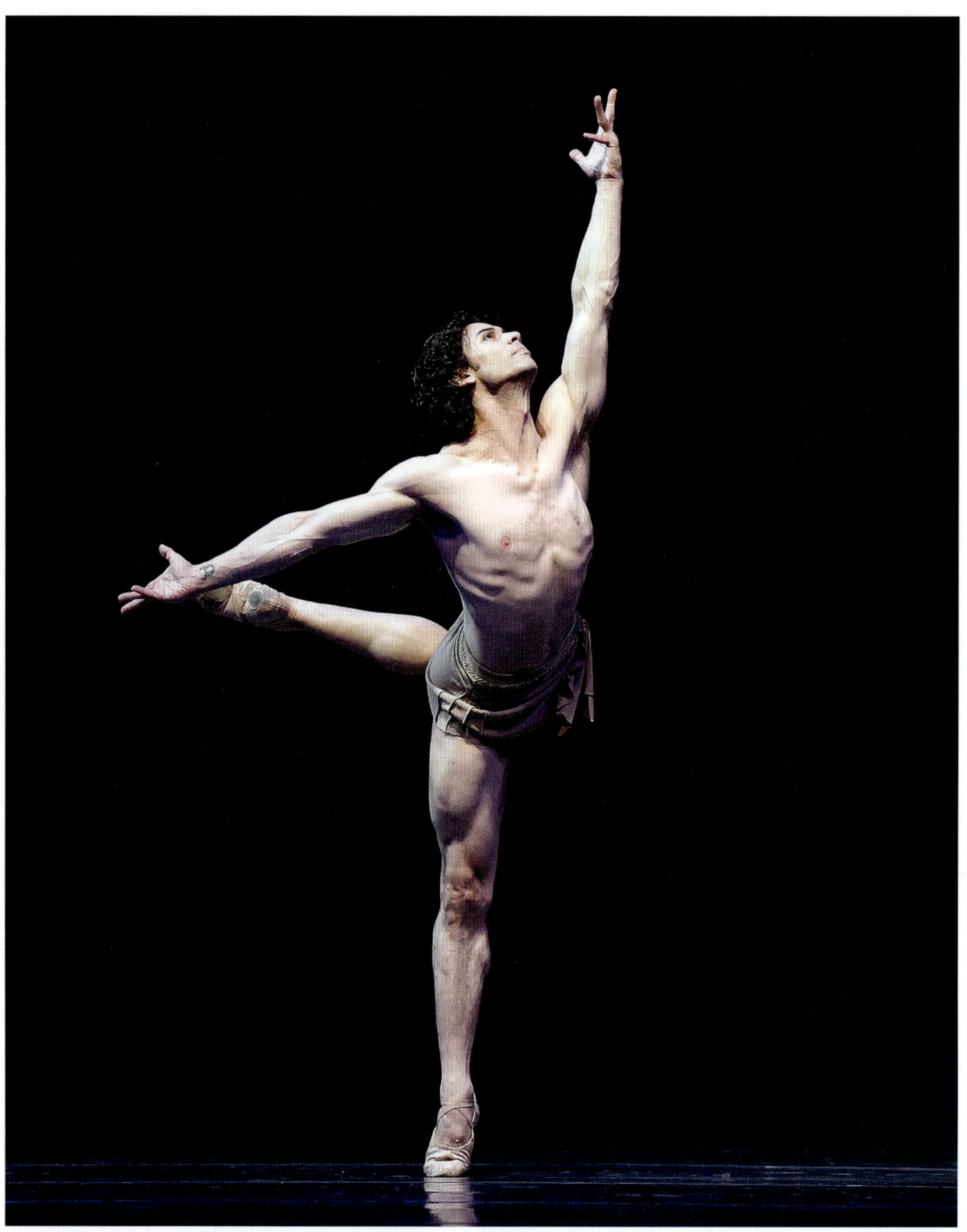

Herman Cornejo in *Diana and Acteon,* Indianapolis City Ballet gala, 2013.

competitions, and was quickly snapped up by ABT. Not long after (and while still in the corps), he was given his breakout role: the Bronze Idol in *La Bayadère*, which led to his promotion to soloist only two years after joining the company. But Herman worried he was destined for a life of typecasting, largely because of the typical height of male principals at that time. To throw off any predetermined soloist label, he kept asking for chances to do different roles, "knocking at the door" to persuade Kevin McKenzie (ABT's artistic director at the time) that he was more than a soloist with beautiful technique. His persistence paid off, though his first three leading roles came about because other dancers were injured.

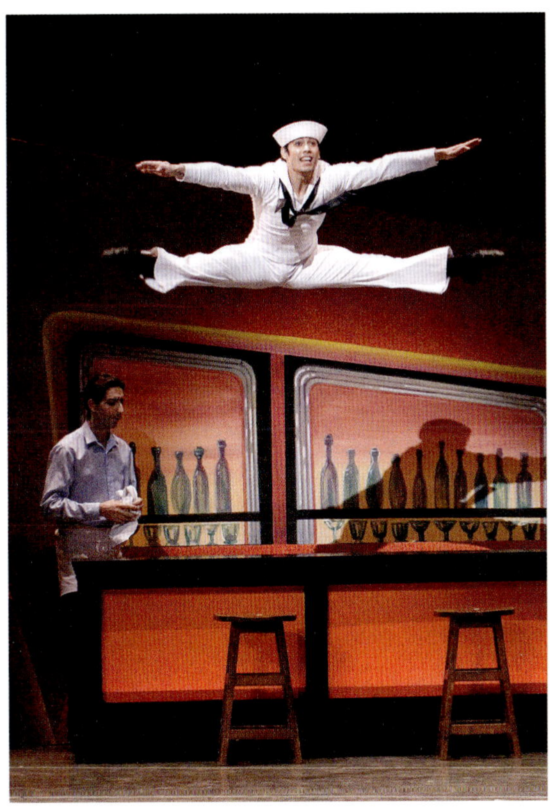

Herman Cornejo in *Fancy Free,* 2006. Photo courtesy of American Ballet Theatre.

It's hard to imagine this dancer—who is today recognized as a leading interpreter of iconic roles, an innovator in dramatic dance and theater productions, and the first choice for contemporary choreographers worldwide—being categorized as a supporting actor instead of the star. Herman thinks fighting for recognition is part of why he did go so far. "I don't know, but sometimes it feels like when the doors open easily for you, you don't push as hard," he said. "When you have one moment to show what you can do, one performance to prove yourself, it gives you the strength to push even further. Luckily, I had a director who gave me opportunities, but I definitely had to work hard to get them."

Why did being a principal matter so much to Herman? It wasn't for the glory or prestige of the title. It was because he wanted to do more than just display dazzling steps, even though his technical ability has been with him from nearly day one (he says he executed a perfect double tour en l'air a

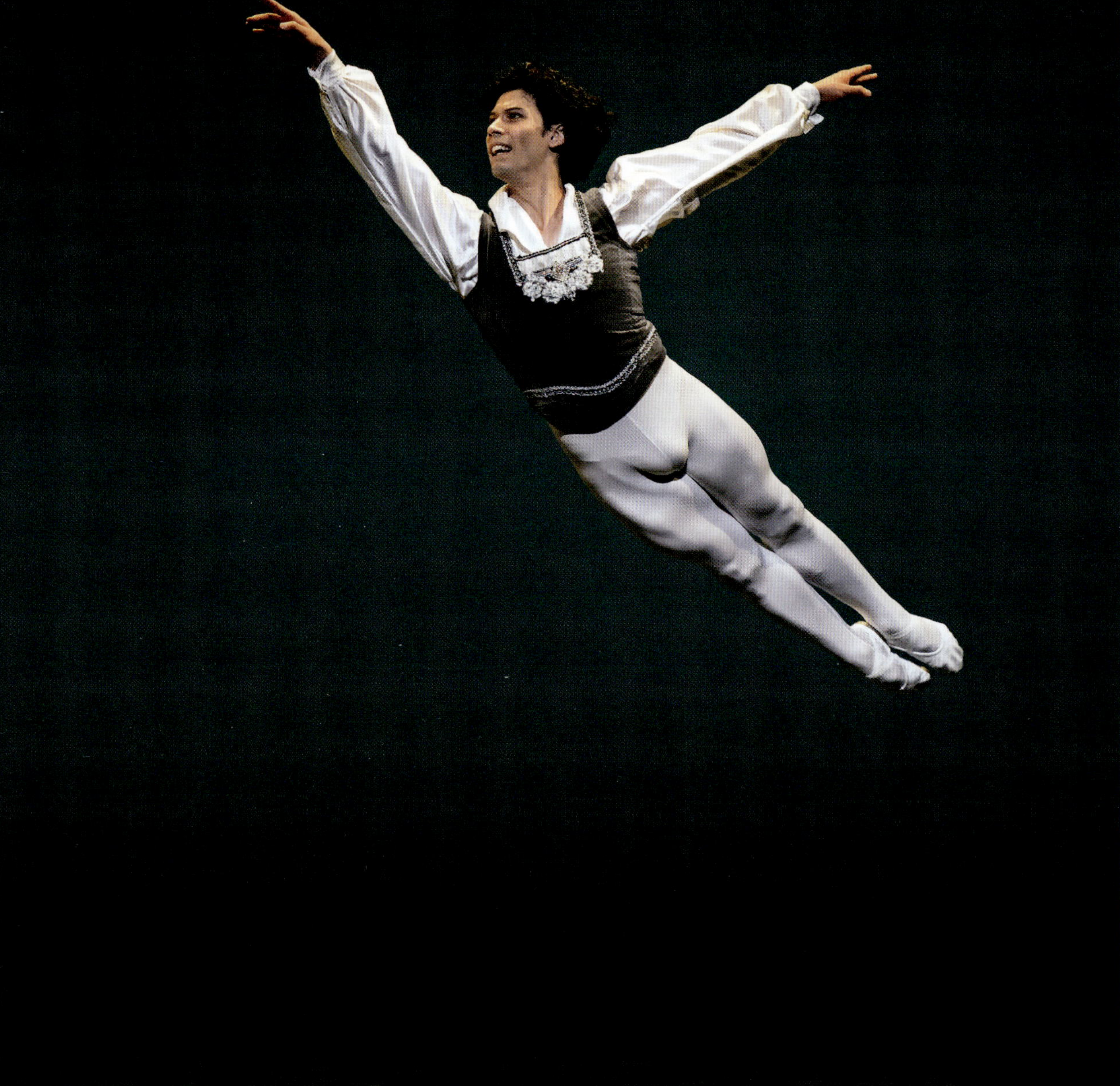

Herman Cornejo in *Tchaikovsky Pas de Deux,* Roberto Bolle and Friends, 2013.

week after his very first ballet class). For him, being a ballet dancer meant being an actor.

"I didn't find that opportunity when I was in soloist roles, where you show technique and then five minutes later you're offstage," he explained. "To be an actor, you have to be the lead dancer, onstage for three hours and carrying the story."

Herman knows that growing into a mature artist with the powers to transfix an audience takes experience, openness, and empathy. Even after his promotion to principal dancer he relished the years-long process of developing those qualities. He also relied heavily on his partners to be equally invested so that they could go deeply into emotions together, like mirrors reflecting each other. Xiomara Reyes, with whom Herman performed almost every debut, was one of his most frequent partners until her retirement in 2015. "When you can relate to each other, trust each other that whatever happens during a show you will be there for each other, it creates something really beautiful," he said. "Other dancers would switch partners throughout the season, but we did every single thing together. Her retirement did tear me apart."

As for his own future, Herman prefers to avoid forecasting and instead, as he wants others to do, focus on the now. "I feel better physically now than I ever did," he said. "I have peace of mind instead of always pushing, wanting, thinking, 'what's next?' It's beautiful to not have a long-term goal. I go day by day, year by year. I'm enjoying the moment."

Jennifer Alexander in costume for *Giselle,* 2006. Photo courtesy of American Ballet Theatre.

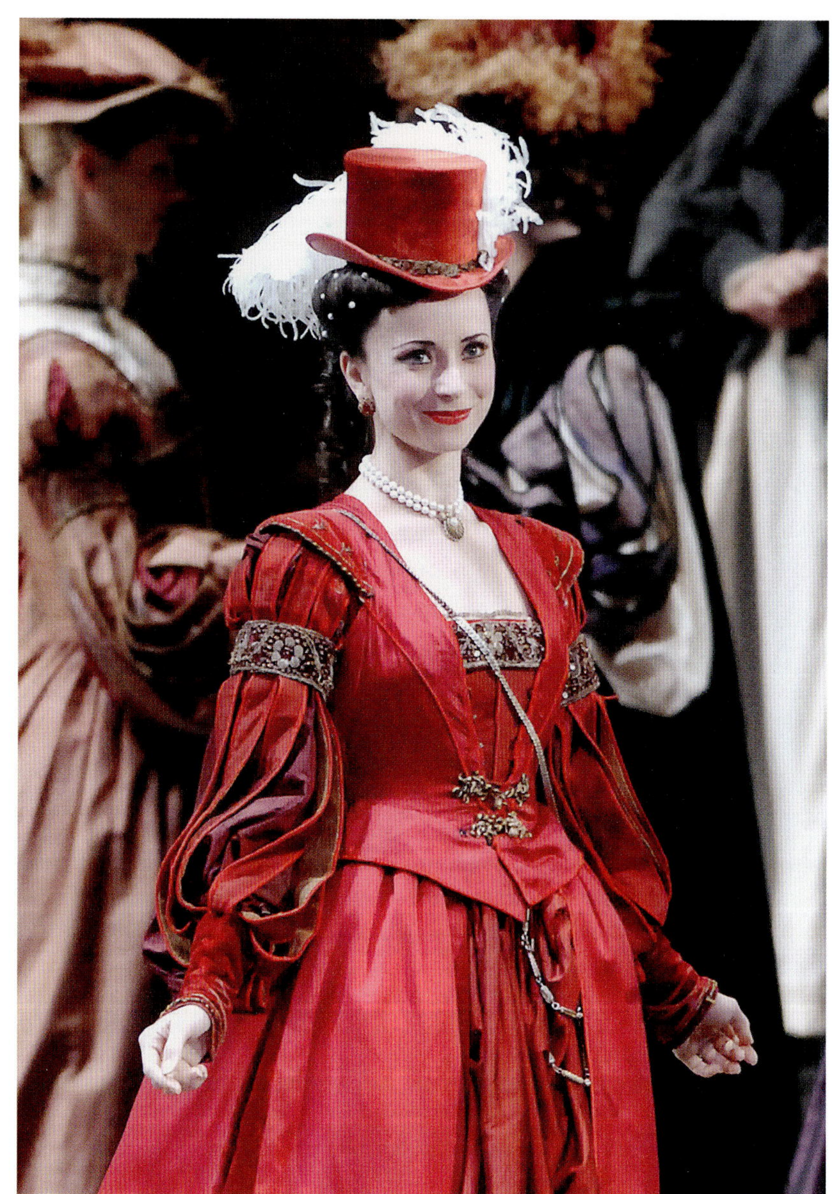

JENNIFER ALEXANDER

This was someone who could have been a principal in another company, but she didn't. She did her corps and soloist roles with a sense of pride and an elegance and dignity that taught me and those around her to see how beautiful it is to be in the corps de ballet. There's a way of being that trumps rank. And that really matters.

ANNE MILEWSKI CARY

IT IS SAID that the way a person dances reflects who they are. Jennifer Alexander was a special sort of dancer, and a very special type of person.

According to her sister, Andrea, Jennifer came from a long line of performers. Their mother, Vanessa, was an actress; their grandparents toured a popular Western-themed vaudeville show around the world. Andrea also thinks Jennifer's instinctive ability to combine graceful movement with athleticism came at least in part from her father, Keith, a golfer in the Canadian Hall of Fame. "Our mom encouraged Jenny from early on," Andrea recalled, thinking about how Jennifer first caught the ballet bug in classes at a neighborhood school in their hometown of Calgary, Alberta. Jennifer loved having an audience right away, too. A favorite family memory is the time she landed on the front page of the local newspaper at about age seven, pictured hamming it up for the photographer at a local event, wearing a little yellow tutu and sunglasses.

From there, things got more serious. By the time she was a teenager, Jennifer's evident talent and drive were strong enough that she moved away from home to study at the Royal Winnipeg Ballet School. After completing her training she joined the Royal Winnipeg Ballet for two years before moving to New York City, following her ancestral roots into musical theater. She performed in *Carousel* and *The Red Shoes* on Broadway but returned to her first love when she joined American Ballet Theatre in 1994. For the next thirteen years Jennifer danced in ABT's corps de ballet, becoming one of the company's most beloved, respected, and reliable members. As a seasoned performer

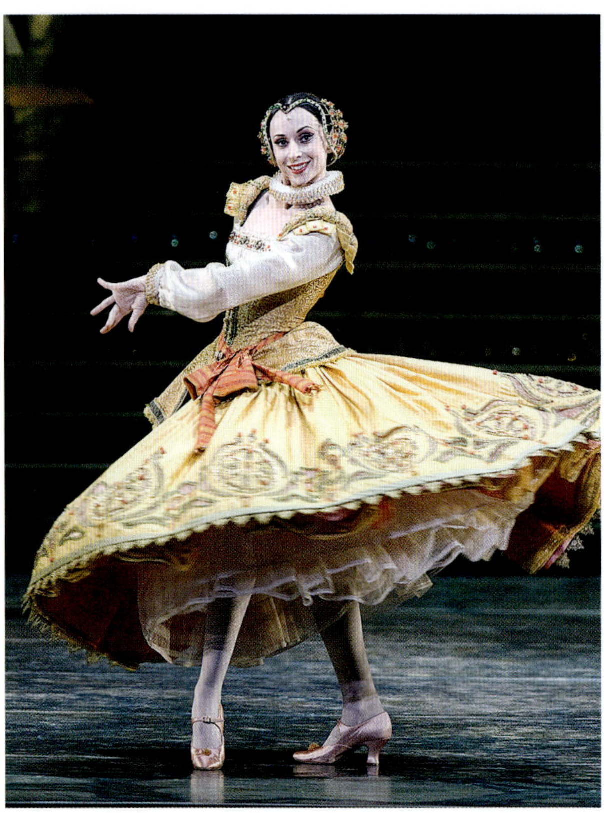

Jennifer Alexander in *Romeo and Juliet,* 2005. Photo courtesy of American Ballet Theatre.

with experience and seniority, she was a generous role model, mentor, and confidante to those just beginning their careers, and choreographers and repetiteurs valued her natural stage presence and polished technique. Jennifer held a place of honor and love in the company that truly became her family.

ON DECEMBER 2, 2007, Jennifer, her husband, and another dancer were returning home from a *Nutcracker* performance in New Jersey. Icy roads caused a multiple car accident, which the group narrowly avoided, but required them to pull to the side of the roadway. While they waited for conditions to clear, another vehicle skidded in their direction, taking Jennifer's life.

Jennifer's death rocked the dance community to its core. The tragically early loss of a person who represented stability, generosity, joy, and a brilliant love of life left everyone who had been in her orbit in shock. For those who had seen and felt her magical way of forging connection with anyone, no matter their age, rank, or position, Jennifer's sudden absence prompted reflection. In a profession known for its competitiveness and adoration of stardom, here was someone who had quietly become a star in the eyes and hearts of the people who, to a dancer, are the most important and discerning audience: their fellow dancers.

IT'S A DISTINCTIVE AND RELATIVELY RARE BREED of dancer who spends a decade-plus career in the corps de ballet. There was a time, in an earlier era of ABT, when it was common to join the corps as a teenager and to see that position as both one's starting and ending place. When Jennifer was hired into the company, she entered a corps full of dancers nearing the end of long careers. She absorbed the pride they took in their work and learned to appreciate the too often underestimated value of their dedication and contributions to the company as a whole. She felt the honor of serving as a group in an industry characterized by its exaltation of the individuals in the spotlight. As ABT's tradition shifted to one of grooming future stars from its corps and promoting from within its own ranks, Jennifer was the link between generations, standing firmly by her mission to carry on the dignity of the career corps dancer.

NOT LONG AFTER Anne Milewski Cary (who goes by Annie) joined ABT, at age seventeen, the company toured to Mexico. Jennifer, who had recently dealt with several injuries and was recuperating from surgery, had not been around the studio much, so the two didn't really meet until they happened to be next to each other in line at the airport check in counter. Jennifer initiated conversation with this very young, very new, wide-eyed dancer whose views of company life were, Jennifer knew, still largely unformed. "What stood out to me was that here was this woman who was struggling so hard to come back from injuries, but all she could tell me was how great ABT was, how I'd fall in love with it, and that no matter what, it was an amazing place to be," Annie remembered. "She said, 'Annie, just wait and see. This is like no other career you'll ever have. You're surrounded by incredible people and talents, and the inspiration you get every day from your colleagues is unbelievable.'"

Annie and Jennifer developed a relationship so close that Jennifer took to calling Annie her "little sister," which, since Jennifer was her family's youngest child, Annie found extra touching. They shared friendship and the deep, collegial bond well known to anyone who's been in a corps de ballet, but Annie also looked up to Jennifer as a role model and mentor who profoundly shaped her thinking about the fundamental question: What does it mean to be a dancer?

As incoming corps members began to see that moving up the ranks of ABT was more possible than it had historically been, their mentality became increasingly oriented toward career advancement, achievement, and promotion—and many were ready to change companies to find that, if

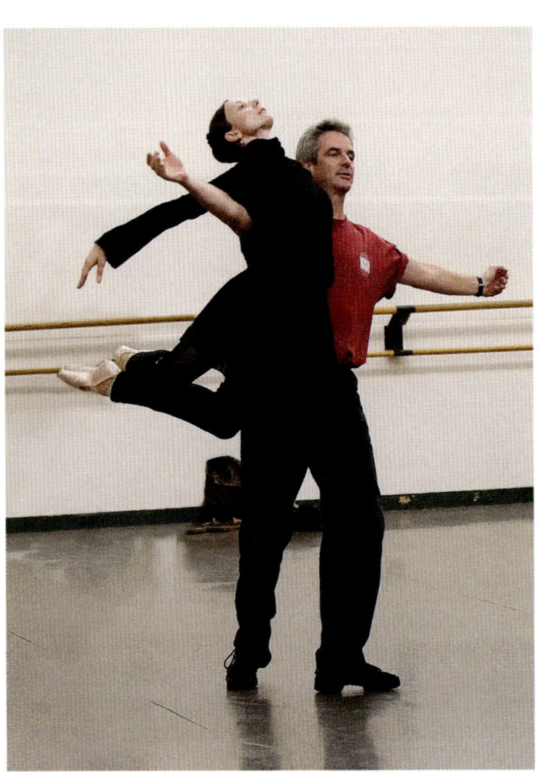

Jennifer Alexander in rehearsal with Kevin McKenzie, 2007. Photo courtesy of American Ballet Theatre.

need be. Jennifer must have had her own doubts and frustrations, even moments of bitterness and questioning about why she remained in the corps—although she did acquire several solo roles in which she shone. She knew she had worth, great talent, experience, and versatility. Annie and other former colleagues talk about Jennifer's striking poise, elegance, and "ballerina aura," which made her stand out even in a line of twenty-four swans. And in a company like ABT where technical standards are so high that, as Annie explained, "Everyone can do everything; we can all do the same steps just as well," being a corps member does not equate with lower ability.

But Jennifer decided to be a principal dancer right where she was, even without an official promotion. With grace, artistry, and respect for herself, her art form, and her company, she showed that there is glory and honor in being a dancer with one's whole heart and soul, no matter your title. Annie said Jennifer's example rubbed off on her fellow dancers. "She made it okay to be in the corps de ballet. Without ever being snooty—she was always so warm, so kind—she carried herself in a way that said, 'I'm in the corps, but I'm a ballerina.' She rose above rank. And I loved that about her. I truly looked up to her for that, and I know others did, too."

Some dancers, if they didn't get promoted, might adopt a sort of "who cares?" attitude about their work, stemming from a feeling that their dancing didn't actually matter as much as that of the soloists or principals. But Jennifer disagreed, rising above rank to show that roles do not define a dancer. Forevermore, Annie wants Jennifer honored through appreciation of the immense talent that surrounds us. "See the everyday beauty," she said. "It's not about how many pirouettes you can do, but how graciously, tall, and proudly you can hold yourself."

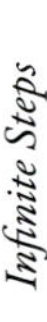

IN NOVEMBER 2007, ABT toured to San Francisco. Annie and Jennifer were almost always roommates on tour, and they were again this time. In a wonderful turn of fate they discovered that they both had the same performance off, so they took the entire day to wander San Francisco, walking, talking, seeing the sights, eating, and talking some more. They covered many topics, from ballet to families to husbands and boyfriends, babies and aging, injuries and what they might do after they stopped dancing. From morning to night, the two walked and talked and shared everything with each other, the hard stuff and the funny stuff, the sadnesses, the hopes and joys. The next month was the accident that killed Jennifer.

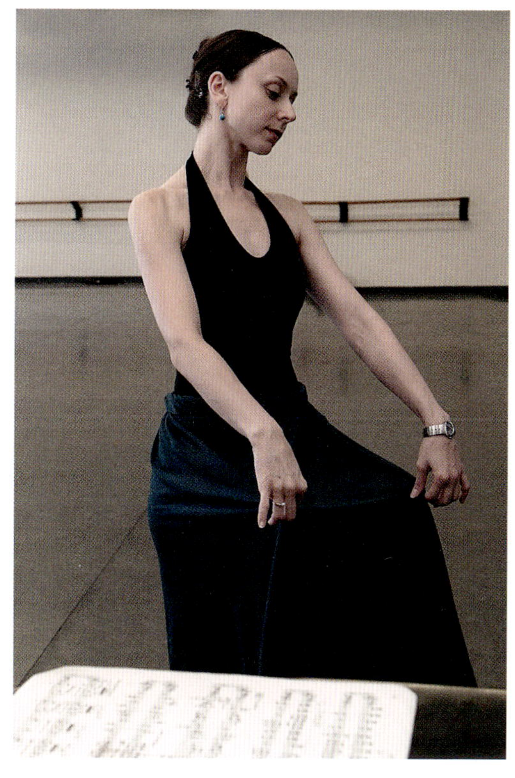

Jennifer Alexander in rehearsal, 2005. Photo courtesy of American Ballet Theatre.

Sometimes things happen that seem beyond chance, and for Annie, this was one of them. "It was the most beautiful day. I keep going back to that day and thinking how grateful I am that we had that. I wonder if there was some . . . it was just meant for us to have that day."

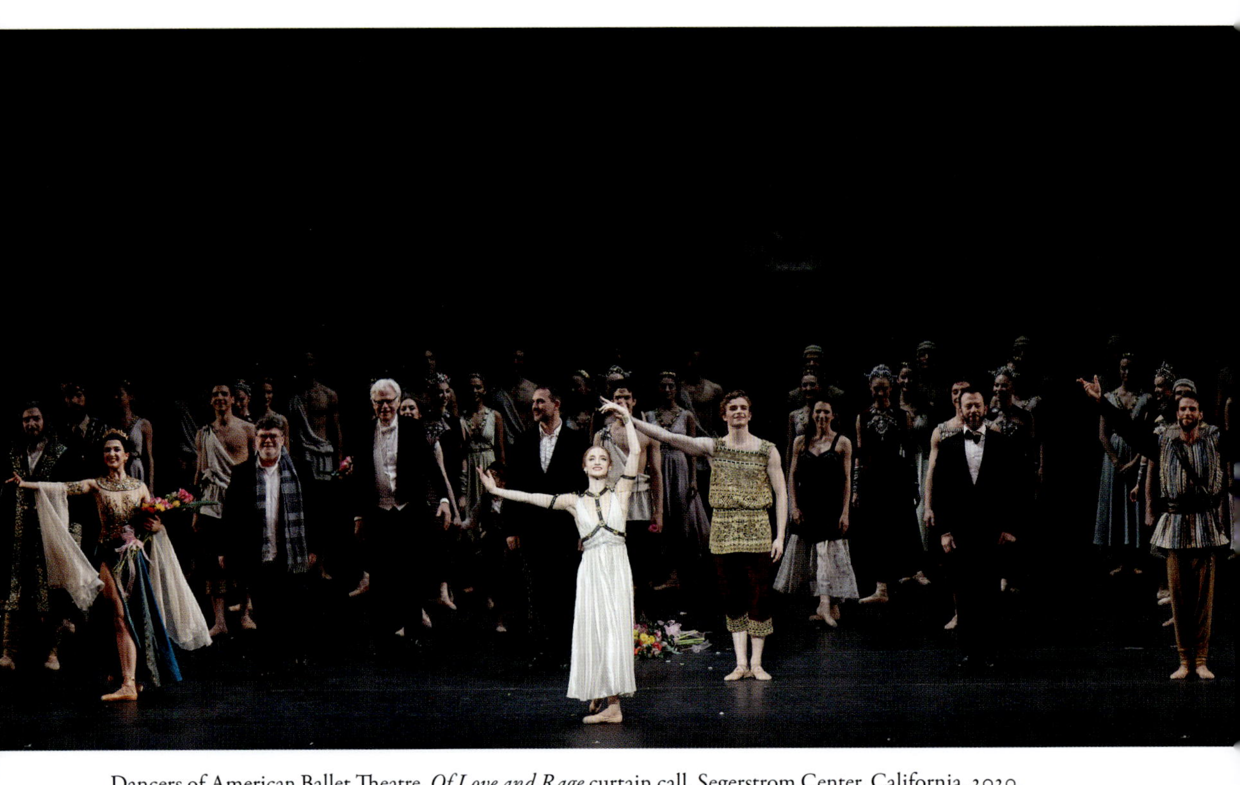

Dancers of American Ballet Theatre, *Of Love and Rage* curtain call, Segerstrom Center, California, 2020. Gene Schiavone's last photograph for ABT. Photo courtesy of American Ballet Theatre.

FINAL CURTAIN

ON MARCH 6, 2020, Gene photographed Alexei Ratmansky's *Of Love and Rage* at the Segerstrom Center in Costa Mesa, California. For the previous twenty years, Gene had accompanied ABT on tours all over the world, and this trip to California was just another stop on a circuit he'd made many times.

That afternoon, he shot dress rehearsal with Hee Seo and Calvin Royal III, two principal dancers Gene had been photographing since they were teenagers in the Studio Company, in the lead roles. The evening's performance was led by Catherine Hurlin and Aran Bell, who represented the generation of dancers beginning to rise into their careers just as Gene—unbeknownst to him or anyone else—was ending his.

After that night's show ended, Gene worked until about 3:00 a.m., editing and formatting photo selections from the performance onto a hard drive to give to Kelly Ryan, ABT's press director, in time for press releases the next day. Since flights were starting to be canceled due to the swiftly spreading fears about COVID-19, Gene flew back home to Connecticut at 8:00 a.m. that day instead of staying with the company in California through the end of their week-long tour.

"I handed Kelly the drive and said, 'See you at the Met,'" Gene recalled, referring to ABT's annual spring season in New York. "But that year's Met season obviously didn't happen."

As the pandemic stubbornly dragged on and the prospect of returning to live, in-theater performances teased like a mirage, Gene felt his energy for the physical work and responsibilities of being the company photographer ebbing. Without the momentum of the performance season carrying him along, he realized that the years of late nights, long commutes, and endless editing had been a grind and taken a large toll. It began to seem like a natural time to move into his second retirement. By the time live performances did resume, Gene had a new project: giving back to the dancers whose lives and careers he'd documented. "It became imperative for me to get out as many photographs as I could," he said. "Dancers need to know what they did, to have representation of this period in their lives. In the end, only the photographs survive."

ACKNOWLEDGMENTS

IN OCTOBER OF 2022, I was invited to coffee by Stephanye Hunter, the dance acquisitions editor at the University Press of Florida. UPF had brought out my first book just a year earlier, but Stephanye began working on the press's dance books after its publication and we had never met. As we chatted about dance, writing, and the intersection of the two in the publishing world, Stephanye told me she'd had an intriguing proposal from a dance photographer and wondered if I would be interested in a possible collaboration. The photographer was Gene Schiavone.

Every artistic project starts with the fleck of an idea. In the case of this one, it took Stephanye's curatorial eye and own artistic sensibility to see that Gene and I could, together, craft his concept into a fully realized manuscript worthy of publication. We are both deeply grateful to Stephanye for bringing us together, for her unwavering positivity, support of and enthusiasm for this endeavor, and for never questioning our ability to do it—even through our multiple requests for deadline extensions. Thank you, Stephanye. Working with you has been a pure joy.

We're honored that *Infinite Steps* is part of UPF's important collection of dance books. We are sincerely appreciative of the dedicated work of the entire UPF staff, who carefully shepherded our book through the many phases of its development that are crucial in bringing a book from our computer screens to a reader's hands.

While this book came into being over the course of only about three years, its seed was planted decades earlier, when Gene first walked into a ballet studio and started taking photographs. Choosing just thirty-three dancers to highlight in *Infinite Steps* out of the hundreds of talented artists who he photographed over the years was a difficult, significant, and emotional process. As we sifted through his (incredibly interesting and quite historical) archives, Gene had something to tell about each and every person, performance, and photo shoot. His many funny, poignant, colorful anecdotes made evident the depth of the personal connection he forged with these individuals and his sensitivity to their passion, drive, courage, and vulnerability. Each and every one of those dancers, whether or not they are pictured on these pages, is part of this book.

The thirty-three dancers of *Infinite Steps* gave us much more than is visible here. They gave us their time—no small donation from the lives of these highly committed people—but even more, they gave us their trust. They went deep into the stories of their lives, sharing not just the known facts of how they got where they are now, but their own, often quite tender, musings on why they made the choices they did along the way. They revealed their vulnerabilities, weaknesses, hopes and dreams, the times they triumphed and where they've fallen short. Every single dancer's generosity of spirit left us humbled and honored to have the chance to reveal the layers of their lives in this book. Thank you all.

A special thank you to Jennifer Alexander's half sister, Andrea Sehmel, and Jennifer's dear friend, Anne Milewski Cary. Gene felt strongly from the beginning of our work on this book that Jennifer's story was emblematic of what we wanted to portray in *Infinite Steps:* full-color portraits of a dancer's spirit and soul. Andrea and Anne revisited painful, yet also very loving and beautiful, memories so that we and our readers could fully know Jennifer as she lived and as she lives on. We all owe them our gratitude.

When we approached "Marie" about being included in this book, she was initially quite hesitant. Her willingness to revisit her difficult past with honesty and candor, reopen wounds that were not fully healed, and entrust us to tell her story was incredibly generous and brave. We are honored and grateful to Marie for giving so fully of herself.

Many people who played significant offstage roles in Gene's photographic career, most especially the staff of American Ballet Theatre during his time as the company's photographer, helped lay the groundwork for *Infinite Steps.* Heartfelt thanks to Kevin McKenzie, David Lansky, Danielle Ventimiglia, Rosanne Forni, Tina Escoda, Clinton Lockhart, Brad Fields, Kyle Pickles, and John Meehan for their kindness, camaraderie, and support of Gene and his work. We deeply thank Susan Jaffe, Susie Morgan Taylor, and Laura Miller for approving of this project and enabling use of the photographs of ABT dancers. We are so thankful for Vicky Shaw's consistently positive and helpful presence throughout Gene's photographic life as well as during the development of *Infinite Steps.*

Kelly Ryan, ABT's former press director, was instrumental in the development of Gene's photographic career through her belief and trust in his ability to capture the artistry of the dancers of ABT. She continued to offer advice, feedback, perspective, editorial suggestions, and moral and practical support as we worked on this book. Her presence throughout this process has been invaluable. We are incredibly grateful to her.

A very warm thank you to the directorship and staff of Boston Ballet, especially artistic director Mikko Nissinen and artistic administrator Elizabeth Olds, for their support and encouragement of both Gene and I over the years. Thank you also to Mariinsky Ballet director Yuri Fateyev, who invited Gene to photograph and allowed continuous access to the company, making possible the historic documentation of the company's artists. We thank Sergei Danillian of Ardani Artists for being an ongoing champion of Gene's photography over the years.

Geoffrey Fallon, thank you for your belief in the importance of dance and dance artists and for your deep generosity that enables us to do our work and share it with the world. Your encouragement and moral and practical support of *Infinite Steps* is immensely appreciated.

It is hard to express just how important my family has been to me during the process of working on this book. Dad, Flynn, Sean, Deb, Ry, Kate—and Mom, as you watch and read from afar—you have been, as always, my sounding boards, receptive readers, and tireless cheerleaders. Knowing you are reliably at the ready to offer advice, perspective, comfort, and motivation kept my confidence from slipping away multiple times and reignited my energy when I felt drained. I love you and thank you from the bottom of my heart.

Lastly, the person to whom we all owe our gratitude: Ellen Schiavone, for igniting the spark that created twenty years of beautiful and historic photographs.

GAVIN LARSEN is a dance writer, teacher, and former professional dancer. Born and raised in New York City, she received her dance training at the School of American Ballet before performing professionally with Pacific Northwest Ballet, Alberta Ballet, the Suzanne Farrell Ballet, and Oregon Ballet Theatre, from which she retired as a principal dancer in 2010. Over the course of her career, Ms. Larsen danced prominent roles in ballets by George Balanchine, Jerome Robbins, Christopher Wheeldon, James Kudelka and Paul Taylor, among others, and originated roles in numerous ballets. Since retiring from the stage, she has been a regular contributor to *Pointe* and *Dance Magazine* and her writing has also appeared in *Dance Teacher, Dance Spirit,* Dance/USA's *In the Green Room, Oregon ArtsWatch,* and the *Dancing Times,* as well as several literary journals, including *Threepenny Review, Page & Spine,* and *The Maine Review.* Ms. Larsen has taught and coached widely around the US and been a guest teacher in Canada and Japan. Her memoir, *Being a Ballerina: The Power and Perfection of a Dancing Life,* published by the University Press of Florida in 2021, received critical praise for its candor and grace. She lives in Asheville, North Carolina.

GENE SCHIAVONE was the staff photographer for American Ballet Theatre between 2000 and 2020. In addition to photographing nearly every ABT performance in New York and on tour during that time, he documented rehearsals and captured compelling candid images of the company's dancers. Mr. Schiavone has also provided photography for major companies and organizations around the world, including the Mariinsky Theatre, Bolshoi Ballet, Miami City Ballet, and Boston Ballet, the Youth America Grand Prix competition, and many international gala performances. A significant part of his work also included studio photography for a generation of dancers from student to professional.

Although he initially pursued a business career, Mr. Schiavone's lifelong fascination with cameras and capturing the moments of life on film led him to a second career in photography. Ballet was not a specific area of interest until his wife, Ellen, became involved with American Ballet Theatre and introduced him to some of the company's dancers, piquing his curiosity about the previously mysterious, foreign world of ballet. Mr. Schiavone began photographing the ABT Studio Company, a group of talented young pre-professionals, and soon thereafter became the chief photographer for the main ABT company.

Mr. Schiavone feels privileged to have photographed many of the world's most noted dancers. His photographs have appeared in the *New York Times,* the *Wall Street Journal,* the *Washington Post,* all the major dance publications both in the US and abroad, and were frequently featured in ABT publicity materials including posters, brochures, and billboards.

In 2020, Mr. Schiavone retired from performance photography, though he continues to work with individual dancers in studio sessions. His intention is to create a lasting testament to the dancers he lovingly photographed over so many years, and whose effervescent art will live on in his images.